Survey Research

Survey Research

Roger Sapsford

SAGE Publications
London • Thousand Oaks • New Delhi

First published 1999

 SAGE Publications Ltd
6 Bonhill Street
London EC2A 4PU

SAGE Publications Inc.
2455 Teller Road
Thousand Oaks, California 91320

SAGE Publications India Pvt Ltd
32, M-Block Market
Greater Kailash – I
New Delhi 110 048

British Library Cataloguing in Publication data

A catalogue record for this book is available from the British Library

ISBN 0 7619 5527 5
ISBN 0 7619 5528 3 (pbk)

Library of Congress catalog card number 98–61884

Typeset by Mayhew Typesetting, Rhayader, Powys
Printed in Great Britain by Redwood Books, Trowbridge, Wiltshire

Contents

Preface

The aim of this book is to provide something readable, useful and informative on survey methods and the place of surveys in the spectrum of research studies, taking account of how research *is* carried out, not just the theory of how it *ought to be* carried out. As a text I hope it will be usable by students, from second-level undergraduates through to research students and students on taught methods courses. It covers sufficient of the technicalities and discusses the ethical and political background to research in sufficient detail to help with examinations and coursework essays. At the same time, it is intended to be sufficiently practical to help with the design and conduct of survey projects and thesis/dissertation research. I hope it will also be of interest to practising researchers. The intent has been to give real insight into how research is planned and conducted and to establish research as an intellectual, moral and political activity as well as a practical one.

The central message is that theory, technique and practical application are not separable when it comes to doing or thinking about research. The book covers the technical questions which have to be considered when planning and carrying out research, but also the ethics and politics of research projects. It starts with a discussion of how research ideas are developed – whether the 'question' is an academic one leading to a thesis or paper, or a practical one leading to a report to a customer or policy-maker – and how the development of ideas goes hand in hand with the development of a research design. At all stages, through to a final chapter on writing up and reporting, practical research issues are mixed in with the issues of ethics/politics, philosophy, sociology and social psychology which surround and underpin them. While major large-scale studies such as government surveys are discussed, the main emphasis is on small-scale projects such as can be carried out by one researcher or a small group. The stance adopted is that of a practising researcher who has carried out both 'academic' and 'practical' research projects, and the book discusses research carried out in constrained circumstances and with unsatisfactory resources as well as 'ideal-typical' studies. (Several of the major examples are from work I have carried out myself or the work of close colleagues, which allows me to 'go behind the scenes' and bring in details which did not appear in the published reports.)

To say that the book is rooted in the practice of research aimed at finding out 'what is going on out there' does not imply, however, that it avoids 'abstract' questions of epistemology. Theoretical perspectives are inevitably a part of practice and, as we shall see, there are good reasons for placing 'what is going on out there' in inverted commas. What do we mean by 'out there'? What kind of 'things' are we 'finding out', and for what purpose? What is distinctive about survey methods and what, if anything, justifies treating them as a style of research separate from other styles? What can we sensibly say about the surveys we carry out or read about, and what may be deduced from them? Most important of all, how do we *do* survey research, in order to have any results to talk about at all?

I should like to offer my thanks to Chris Rojek, who suggested the book and commented on drafts, and Pascale Carrington and Kate Scott who steered it through. Beyond that, all academic life is a (generally unacknowledged) collaboration. I ought to thank many people, but particularly Pamela Abbott, Charlotte Banks, Martyn Hammersley, Betty Swift, Ray Thomas and Michael Wilson, from each of whom I have learned a great deal, and I am particularly grateful to Martin Levoi for his advice.

PART A

INTRODUCTION

---

1 What *is* survey research?

What *is* a survey?

What do *you* mean by the word 'survey'? List some of the different ways in which the word can be used.

- Standing on a hilltop, I *survey* the surrounding countryside – I look out over it and see what is there.
- The original Norman 'Domesday Book', in the eleventh century, *surveyed* the manors and farms of England – it aimed to list and describe them all.
- The decennial Census of Population (see Example 1.1) *surveys* the population of England and Wales – it provides a detailed description of all people and households.

A survey describes a population – it counts and describes 'what is out there'.

- When an architect or engineer does a survey of a house or a tract of land, something more is suggested by the term than just a general description or list of attributes. A survey of a tract of land involves a precise mapping of all the major features, but especially those which are of relevance to the survey's purpose: the lay of the rock, clay and water, if houses are to be built; the formation of the rocks, if mining is intended.

A survey in this sense is a detailed and quantified description – a precise map and/or a precise measurement of potential.

- The Census can be seen as a survey in this more detailed sense also. What it measures is the nature of the 'human stock' or 'human resource' – the population to be governed and put to work, its housing, its employment, its level of education and training, and so on.

Censuses and surveys of this sort originated during a conceptual transition from population as a collection of people to population as a resource, during the industrialization of society in the late eighteenth and nineteenth centuries. (The first British Census took place in 1801.) If we want to exploit the agricultural land of a region with maximum efficiency we need detailed maps of land use and land potential. If we want to exploit mineral resources, we need detailed geological maps. In the same way, we need a 'mapping' of the human population if we want to make best use of it in industry and to provide the services that it needs. We need to know its geographical distribution, its distribution by age, how many are of working age, what children are coming forward as replacements, how many older or disabled people will need support, how adequate the housing stock is for the use to which it is put, and so on. The Census 'maps' population, for purposes of planning and forecasting, in the same kind of way as the geologist maps potential mineral deposits or the surveyor maps possible uses of land.

Example 1.1: The decennial Census of Population

The British Census has taken place every 10 years since 1801, except for 1941, and aims to provide a complete count of every person resident in England and Wales on a particular night (there are separate censuses of Scotland and Northern Ireland) and of the households or institutions within which they live. The Census of Population in the United States is even older, having been held every 10 years since 1790, and the first Swedish Census also dates from the late eighteenth century.

The British Census cost about £135 million to administer in 1991 and required the services of 118,000 'enumerators' (basic data collectors). Twelve miles of shelving were required to hold the completed forms at the input processing stations (Dale and Marsh, 1993).

Before the event, Census enumerators go round their allocated districts identifying every house or other dwelling-place, and they attend briefing meetings in which they receive standardized instruction on the use of the Census questionnaire and the nature of their duties. At these meetings perceived ambiguities in the questions and procedures can be explained. During the week before Census night the enumerators then go round their districts delivering a form to every residential household. (Institutions such as nursing homes and hotels are dealt with separately.)

One person in every household is charged with filling in the form, about everyone resident in the household on the night of the Census (plus details of people normally resident but temporarily absent). The first decision the enumerator has to make, therefore, is what constitutes a household – in other words, how many forms to leave at a given address. A reasonably precise definition will have been given – for example, that people constitute a household if they are normally resident at the same address and share the majority of meals. 'Nuclear family' households are not normally a problem for the enumerator, but he or she may have to take decisions about, for example, establishments such as shared flats, which may contain one household or several.

Informants then fill in the Census form. This asks for names of everyone resident or normally resident in the household. For those resident it will ask a number of personal details – age, gender, employment, previous address and so on. Questions are also asked about the house or flat: for example, ownership, number of rooms, facilities such as bathrooms available, whether there is a car available to household members, etc. In the 1991 Census, after 20 years of thought and consultation of minority ethnic communities, a detailed question on ethnic origin or grouping was included for the first time, which has made it possible to look in detail at the employment and housing of people in these groups.

After Census night the enumerator returns to the household to collect the completed form. A few simple checks are performed at the time of collection – that all questions have been answered, that some key questions have been correctly understood (for example, the count of rooms and whether kitchens and bathrooms are to be included) and that key linked questions have logical answers (for example, that where a spouse's occupation is entered on the form, there is a spouse for him or her to be partnered with). The forms are then taken away and checked again in more detail; if necessary, the enumerator will return to some households to clear up ambiguities and mistakes. The enumerator then does some preliminary coding – enters numerical values for some of the key answers on a machine-readable sheet – and sends the coded sheets and the forms off to the central office, where the coded sheets are processed for quick analysis and the rest of the form is coded and entered on computer for subsequent more detailed examination. Before the rest of the form is coded, further checking is done, and it may be necessary to contact some informants if mistakes have been made. (The entirety of the form, including 'difficult to code' items where there is a high proportion of handwritten answers, will be coded for only a 10 per cent sample of forms.) Finally, an officer of the Office of Population Censuses and Surveys (OPCS) visits a sample of households in a follow-up survey, to check on the work of the enumerators. Figures are also compared with other data sources, including extrapolations from the previous Census, to check that the counts are plausible. In 1991 such checks revealed a probable under-count of about 4–5 per cent of population.

Responses from institutions – hospitals, prisons, hotels, nursing homes – are also entered centrally. There is even an attempt to provide at least a count and some basic descriptive information for those who do not live in households at all: police officers tour metropolitan areas and try to count and briefly interview those who are 'sleeping rough'.

The Census provides a snapshot of the population on a particular night. A sample of 'anonymized' records is available for analysis by researchers. By comparing current and past responses for a nominated panel of households, it is also possible to publish longitudinal figures which show what has happened to a sample of households over a period of time; the results of such examinations since 1971 are published as the OPCS Longitudinal Study.

The Census provides a general description, but there are many other government surveys which examine particular aspects of the life of the population in more detail and with greater frequency. Specific surveys are also carried out by commercial organizations, government departments and groups of academics, to find out more focused information about the population for particular purposes. Counting people's age, location and work status was only one aspect of the growth of 'the managed society'. Tools were developed during the first half of the twentieth century – the ancestors and close relatives of psychometric instruments still in use today – to measure intelligence and capability, personality, skill and aptitude and a wide range of characteristics relevant to designing and recruiting to schools and factories. Even more extensive is the growth since the middle of the century in surveys to measure beliefs, opinions, preferences and habits – so that government and other directive organizations can respond to popular wishes, or to test whether government policies will be acceptable to the electorate, or to forecast the outcome of national events (such as general elections) or reaction to local events (such as the intention to site a prison or psychiatric hostel in a particular locality), or most often to assess the market for products and the effectiveness of advertising for them. Measurement of population by means of surveys has become a major resource for planners and for commerce. Wherever we need to know the characteristics of a population, or its resources, or its needs, or its opinions, the natural thing to do is to go out and ask questions or to count what we need to know about it by direct observation.

Quantification

What differentiates surveys from other kinds of research project?

Surveys involve *systematic* observation or *systematic* interviewing. They ask the questions which the *researcher* wants answered, and often they

---

Box 1.1: Population

In ordinary language populations are usually made up of individual people –
we talk about 'the population of London', meaning all the people who live
and/or work in London. The term is also commonly used of the animals or
plants to be found in a given locality. In statistical terminology and when
used in survey research, however, a *population* is *the entire set of objects
about which we wish to speak or make generalizations*. This may be (and often
is) people, but objects or institutions may also be populations – a survey of
British schools, for example, would want to generalize about 'the population of British schools' (that is, to say what is true of all of them).

Clear definition of the population to which the results are to generalize
is essential in survey research and not always obvious. 'The population of
London' is a case in point: do we mean just those people who *live* in
London, or all those who are to be found there on a weekday (including
those who work in London but live outside? those who are there on
holiday? those who are passing through to some other destination?). Or
do we have some more limited and closely defined subset in mind – for
example, 'the population of people using the London transport system on
a given day'?

---

dictate the range of answers that may be given. Standardization lies at the
heart of survey research, and the whole point is to get consistent answers to
consistent questions. We ask everyone precisely those questions that we
want answered. More than this, we try to ask the questions in precisely the
same way in each interview – to *standardize* the questionnaire as a
measuring instrument. (Not all surveys involve asking people questions, of
course – systematic observation is a form of survey research – but the
same issues apply: we try to define precisely what is to be observed, to
observe it in every case or setting or location and to train the observers so
that they apply the criteria consistently and reliably.) From being just a
counting exercise, like 'Domesday Book', surveys have developed into
exercises in *measurement*. A substantial technology has grown up around
the notion of *validity* – the extent to which a test or question measures
what it is intended to measure. This is the first of the three 'technologies of
research' which we shall consider in this chapter. They are not unique to
survey research – all research has to demonstrate validity, for example –
but they are well developed in particular ways in survey research.

Sampling

The Census is nearly unique among large-scale surveys in collecting data
on every single case within a population; most make do with a sample.
Read Box 1.2, and then try the following question.

Box 1.2: Census and sample

A *census* is a *study which includes every member of a given population*. With a capital letter, 'Census' usually means the decennial count of every member of the country's population. However, every 100 per cent study is correctly described as a 'census'; for example, an interview study of every prisoner on a given prison wing is a census of opinion on that wing.

A *sample* is a *subset of the population* – usually with the implication that the subset resembles the population closely on key characteristics (is *representative* of the population). If the sample is representative of the population, then what is true of the sample will also be true of the population (within a calculable margin of error).

Why, do you think? List some possible reasons for sampling rather than collecting data from the whole population.

There are many reasons. One is sheer cost and the time involved in counting every case of a large population. With all the resources of government, the Census can be run only once every 10 years, and it requires a vast army of enumerators nation-wide. Until recently the results have taken several years to process, so that detailed figures were always several years out of date by the time they were released; modern computing resources have speeded up the analysis of preliminary figures, but the operation still takes 2–3 years to produce detailed analyses. The second reason is coverage: a very large survey, particularly if it is to be made compulsory (as the Census of England and Wales is), has to be limited in what it asks, while a smaller-scale operation may be able to ask a longer list of questions. (It may also be able to ask questions about more sensitive areas, because more interviewer time can be devoted to each case.) The third reason is training: a relatively small-scale survey can be carried out by the researchers themselves or by a relatively small number of interviewers who can be trained and briefed in some depth. For all these reasons, Census figures are supplemented by more frequent collection of more detailed data from a sample of the population, in surveys such as the annual General Household Survey (Example 1.2).

Example 1.2: The General Household Survey

As well as organizing the decennial Census, the OPCS has also carried out a *General Household Survey* every year since 1971. A random sample of 15,000 households are approached, yielding an eventual sample of some 12,000 households after some have refused to take part – which means data on over 30,000 people. The purpose was aptly described in an early report (OPCS, 1978):

It aims to provide a means of examining relationships between the most significant variables with which social policy is concerned and, in particular, of monitoring changes . . . over time. It is thus of particular importance as a source of background information for central government decisions on resource allocation between social programmes.

The sampling pattern is not a simple random one, but a complex stratified design which aims to produce as good as possible a representation of the population, including people in rare but important categories. Until 1984 the sampling frame employed was the electoral registers, but since then these have been replaced by the Postcode Address File. A two-stage sampling design is used. First, postcode sectors are allocated to strata on the basis of region and type of area, 22 such major strata being created. Second, within the major strata, postcode sectors are stratified according to economic and housing indicators derived from the most recent Census to yield groups which are relatively homogeneous with respect to proportion of private sector renting, proportion of households renting from local authorities and the socio-economic class of heads of household. This process yields 576 groups of equal size, and one postcode sector is chosen randomly from each group. Up to three households will then be interviewed at each address, if there is multi-occupancy. The response rate is around 72 per cent, or 82 per cent if partially completed interviews are included (OPCS, 1996). About a sixth of non-response is due to failure to contact the household, and the remainder is refusal to participate.

The interviews are conducted throughout the year. Interviewers undertake a three-day initial training course and are briefed before starting the survey, and new recruits are accompanied by a training officer during their first interviews. Interviewers are also monitored regularly in the field.

The main areas of enquiry are population (numbers of people by age, gender, family relationships and so on), housing, employment, education and health. As well as a bank of permanently present questions which allow comparisons over time, the survey also asks specific blocks of questions from time to time in order to illuminate particular areas; notable examples have been smoking and drinking, crime victimization, housing costs, experience of long-term unemployment and information about older people in private households.

Unpublished General Household Survey data can be made available to researchers, for a fee, provided the anonymity of informants is preserved.

Clearly, if the figures are to be useful then we must be confident that they actually do describe the population, and it would be all too easy to question even a very large sample and still obtain unrepresentative results. If the sample were confined to one region of the country, or if it over-represented males or females, or the young or the old, or the rich or the poor, the results would not give us a fair and useful picture of the population as a whole. To guarantee representation, a substantial technology has grown up around the business of sampling. Broadly, two approaches to this problem are possible.

On the one hand, we can deliberately construct a sample which is representative of its population in this respect: using census figures as 'facts about the population', we can construct our sample to be distributed in the same proportions as the population by age, gender and anything else that strikes us as of importance. This by itself does not guarantee a properly representative sample, however, because our sample may differ from the population in ways which did *not* strike us as important but turn out to be so with hindsight or, worse, distort the figures without our ever realizing they are doing so.

The alternative approach is to select our cases randomly, so that pure chance determines who is approached and every case has an equal chance of being selected; this maximizes the likelihood that there will be no systematic bias in the sampling. However, random samples *can* turn out to be unrepresentative – taking a sample from a pack of cards, there is no absolute guarantee that any given sample will contain equal numbers of red and black ones, though the likelihood of this increases if the sample is large.

The General Household Survey (Example 1.2) in fact combines these approaches in a *stratified* sampling pattern, taking random samples but within subsets of the population (by region, class and so on) so determined that the sample will definitely be representative of the population in these respects. The technology of sampling is discussed in depth in Chapters 3 and 4.

Comparison

Most surveys are not just about describing populations, but are to be used to test some conclusion or at least to find out how one group differs from another. Thus a prime purpose of survey data is to make planned *comparisons*. If we are looking at changes over time, we need to compare later periods with an earlier one as baseline. If we want to evaluate the effects of a change in practice or policy, we need to compare 'before' with 'after'. If we want to know the effects of some common behaviour – for example, smoking – we need to compare those who indulge in it with those who do not. Even if all we are interested in is describing some group and their particular needs – older people, perhaps, or lone parents – we often need to be able to say not just that a certain number need X or Y, but that their deprivation of X or Y is greater than, or less than, or much the same as other groups.

Comparison is the third of the 'technologies' of survey research (or perhaps the word 'logic' might be more appropriate here). For every question that needs answering on the basis of survey data we have to ask ourselves whether a comparison of some sort will be involved (it generally will) and whether the comparison will be possible from the data which we are planning to collect. Often the basis of comparison is figures already collected for some other purpose: is this group housed better or worse than the general population, as measured by the Census or the General Household Survey, for example? More often we will be collecting both the 'target' data and the data for comparison, and we need to ensure that the groups are constituted on the same basis so that they can validly be compared. It is no use, for example, comparing men's and women's occupations using a random sample for the men but the wives of those who happen to be married as the sample of women. Convenient as this would be in terms of data collection, the comparison would be invalid because it excluded women who were not married. Properly designed comparison lies at the heart of survey analysis.

The technical term for all three of these 'technologies' is *validation* – establishing the *validity* of the research (see Box 1.3). To ask whether a study is valid – or rather, the *extent* to which it is valid – is to ask about the status of the evidence. We are asking whether what is presented as evidence can carry the weight of the conclusions drawn from it, or whether there is a logical flaw (in measurement, in sampling, in comparison) which makes the conclusions doubtful or at least detracts from our belief in them. The reader asks 'Why should I believe these conclusions?', and it is the job of the survey report to provide good reasons for belief. The rest of this book examines how such reasons can and should be built into the design of surveys.

Box 1.3: Validity

A research argument is said to be *valid* to the extent that the conclusions drawn from the data do logically follow from them. Questions we must ask of every survey to test this involve:

1 *validity of measurement* – the extent to which the data constitute accurate measurements of what is supposed to be being measured;
2 *population validity* – the extent to which the sample gives an accurate representation of the population which it is supposed to represent;
3 *validity of design* – the extent to which the comparisons being made are appropriate to establish the arguments which rest on them.

Is a survey appropriate?

'Survey' is given a very wide meaning in this book, but it is only one form of research. The question has to be asked: 'Is a survey what I want to do?' This breaks down into five questions, which are covered in the rest of this book:

1   Is research feasible at all in these circumstances?
2   Is survey research the right way to approach the problem, to obtain the kind of answers that are required?
3   Is a survey feasible here – would it yield valid conclusions?
4   Is it ethically appropriate to use survey methods here rather than some other approach?
5   Is it ethically and politically appropriate to carry out any form of research, given the research questions and the social context?

The technical and formal questions (questions 1–3 in the list above) inevitably take up much of this book. The first question concerns not how the research is carried out, but whether research can be carried out at all to provide the answers which are required, and this will depend not on the design of the research in the first instance but on the nature of the questions. Chapter 2 looks at problem formulation and setting up questions which are capable of being answered by research. Most of the rest of the book is concerned with technical issues – with how surveys *should* ideally be run, and with how they *could* be run (and *are* run) in less than ideal circumstances.

The other two questions, questions 4 and 5 in the list above, receive less specific coverage in the book but are equally important. We have to ask ourselves what harm could be done by our research and to design the research to avoid it. It is in the 'contract' between researchers and their subjects, respondents or informants – the set of 'reasonable assumptions' which both sides bring to research – that researchers are responsible professionals who will exercise their responsibility by protecting those with and/or on whom they work. We have also, as social theorists and critical thinkers, to be aware that research is not an asocial process but itself a part of the social world. Like any other activity in which we take part, we ought to be aware of and influenced by the likely consequences of our thinking and our actions for people, groups and social processes and to have some inkling that our work is a continuation of social history and a contribution to creating the history of the future.

Further reading

(The role of further reading in this book is to expand on the subject-matter and arguments, to offer alternative points of view and, in the 'technical' chapters, to provide sources of reference for those who need to explore a topic in more detail than is possible here. It will also include follow-up reading on studies used as major illustrations.)

Good general introductions to surveys and survey design include Chapter 1 of Hakim (1987) and Chapters 1–3 of Oppenheim (1992).

For further reading on the Census, see Dale and Marsh (eds) (1993); Hakim (1979); and Office of Population Censuses and Surveys (OPCS) (1980). Barrett (1994) is a useful coverage of the U.S. Census.

A good introduction to the General Household Survey is the original one – OPCS (1973).

2   What's the problem? Developing ideas

The final product

Any piece of research starts with a question or problem and proceeds to a solution based in part on the interpretation of evidence which the writers claim is valid for the purpose. (Just how research questions get on to the agenda is a wide topic and beyond the scope of this book – but see the comments on 'political' factors later in this chapter and elsewhere.) The stages of a final report are the stages which we have to go through in order to plan a research project. We need to know what the problem or question is – in general terms at first, and then with increasing precision as we go through the stages of planning. We need to have some idea about what *kind* of answer will count as acceptable. We need, given these, to plan an argument which will get from the problem to that kind of answer. Thence we can tell what kind of evidence we shall need and can plan the sampling and methods of collection so that this kind of evidence can be procured (and that its validity can be demonstrated to the reader). Demonstrating the validity, in turn, will mean building in 'checks and balances' within the study. So, thinking about what we shall have to put into the final report has given us a list of questions we need to ask at the very beginning:

- What's the problem?
- What kind of answer am I looking for?
- What kind of an argument might lead from the question to the answer?
- What kind of evidence will I need to sustain this kind of argument?
- How is this kind of evidence to be collected, and from/about whom or what?
- How shall I demonstrate to the reader that the evidence is valid?

These questions hold for all kinds of project. If you are working for a client – a commissioning agency, a customer of research, a newspaper, an institution – you are thinking at this point about what *their* problems are, what kinds of solution are likely to be useful to them and what methods they will understand and find convincing. If you are doing a purely 'academic' project – for an end-of-year assessment, for example – then your audience is those who will be reading and marking the work. If you are doing a project as part of the process of developing knowledge and theory about a topic area, your audience will be other academics and researchers – and separately, quite likely, practitioners such as doctors or social workers or nurses or administrators who work within the topic area. There is *always* an audience, however. Research may be an enjoyable activity in its own right; however, it is not the enjoyment which makes it research, but the sharing of conclusions and evidence with others in a target audience.

At this point we should note two paradoxes – or, if not paradoxes, at least areas of potential conceptual confusion. First, I appear to be saying here that pleasing an audience is more important than finding out the truth. This is *not* what I meant to say. I take the same position as Hammersley (1993) – that the first aim of research has to be finding out true things about the world, because to say otherwise is self-defeating. However important political/social engagement may be, there would be no use for the results of research unless we believed they were dictated by 'the nature of the world' rather than the political or social beliefs of the researcher. (What differentiates research from polemic, indeed, is that it is designed so that the researcher's beliefs could be falsified by the evidence.) Having said that, however, it remains true that research is always carried out – and certainly always written up – with some audience in mind. It is also my own belief that research should have some impact on the social world. Second, I appear to be saying that you decide what the results are going to be *before* you carry out the survey. Again, this is not my intent.

Why, then, do you suppose I have talked so much about anticipating the answers?

Because survey research is highly structured, it is true in general that you are unlikely to discover anything from it which you have not in some sense anticipated. Knowing what sort of answer you need in order to develop your theory – or what sort of answer your client needs for the development of policy or practice – you know to make sure that it is possible to obtain this kind of answer from the study.

Validating evidence

Given an adequate definition of the problem – which means at least a fair idea of the kind of conclusions to which your report will want to come – the rest of the planning stage involves obtaining valid evidence for the conclusions and demonstrating its validity (look back at Box 1.3). You will want to think about the population from which your sample will be drawn, for example, to avoid excluding cases which may be important for the argument. Sometimes theory gets in the way here. A whole generation of studies of changes in the labour market and the class structure, important not just to class theory but to our understanding of Britain and the USA as democracies, was bedevilled by a blindness to the fact that women as well as men have jobs and opinions and stand in a relation to the social order beyond that of their potential roles as daughters, wives and mothers (see

Abbott and Sapsford, 1987). The converse also occurs – persistently seeking differences where the balance of the evidence suggests none exist, because 'there *must* be differences'; for examples, consider the history of psychological research into gender or 'race'.

Your report will consist of measurements or counts of what you say exists 'out there' – counts of objects or people, or characteristics of people, or behaviours, or attitude statements or scores on tests, for example. Another important part of survey design is showing that your measurements are accurate and trustworthy (*reliable*) – that someone else using the same measurement tools would have obtained the same or similar results. Yet another, equally important, is showing that what you measured *does* mean what you *say* it means – that you have succeeded in measuring what was needed for the argument. This may involve showing merely that the counts are accurate – for example, that the number of refrigerators in the household was properly counted and that you have not overlooked the occasional one lurking in the garage. It may involve a more complex argument about why you counted the number of refrigerators in the first place – are they, for example, an adequate indicator of wealth, or would it have been better to assess the wealth of the household by some more complicated means? Often philosophical questions come into play: when people say they believe this or would do that in certain circumstances, does that have any bearing on their actions? Alternatively, is it a *rhetoric*, not closely aligned to people's actions but capable of independent explanation in its own right? It is important that as many objections as can be foreseen are dealt with at the planning stage, because it may not be simple to counter them after the data have been collected.

Finally, the underlying 'validity' question is the honesty of the researcher, and here there is not much to be done. All research depends ultimately on our trust that the researcher is at worst incompetent or 'short-sighted' but not positively mendacious. We build checking procedures into our surveys so that we can assure ourselves that particular stages of the data collection were carried out in the way described and/or that key choices were made by predetermined criteria which are demonstrably independent from even unconscious bias. We can never demonstrate, however, that inevitable preconceptions and prior values have not in some way shaped the results; the best we can do is to declare them, where known, so that the reader can make allowances. Replication by other people is the only safeguard against deliberate dishonesty.

Defining the problem

The most important part of the survey project is prior analysis of the 'question', and at the same time the most important problem is preconception, as was suggested above. Survey research tends on the whole to require a higher degree of prior planning than other approaches. Most surveys involve a considerable investment in time and/or money to collect a

---

Box 2.1: Reliability

An aspect of validation, *reliability* is the *stability of the measures* - the extent to which repeated measurement yields constant results (over a reasonably short period of time, during which change would not be expected to occur), or supposedly identical measuring instruments yield identical results. The metaphor commonly used is that of the yardstick and the tape-measure: a wooden yardstick yields the same measurement for length when the distance between the same two points is measured twice; a cloth tape-measure may stretch a little, depending on how it is held, so it may not give precisely the same reading twice. The former is said to be a reliable instrument, and the latter a less reliable one.

In the simplest of cases, reliability is checked by literally measuring twice and looking at the agreement of the two measures. Where this is not possible or appropriate, a number of other ways of approaching the problem may be used: using two parallel tests, or comparing random halves of items from a test all of whose items are supposed to be measuring the same thing. When looking at the human observer as a measuring instrument – judging quality of performance, for example – a common method of checking reliability is to use more than one judge and to compare their results.

Reliability is essential for validity: if you are not measuring *something* reliably, then you cannot be measuring the *desired thing* reliably. Measures can be reliable but invalid, however; they can measure *something* reliably but not the *desired thing*. An example would be a miscalibrated yardstick, which reliably gives the wrong length.

---

large amount of data in a single 'pass' through the field. This expenditure will be partly wasted if mistakes and truisms are built into the original design, and it will be totally wasted if it turns out that the data are not what are needed to answer the original question (or what the original question should have been).

The first stage, then, is looking carefully at what kind of answer will be required and using this analysis to help define the original problem. We want to know about prison conditions, let us say, but what do we want to report? Are we interested in how conditions are experienced by prisoners, or by staff? Are we interested in effects of prison conditions – on mood or mentation, or subsequent criminal acts, or later employability and social integration? Or do we have a 'social policy' interest in others who are affected – for example, the families of prisoners, or specifically their children? Or is our interest wider and more 'societal' – a concern with the place of prison in the criminal justice system, with why prison sentences are awarded and with the function of the penal system within the complex of law and policing? Or is our interest in the ethos and practice of prison management, as a case-study of managerialism in non-commercial institutions? Or is the 'range' of our interest more limited and specific – prison visiting, or internal arbitration procedures and prisoners' rights, or prison work, or prison education? Is the aim just 'to describe', or to test and extend social or psychological theory, or to change prisons, or to perhaps to make a case for their abolition? We cannot just 'survey prisons' or 'survey prisoners'; each of these interests leads to a different kind of survey, requiring differently designed procedures of data collection to gather different kinds of information.

Often in market research the most important stage of planning, and the one where the research consultants really earn their money, is the series of initial consultations with the client. Someone may want a survey 'to look at the impact of our coffee advertising'. But what is meant by this, in terms of survey design? Is the interest in how widely the advertising has been noticed, and/or by whom, to see if it is effectively disseminated to what may reasonably be seen as the target audience? Does the client need to know whether it is reaching *new* potential customers? Is he or she interested in what change it makes in 'attitude', or in the salience of a brand name (how readily it is named by potential customers) or its image (what kind of a product it is seen as naming)? Is 'attitude' enough, or do we need to measure intent to buy, or whether the product actually was bought? (The latter would obviously be better if what is being advertised is an existing product, but we might have to settle for the former if what is being explored is whether a new product would command a market if released.) Is it the advertising which is the focus of the study, or the product? (The advertising has succeeded in its purpose if it brings the product to attention and perhaps induces people to buy it and try it out. If the real focus is the product, however, it may be that we need to look for repeat buying and changes in buying behaviour over time.) The underlying question may not be immediately apparent to the client; he or she may need to 'talk out the problem' in order to commission the most useful kind of research. A second question which a good group of consultants would ask themselves is whether the right person is defining the problem. Initial consultations would be with a director or supervisor or with an advertising department, but the 'problem' might concern some quite different department – the sales organization, for example, or the production departments.

The need for this kind of consultation is most clearly evident in commercial research, but the same process is needed in applied social research as well. If you were researching prisons or prisoners in the interests of the prison authorities – to continue with the example started above – you would need to formulate the questions which the authorities needed answering in such a way that there was maximal chance of the information being useful and used. This would require considerable prior analysis. You would need to know what the 'customer' thought the results would be useful for, and either design the research with this use in mind or warn from the start that the objectives were not fully achievable. You would need to talk not only to the department which commissions research but also to the departments which use it, in order to make sure that the 'customer' had correctly understood what was feasible and desirable at the operational level. You would want also to talk to local hierarchies and to staff 'on the ground', to enrich your analysis and to forestall hostility.

Beyond this, it is at this stage that you would have to consider the ethics and politics of the research. Whether it is ethical to help sell coffee is not a major problem for the researcher (though some researchers have been worried about their results being used to sell tobacco or alcohol). When dealing with social problems, personal need and the actions of the state, however, the researcher becomes part of the 'apparatus' and acquires a responsibility for its actions. It is at this stage that you would need to consider whether individuals could be harmed by their participation (or non-participation) in the research, and more widely whether the way in which the problem is being formulated prejudges important issues to the detriment of those who are most vulnerable.

At all these levels of consultation and prior analysis the enemy is pre-supposition. Where research is commissioned and applied, the 'customer' will have preconceived notions of what the question ought to be and what kind of answers may be needed, but that is not necessarily the most fruitful way of considering the problem. Research into shoplifting, for example, might focus on how customers are to be prevented from purloining goods, because this is the 'obvious' question, and it would then come up with recommendations in terms of layout, anti-theft technology and the policing of customers. Ask the question 'Who does the stealing?', however, and we would probably find that there was more theft by staff than by customers. Reframe more widely, in terms of costs, and we might find that the financial cost of anti-theft devices or the cost in terms of staff goodwill of intensive policing exceeded the value of the goods purloined.

In such cases the researcher often acts as 'the outsider who sees more'; being free of the local preconceptions, he or she can sometimes help get the question fruitfully reframed. Some of the best 'academic' research (and extremely practical, in its outcomes) has looked at old problems from a new theoretical perspective and shown that they become more tractable when thus reconceived. An example here might be the shift in Home Office research in the late 1970s and early 1980s from how to change offenders to how to make theft less appealing and physically more difficult: see Clarke (1980), Clarke et al. (1978) and Mayhew et al. (1976). This involved a reframing of the question from 'How do we change/deter thieves and vandals?' to 'How do we cut down the incidence of theft and vandalism?', a simple shift of perspective but one with far-reaching consequences.

All research involves a paradoxical mix of involvement and detachment, however. (We say this most often about qualitative research – for example, participant observation – but it holds true for other styles as well, at least at the stage of planning and problem definition.) It is the outsider who can best see past local preconception to reframe questions in 'non-traditional' ways and whose lack of prior involvement acts as a guarantee of objectivity (a term we shall have occasion to discuss in more detail later in the book). However, it is the insider who knows what is actually done on the ground (by him or her, at least, even if not more widely), who sees immediate consequences of the actions taken and who has gone beyond the popular level of preconception to something more grounded in practice and personal experience. Good research needs both kinds of input. Norbert Elias suggested that the ability to see beyond local norms to the different experiences and beliefs of others was a defining characteristic of sociology, and the same can be said for all the social science disciplines and for good research into professional practice.

Beyond this kind of preconception again comes the level of 'political' (or ethical) preconception which concerns what is defined as a problem in the first place. This is exemplified in the change of focus in 'theft' research discussed above; by side-stepping a formulation which necessarily focuses attention on the offender, difficult ethical questions about the treatment of offenders can be avoided and, possibly, greater changes in the amount of theft committed can be brought about. If you are looking at adolescent smoking, you can focus on 'youth' as 'the problem' and try to change 'youth's' behaviour. Doing so has two consequences, however. One is that it distracts attention from the behaviour of tobacco producers, tobacco retailers, tobacco advertisers and a government which controls all these to only a limited extent and profits from the revenue which tobacco sales bring in. The other is that it re-creates the category of 'youth' as 'a problem'; it is all too easy to focus on changing youth's behaviour rather than looking at what young (and other) people do and why they do it. This point is made very well by Hilary Graham (1993) when she looks at the reasons why working-class women smoke as part of the way they cope with limited and difficult lives rather than as some sort of thoughtless psychological aberration.

Case studies

The discussion so far has been somewhat abstract and general. We can sharpen it up and see better the nature and diversity of problems that have to be faced at the design stage if we look at some concrete examples of surveys that have been run.

Travelling for heart surgery

In the late 1980s, the University of Plymouth in the South West of England was approached by a local consultant surgeon who had obtained money for a research assistant and had a problem into which he wanted to carry out research. Plymouth had a large district general hospital where most kinds of surgery could be carried out, but for certain rare operations it was necessary for patients to travel to London. The doctor was particularly interested in patients travelling for heart surgery.

Pamela Abbott and Geoff Payne at the University of Plymouth were the people who undertook the planning and supervision of the research, and Abbott (1992a) wrote an article on the planning stage which outlines some of the decisions which had to be taken. The first was definition of the problem, reaching beyond the immediate task and looking for what the consultant hoped ultimately to get out of the research. The immediately declared purpose was to gather information for dissemination in a booklet for patients and their spouses, identifying problems and sources of stress and passing on solutions at which others had arrived.

> However, it quickly became evident that the consultant had a 'hidden agenda': he was obviously interested in obtaining evidence to use in a campaign to procure open-heart surgery provision at the District General Hospital, and he hoped the research would begin to provide a basis for evaluating patients' experiences of 'internal markets' within the NHS. (Abbott, 1992a: 70)

In other words, the surface reason for the research was to reduce the pains and risks of travelling, for patients and their spouses, but a desirable outcome would be the opposite – evidence that these pains and risks were irreducible and that some other solution was to be preferred.

Facing up to this potential conflict of interest, the researchers provide a nice illustration of the difference between 'commitment' and 'bias':

> Those commissioning the research may have a political agenda, which may or may not be shared by the researcher. Provided the researcher does not have ethical objections to the purpose of the research, however, politics have to be kept outside the planning and conduct of the research. . . . we may hold a political position and have hopes for the outcome of a piece of research but are required to design it to allow the possibility that the opposite position could be upheld by it. . . . we tried to design the research so that our politics did not influence the research process or dictate the outcomes. (Abbott, 1992a: 69–70)

The outcomes to be sought, therefore, cover what the problems of travelling for this kind of surgery are, for both the patients and their spouses, and how (if at all) they might be overcome. The last element cannot be answered properly by a study of problems which looks backwards at problems experienced; it would require experimental or action research, trying out solutions and seeing which worked. However, an account of what the problems are would at least indicate what it is that requires attention, and collecting material on how past patients have coped with problems gives some basis for advising future patients. The nature of 'problems' to be examined is undefined in the brief. After listening to a discussion of their experiences by four former patients and their spouses, the researchers decided to concentrate on (1) what happened to the patients and their spouses and how they felt about it, and (2) on what information was provided for them, by whom and how useful it was. The decision to adopt survey methods was therefore taken, and a questionnaire was devised after group discussion with former patients (and their partners) and discussions with the consultant and the ward sister on the cardiac unit. To retain some element of the advantages of qualitative methods while also benefiting from the rigour and wide coverage of a systematic survey, questions were kept as naturalistic as possible. That is, the questions dictated the subject-matter of the answer, but they often did not prescribe a restricted range of choices within it, leaving informants free to define their own answers.

Initially the intent was to carry out a postal survey, sending questionnaires out to patients and their partners for self-completion. This would be cheaper than using an interviewer and allow wider coverage. However, drafts of the questionnaire were sent out to the patients and partners who had participated in the group discussion, and from their responses it became clear that the area was too complex to be explored satisfactorily without an interviewer to explain, prompt and ensure complete coverage. It was agreed that interviews could take place at the hospital, when patients came in for routine examination. They were, of course, to be voluntary and divorced as far as possible from the diagnostic and treatment routines. An interviewer was trained, and she then tried out a small number of interviews at the hospital, on the basis of which further minor modifications were made to the questionnaire.

A further major area of decision concerned the comparisons which should be made to control for 'extraneous explanations'. What was of interest here was the problems and experiences specific to *travelling* for surgery. However, if the questions were asked just of the patients and their partners, it would not be possible to separate out these specific data from the wider problems and experiences associated with having heart disease and having to undergo surgery, which would not be associated specifically with having to travel for it. It was therefore necessary to find some kind of 'comparison group' who had a similar complaint and underwent surgery but did not have to travel for it. An ideal comparison in some ways would have been Londoners scheduled for the same operation in the London hospital to which the South West patients travelled, but the London population was demographically very different from the South West patients. Some kind of matched sample might have been possible, pairing each South West patient with a similar London patient, but matching on a number of characteristics tends to be difficult, so the result might have been small and untypical samples. Further, the facilities and access for interviewing which had been negotiated in the South West were not available in London. It was therefore decided to use a group of South West patients who had a similar complaint and were treated in the District General Hospital. The consultant suggested a group suffering from a different kind of heart problem as reasonably similar to the target group.

A final question was numbers – the size of the sample. Here the major constraints were time and the purpose of the study. Four groups suggested themselves initially – travelling patients; patients with a similar complaint who received surgery in the South West; and their respective partners. To obtain information about factors such as initial expectations and information available before travelling, uncontaminated by lapses of memory and the effects of subsequent experience, the study had to be a prospective one, asking questions before travelling and then following up with a further questionnaire after the experience. A year's worth of referrals from the South West to the London hospital would give about 200 cases, which was a sufficiently large sample to allow formal statistical comparisons to be made (see Chapters 9–11). However, material for an information booklet for patients was required more swiftly than this time-scale would allow, so interviews were also carried out with patients who had received surgery during the past year, to give preliminary answers which would be contaminated by memory but still better than nothing as interim information.

Care for older people in the community

You should now read the account of Abbott's community care research presented as Example 2.1.

Example 2.1: Community care for older people

This is a piece of applied social research commissioned by and undertaken for social care authorities in Cornwall, in the far South West of Britain. The stimulus for the research was the impending implementation of the National Health Service and Community Care Act in April 1993.

> In preparation for the implementation of the Community Care legislation, Cornwall Social Services, Cornwall FHSA [Family Health Service Authority], Cornwall and Isles of Scilly Health Authority and Cornwall Community Trust were concerned to examine in detail the skill mix involved in providing community care for chronically sick and disabled people and the elderly. Their concern was that personnel should be used as appropriately as possible, and that qualified personnel should not be undertaking tasks that could be undertaken by others in providing services for these client groups. (Abbott, 1992b: 1)

The purpose of the research was to document what statutory and other services were provided for the client groups, and particularly for older people, in this remote part of England where population density is low and population dispersal high. A particular focus of concern was the management of the small number of cases where needs are complex and may be provided for by more than one source. Within this remit a more specific purpose still was to examine the overlap between district nurses and home helps in the provision of social and personal care and the efficient use of trained nurses as a resource.

Three general practitioner (GP) health practices were selected as a focus, in three different kinds of area. The research proceeded in several phases, involving a range of data-collection techniques:

1 The three areas were 'cased' by observation and talking to key informants, with the aim of identifying every elderly or disabled person on the GPs' books who received home help or district nursing care and every provision in the area which catered for old people's needs. An initial report on the available provision was made to the client.

2 Questionnaires were administered in their own homes to all the identified older/handicapped people and, where there was one, to the 'informal carer' (co-resident spouse, relative, etc., providing care). None of them refused to co-operate, though not all questions were answered satisfactorily by every informant. The questionnaire asked what kind of service providers had visited during the last year and how often, which of a list of duties or services had been received, what other services the informants used, how satisfied they were with provision, and basic questions about age, gender and whether they had living (and visiting) relatives in the locality. The degree of isolation of their home was also noted by interviewers.

3 District nurses and home helps were sent a similar questionnaire, asking what tasks they performed for each client and how they saw their role. Eleven of the 16 potential district nursing respondents returned the questionnaire, and 31 of the 37 home helps.

4 One of the researchers accompanied home helps and members of the district nursing teams when they visited clients, to talk to them less formally and to observe the work they undertook and how they interacted with clients.

5 Later, district nursing team leaders and home help organizers across the county were sent a questionnaire on the allocation of responsibility for different kinds of client and different kinds of task. This questionnaire included *vignettes* – short descriptions of cases accompanied by questions about who should be responsible for various care tasks in each case. Nineteen responses were received from home help organizers and 28 from district nursing team leaders.

One hundred clients were interviewed (all the users of district nursing and/or home help services, plus three identified users of day-care services). Just over 10 per cent received both district nursing and a home help service; the others had one or the other, in roughly equal numbers. Just under half had an informal carer – generally a spouse and mostly themselves over 75 years of age. The survey identified a range of services received by clients. Home helps performed domestic and social care tasks (cleaning, for example, or helping clients shop or collect pensions). District nurses performed most of the medical tasks such as changing dressings. Both services provided personal care (bathing, dressing, washing hair, and so on). Where clients received both services there tended to be a clear division of tasks, but district nurses often provided personal care on days when the home help was not visiting. District nurses were concerned about the ability of home helps to handle personal care without training. Home helps were annoyed at the lack of recognition of their skills, acquired from years of caring for their own families and relations.

Both district nurses and home helps admitted to performing tasks for patients which were not on the nursing/home help care plan agreed for the patient. For nurses these included minor social, personal and occasionally domestic care, but they were rarely performed on a regular basis. The home helps performed heavy domestic work or 'client-sitting' while the carer went out. Two-thirds of the home helps said clients telephoned them at home – mostly to ask for shopping to be done, but in five cases for other reasons, such as that they had fallen over. Several of the home helps said they sometimes made unscheduled visits to their clients, to see they were all right when they had seemed ill.

Despite poor pay and irregular hours of employment, there was a high degree of job satisfaction among home helps. Far from feeling exploited, most regarded their job as one requiring skills which they had acquired during a lifetime of domestic, personal and social care in their own and their parents' homes. The job was seen as rewarding and as deserving a higher image; several thought the title of 'home help' was inappropriate, preferring something with 'carer' in the title.

From the questionnaire to organizers and team leaders – those currently responsible for the allocation of services – we can see that the expected division of labour is seen as appropriate by both, with home helps allocated to domestic tasks and district nurses to medical/nursing ones. Personal care allocation overlaps, but the responses confirm that each 'profession' is likely to see it as somewhat more appropriately allocated to their own staff than to those of the other service. Both are likely to regard continuing domestic tasks – cooking, light cleaning – as appropriately allocated to the spouse, however old and infirm, but this is less likely to be the case if the spouse is male. It is also seen as appropriate, by both, to assume (without any check on the feasibility of this) that some domestic and personal care tasks will be performed by neighbours or visiting relatives (for example, daughters living within 10 miles).

Further reading

For fuller results of this study, and more on its design, see Abbott (1992c; 1994; 1997) or Abbott and Sapsford (1993).

This was another piece of commissioned research, called for at a time when a reorganization of community care for the elderly was impending and required to provide data to aid in that reorganization. The surface 'problem' was general and descriptive – to see what care older people (and a small number of the chronically sick and disabled) were offered. A particular focus, however, was to be the practice of the home help and district nursing services. Underlying the original request of the research was a notion that qualified nurses should be doing only nursing which requires appropriate qualifications, with other tasks carried out by unqualified personnel. It was envisaged that most of these would be friends, relatives, neighbours or the home helps, but in the event it turned out that unqualified staff attached to the district nursing service – nursing auxiliaries – also carried out some of these tasks.

The problem was therefore clearly defined from the outset. However, the academic commissioned to carry out the research was also interested in the nature of women's work and specifically the work and working conditions of home helps, so the design of the study had to include material relevant to this as well. An initial preconception, natural for a feminist, was that home help work would emerge as exploitative and demeaning. In many ways this was also the outcome; home helps are paid little per hour for an unreliable number of hours per week and are heavily controlled by organizers in determining the formal scope and content of their work, which may be taken as evidence of exploitation. However, the research was also able to show that the women enjoyed and valued their work and that it drew on a considerable (unacknowledged) skills base. That it was able to show this is due to the original design, which was kept open enough that unexpected findings could emerge. While tight and precise problem definition is necessary for tight and precise answers, an over-tight design leaves you unaware of other factors which might be important. (Worse, it may leave you suspecting the importance of other factors but without the evidence to explore them.)

The nature of the sampling was more or less dictated by the resources available through the commissioning agencies. A county-wide survey would have been more representative of the county's practice as a whole but might have been complicated by differences in policy or practice between different areas. To ensure that where differences emerged the samples were big enough to allow adequate analysis, it was necessary to take a cluster sample, nominating areas within which the whole case-load would be approached. Three GP practices would yield about 100 cases, an adequate sample for analysis and within the resources available. Practices were therefore picked which typified particular *kinds* of area and between them gave an idea of the range of working conditions and locally determined needs.

From the start the questionnaire to older people was going to be interviewer-administered – it was quite long and complex and not suitable for self-completion, particularly by people who might be quite frail and easily tired. Asking the older people themselves (and their 'informal' carers) was an obvious starting point in exploring what services were provided and ensuring that the full range of providers appeared in the research. For the more detailed study of what home helps and district nurses provided, however, it was obviously necessary to ask the providers. This allowed a check on the validity of answers from the clients and opened up areas for discussion where the providers' answers differed from those of the clients. It also permitted exploration of actual as opposed to formal practice – what extra duties home helps and district nurses performed and the extent to which their help was called on outside the formal framework of the visit (for example, by the client telephoning them at home). Here a self-completion questionnaire was used, and the main problem of self-completion questionnaires was inevitably encountered – that not all informants complete and return the questionnaire. This is a problem because those who refuse or cannot be bothered may be different kinds of people from those who comply, leading to biases in the sampling. Often it is necessary to build in some way of controlling or at least identifying these biases.

The questions were highly structured for the most part, consisting, for example, of lists of duties which might have been carried out. This limits the breadth of the information – it is always desirable to have an 'other' category under which informants may record items which had not occurred to the researcher before the event – but it is necessary in cases such as this in order to obtain comparable information. If we want to be able to say that home helps and nurses carry out non-overlapping sets of duties, or that one category does tasks which might be seen as the preserve of the other, then we need to be sure that people in each category considered and selected or rejected the same list of tasks on the questionnaire. (The list was as comprehensive as possible; it was compiled from the job descriptions of the two categories of provider, plus items which came up in early conversations with them, plus items drawn from previous research on the care of older people, plus anything else which occurred to the research team as relevant.) The questionnaire also included more 'open-ended' questions on job satisfaction and the nature of the job, however – general questions to which the informants gave extended written answers rather than just picking from a pre-specified list – which is what permitted new ideas about the jobs to emerge.

Clients and providers are the best placed to tell us what services are provided, and the providers can also give us information about how they feel about their jobs. In addition, the providers can report on policy, as they see it. The allocation of work and allocation policy are determined not by the immediate providers, however, but by their 'controllers' – the team leaders for district nurses and the organizers for home helps. A further questionnaire was therefore seen as desirable, to those who allocated work and implemented allocation policy. There are relatively few of these, so it was necessary to mail county-wide in order to obtain a reasonable sample size (and even then the numbers of completed questionnaires would be too small for formal statistical analysis). This questionnaire consisted mostly of open-ended items asking about policy, resources and constraints on allocation. Because there is a difference between what people might say is policy in general and what they might do in particular cases, however, some more realistic element was needed. It would have been possible to take actual cases and see what allocation was made, and to question the organizers or team leaders about why, but this would have been time-consuming and expensive, and there might have been ethical problems about discussing real cases. What Abbott did, therefore, was to construct fictional cases on the basis of real ones which she had encountered – vignettes – and ask the organizers and team leaders which of a list of services should be provided and by whom. This yielded useful data about the notional split in duties between home helps and district nurses, about differences in the ways in which the two services said they would allocate resources and about the extent to which each service thought friends, neighbours, non-resident daughters and (often frail and elderly) spouses should be responsible for some elements of the care.

The major 'political' issue in the research was that there were conflicts between providers which were not apparent at the start, and the district nurses felt under some threat from the impending statutory reorganization and any research which emanated from it:

> The home helps wanted to retain personal care and do more of it because they wanted to maintain or increase the number of hours they were employed. The [district nursing] auxiliaries felt that if home helps took on more personal care their own jobs were endangered . . . The district nursing sisters certainly justified their taking on clients who required only personal care, in part, as protecting the jobs of their auxiliaries, and I was certainly seen as a threat – a researcher who might recommend that auxiliaries were no longer required. (Abbott, 1994: 303)

The element of threat was overcome, fortuitously, by the openness of the design: as well as 'cold' precoded questionnaires there were plenty of personal interviews and opportunities for conversation and plenty of room on the staff-directed questionnaires for informants to talk about what was important to them as well as answering the researcher's specific questions.

Causes and effects of alcohol consumption

For our third and final case study in this chapter we shall look at a North American survey of drinking among women.

Now look at the description of this presented as Example 2.2.

Example 2.2: Antecedents and consequences of women's drinking

In the autumn of 1981 a research group at the University of North Dakota conducted a national survey of drinking and drinking problems among women. Four major sets of possible antecedents were explored in the questionnaire: personality variables and childhood experience; environmental circumstances (including the drinking behaviour of significant others, extent of social support, and the characteristics of the main interpersonal relationship); gender-specific stereotypes of drinking; and life-history events (both stressful events and more specifically sexual experience and dysfunction and obstetric and gynaecological disorders). There were also a large number of variables to do with consequent problems, including those which might be taken as particularly relevant for women – for example, impairment of household role performance, problems in relating to children, and accidents in the home. Following the lead of earlier surveys, questions were asked about driving while intoxicated, behavioural problems at work or loss of competence, and spouse's or partner's complaints about drinking or drunken behaviour.

The number of different problems experienced in the year preceding the survey was taken as an index of problem consequences. An index of alcohol dependence was also constructed, based on symptoms such as drink-related memory lapses, rapid drinking, drinking in the morning, inability to stop drinking before becoming intoxicated, and inability to reduce consumption over time; the number of different symptoms experienced in the preceding year formed the index. The questionnaires also measured demographic characteristics such as education, household income, marital and employment status. The main survey questionnaire was pretested on 100 randomly selected respondents in three cities.

Particular care was taken to select questions and phrase them in such a way as to maximize their relevance to *women's* lives. Care was also taken 'to maximize the validity of self-report. For example, drinking questions in the screening interview included a wide range of response categories and implied that frequent or heavy drinking was acceptable and normal' (Wilsnack et al., 1987: 92). Questions on potentially sensitive topics were asked towards the end of the interview, to allow some prior rapport to develop with the interviewer. Questions on sexual experience were presented in self-administered handouts which were then placed in sealed 'privacy envelopes' so that the answers remained unseen by the interviewers. It is notable that only four of the 1317 respondents refused to continue to the end of the interview once they had started it.

There were three main measures of alcohol consumption:

1 Thirty-day frequency – how often during the last month the respondent had taken a drink of wine, beer or 'liquor' ('spirits', for British readers). From this an estimate was made of the quantity of alcohol consumed per day (roughly two glasses of wine or just over two glasses of beer or shots of liquor). The main purpose of this measure was comparison with earlier surveys.
2 This estimate was refined, taking account of more detailed information (for example, on the use of 'regular' or fortified wine, on the usual size of the person's drinks, and so on). This refinement made a slight difference to the figures, moving a few of the 'moderate' drinkers to 'light drinker' status.
3 The first two estimates were based on what respondents said in answer to a question about their 'typical' drinking. The third estimate was an upward revision of these on the basis of answers to questions about occasional incidents of heavy drinking (six or more drinks in a session) which respondents may not have included in their report of 'typical' behaviour.

The sampling design deliberately over-sampled heavy drinkers, giving a larger subsample of such women than any previous survey. National surveys in the 1970s suggested that about 20 per cent of the North American female population took four or more drinks per week, and about the same proportion of the female population reported one or more problems connected with drinking – see, for example, Clarke and Midanik (1982). Sampling was carried out by the National Opinion Research Centre, which selected over 4000 private households from its pre-existing national probability sample, in about a hundred geographical clusters throughout 48 states. All women in these households were approached to ascertain their age (only people aged 21 or older were to be interviewed) and the extent of their drinking, and samples of moderate-to-heavy drinkers (500), light drinkers/abstainers (378) and former problem drinkers (39) were selected and interviewed. There was also a sample of men (396) for purposes of comparison, even though the main focus of the research was on women. Response rates as a percentage of individuals eligible for interview were 89 per cent for heavy or former problem drinkers, 83 per cent for light drinkers or abstainers and 66 per cent for men. (A major cause of 'refusal' among men was that full-time employment made them less available for interview.)

Data were collected by 120 interviewers employed by the National Opinion Research Centre. All but four were women, and none had any history of alcohol-related problems. There were three questionnaires in all.

1 A *household enumeration schedule* was completed by some responsible person in the household, listing the names, sex and age of all persons over 21 in the household.
2 A five-minute *screening interview* was administered to every adult woman thus located, with questions on drinking embedded in a series of questions about social and recreational activities, health and use of coffee and tobacco. On the basis of this each woman was classified as a problem, heavy, light or infrequent drinker (abstainers falling in the last of these categories).
3 The main *survey questionnaire* was administered to all moderate, heavy or former problem drinkers and to a random selection of light drinkers, abstainers and men. The interviews were carried out in private and took between 90 and 120 minutes. They were completed between September and December 1981, before the onset of the Christmas festivities.

From the data, weighting procedures were used (see Box 2.2) to estimate distributions and relationships in the population. The headline conclusions were:

1 Men, on average, drink more than women and are more likely to report alcohol-related problems.
2 Contrary to the popular belief of the time, there had not been any dramatic increase in women's drinking between 1971 and 1981 when figures from this survey were compared with the results of an earlier one. However, there were suggestions that women aged 35–64 had increased their drinking over the period.
3 There were strong indications that certain subgroups of women were at greater risk than others of becoming heavy drinkers and/ or developing drinking problems – those aged 21–34, women who had never married or were divorced or separated, unemployed women seeking work, and women cohabiting with 'quasi-marital partners'.
4 Depressive symptoms and depressive episodes appeared to be related to regular heavy drinking rather than to episodes of excessively heavy consumption.

5 Heavy drinking was linked with a variety of obstetric and gynaeco-logical problems, ranging from heavy menstrual flow to miscarriage or stillbirth.

6 Women who were heavy drinkers reported that alcohol improved their sexual experience. There was some indication that this may be a genuine effect, not just a matter of perception, but that the relationship may have been curvilinear, with most disinhibition at moderate levels of consumption and some dysfunction among heavy drinkers.

7 Young women drinkers (aged 21–34) were most likely to report alcohol dependence symptoms, drink-related problems, if they *lacked* stable marital and work roles. Women aged 35–49 were most likely to report these if they had *lost* such roles – for example, through separation or divorce or through children leaving home. Women aged 50–64 were most likely to report them if they were married with no children at home and had no paid employment. Women aged 65 and over were unlikely to report them at all.

8 There was no support for the claim of earlier studies that heavy drinking was correlated with discrepant gender-role orientation.

9 Multivariate analysis suggested moral/religious beliefs, availability of drink at home and association with others who drank as major predictors of drinking or abstention. The amount drunk was pre-dicted by association with others who drank, disruption or reduction of household roles and (surprisingly) the existence of a stable relationship in which the woman could 'talk out' her problems and feelings. Multivariate analysis of problem consequences suggested that those most likely to experience them were not just the heaviest drinkers but also the youngest and those with fewest household and work roles (contradicting a current belief that women who take on too much are likely to experience drinking problems). Reasons for drinking were also associated with whether consequences were experienced as problematic. Symptoms of alcohol dependence were best predicted by history of depression or anxiety. *How* the women drank was also predictive: heavy use of alcohol at home was strongly associated with dependence symptoms.

10 We should note, therefore, that different drinking behaviours can be seen as having different patterns of antecedent cause.

11 The amount drunk, and whether it led to the experience of prob-lems, was relatively independent of the number of stressful life events experienced.

Further reading

For fuller accounts of this research, see Klassen and Wilsnack (1986); Richard Wilsnack et al. (1984a; 1987); and Sharon Wilsnack et al. (1984b).

The 'problem' was to explore the antecedents and consequences of women's drinking. At the time when this research was carried out, American research on drinking and its consequences had tended either to make little distinction between men's and women's drinking or, if founded in a criminological tradition, to concentrate on the public drinking of men. Such useful research as there was on the antecedents of problem drinking consisted mainly of clinical studies of women in treatment for alcoholism – whose results were not typical of the general population of drinkers – or epidemiological studies of the general population which had representative samples but therefore tended to include only a very small proportion of problem drinkers. Existing studies also tended to focus on one kind of variable – personality traits, say, or environmental factors – and so give no picture of how different factors *interact* to produce drinking as a problem.

What was wanted was a sample scattered randomly across the entire United States and large enough to contain a wide range of drinking habits, from total abstainers and those who just have the occasional glass to heavy drinkers, and including some who have had problems in the past so that results for them could be compared with earlier work. This scale of sampling would not be feasible for even a large research team working alone, so they bid for and obtained research money from a national institute and hired an opinion research firm to carry out the interviewing. The institute already had a large preselected 'panel' of potential respondents, randomly distributed across the nation, and from this a set of subsamples of households were drawn, clustered geographically to help keep down interviewer travel. Screening interviews identified the women in the household and the amount they drank, and this information was used to draw samples of light/non-drinkers, moderate/heavy drinkers and former problem drinkers. This sample was *not* representative of the female population; deliberately, it included too many heavy drinkers. Note, however, that this was not a problem, as far as describing the distribution of traits was concerned (see Box 2.2).

The question of comparison arises almost immediately: if we want to know about *women* drinkers, how do we ensure that our results are descriptive of *women* and not just of drinkers irrespective of gender? The obvious course is to sample men as well, and this is what the researchers did.

A great deal of thought had to go into the screening interview and the main survey questionnaire. Past research was examined to yield questions worth asking about the amount consumed, about factors which have been indicated as possible causes or predictors of drinking and about possible problem consequences. To the long list of possible factors the researchers then added problems and stress factors which had not been much considered in previous research but which might be important specifically for women drinkers: 'domestic sphere' issues; life changes such as separation, divorce or children leaving home; and issues of sexuality and relationship. 'Tests' had to be found for psychological traits and states.

Box 2.2: Weighting

If you know that your sample is unrepresentative of the population because it is wrongly distributed on some variable – it has too many women, for example, compared with the population – you can make the figures representative of the population in this respect by *weighting*. This is best explained by an example.

Sex	Number in sample	Proportion in sample	Proportion in population	Weight	Weighted sample
M	200	20%	50%	50/20 = 2.5	500
F	800	80%	50%	50/80 = 0.625	500

Suppose you have a sample of 1000 people, 200 of whom are women, and the population has an equal number of men and women. You work out a weighting factor by dividing the desired percentage by the obtained percentage, and multiply your number of female cases by this factor; in this case the weighting factor is 2.5, so the number of women there should have been in the sample is 500. You do the same for the men.

Ways of asking questions had to be found which would not embarrass informants by asking them to discuss intimate details of their private lives with friendly strangers. (The procedure adopted in the end was to have questions on sexuality and sex life, and also questions on violence and illegality, presented to respondents on a printed sheet, to be filled in and sealed in an envelope, so that the interviewer did not know the answers.) Even the questions on drinking behaviour and amount drunk had to be tactfully phrased so that the respondent did not feel attacked by them – treating heavy drinking as normal behaviour, not as some kind of deviation to which the respondent was asked to confess. The questionnaire as a whole was tried out (*piloted*) on a separate sample of respondents, to check ease of completion and whether the procedures had the desired effect.

This kind of detailed attention to measurement and procedures is entirely typical of good survey work. Collection has to be systematic – every person has to be asked the same questions, in the same order – so that differences between people or groups are not ascribable to differences in the ways in which the measures were taken. They also have to be framed with the thought in mind that how a question is asked is at least partly responsible for how it is answered. As respondents we react to the apparent intent of the questioner, trying to make sense of what is being asked of us and looking for hints as to what is required and what the 'right answers' are. If a questionnaire implicitly says to us that drinking is something to be disapproved, we are likely to respond (even without knowing we are doing so) by understating the amount that we drink. We are also embarrassed by talking about some topics, unwilling to discuss them with strangers or even annoyed at being asked to do so, and unwilling to put ourselves in a bad light. Some topics probably cannot be tackled by interviewer-presented survey questions. The researchers in the drinking study decided that questions on sexuality were of this kind and opted for a self-completion form which gave some degree of privacy to the answers.

What was taken for granted in this research, however, was that you can obtain a valid measure of how much somebody drinks just by asking them. This had been the practice in all the previous research, but it is open to doubts about the accuracy of memory – our own knowledge of how much we drink and our ability to report on it. Another problem arises from the sampling in this study, which is confined to people in private households and excludes the homeless and those in institutions. It is possible that these excluded people, who may include some of the heaviest drinkers, may display effects seldom or never seen in the 'domestic' population. For overall estimates of women's drinking their exclusion is important, particularly as 'selection' for homelessness or institutionalization may not be the same for the two genders. See Godfrey (1986) for a discussion of these and other problems.

Practicalities

Problem definition

Thus there are four elements involved in the initial planning and definition of a survey, illustrated in Figure 2.1: problem definition; sample selection; design/selection of measurements; and the questions of social and ethical responsibility which I have brought together under the heading of 'concern for respondents'. They are shown as multiply interlinked in the diagram for two reasons – any of them can be the starting point of the process; and decisions made within any of them may have consequences for all the others.

We generally think of 'problem definition' as the first stage of any research – it comes first in any report of research. Not all research follows this idealized pattern, however. It may be that the idea for research starts not with problem definition but with sample selection. You may, for example, be a student required to carry out a project as part of your course, in which case your first concern may be to what situations or groups of people you can readily gain access, selecting theory to test or problems to explore which can be handled by research into *these* people or situations. Alternatively, the data-collection procedures might be the driving force of the particular project: this is often the case with research

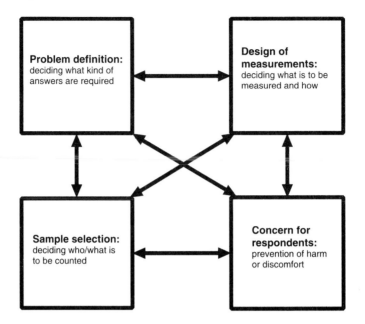

FIGURE 2.1   *Overall design of a survey project*

into personality or intelligence, for example, where instruments which have been devised have to be tested and standardized on large and varied populations.

Figure 2.1 is deceptively simple; each of the boxes can contain a list of disparate questions which have to be answered at the planning stage, any of which could have implications for decisions made under the other headings. Figure 2.2, for example, shows what might lie inside the 'problem definition' box.

Before reading on, spend a few minutes thinking what more detailed questions you might want to put in this box. Then compare your answers with mine.

My version of the box contains the obvious questions about 'what the problem is'. In the case of commissioned research we ask what it is the customer wants – and what he or she *ought* to want, as the question which is presented may not lead to the kind of answer that is needed. In the heart research discussed above, for instance, the immediate 'problem' was to gather information which would ease the lives of patients and partners travelling for surgery, but additional agenda items quickly became apparent: gathering evidence to support the creation of a local facility and making a contribution to the debate on 'internal markets' in the health service. Policy/practice research may not have an immediate customer but is similarly focused on producing information which will be useful (and

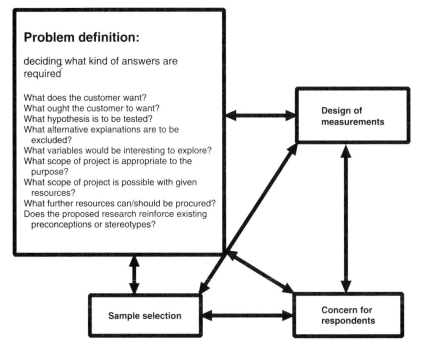

Problem definition:

deciding what kind of answers are
required

What does the customer want?
What ought the customer to want?
What hypothesis is to be tested?
What alternative explanations are to be
 excluded?
What variables would be interesting to explore?
What scope of project is appropriate to the
 purpose?
What scope of project is possible with given
 resources?
What further resources can/should be procured?
Does the proposed research reinforce existing
 preconceptions or stereotypes?

**Design of
measurements**

Sample selection

**Concern for
respondents**

FIGURE 2.2   *Design of a survey project: problem definition*

used) by practitioners and/or policy-makers. In 'pure' research there will be areas which need to be explored for a purpose, or hypotheses which need to be tested on the survey information. Under this heading we might also consider the question of preconception – are we limiting the scope of the research, and therefore of the answers it might produce, by 'falling for' a traditional or ideological construction of the topic area which closes off certain ways of thinking? (An example would be Hilary Graham's work on smoking, mentioned above, which treats it not as a pathological bad habit but as a reasoned behaviour in the face of certain kinds of routine adversity and thereby sheds additional light on it.)

An immediate further question is what 'alternative explanations' will need to be controlled in the design – what could shake the readers' faith in the hypothesis test or make them want to interpret observed correlations in a different way from that adopted by the researcher. This will have obvious implications for the selection of samples and the list of variables to be measured. It may also have implications for *how* samples are selected and variables measured; to ensure a valid conclusion, validity of design and sampling have to be built in from the start, and this is a form of 'control for alternative explanations'.

Finally, there are the sheer practicalities of scale and resource. Part of problem definition always consists of cutting the project down to size and addressing an aspect – or a level of approximation – which can be handled

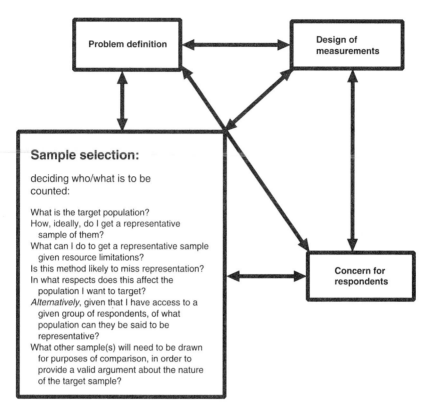

FIGURE 2.3   *Design of a survey project: sample selection*

with the available resources. This necessity is in perpetual tension with the need to design a project which will actually deliver conclusive (or at least strongly suggestive) and actionable results.

'Sample selection', similarly, breaks down (Figure 2.3) into a list of disparate questions.

Again, spend a few minutes thinking up your own questions and then compare your answers with mine.

We need to identify the target population – 'women', say, following Example 2.2 above, so that we can explore women's drinking habits. We can then think of a rigorous way of drawing a representative sample of them – which usually means some form of *random* sampling (see Chapter 3).

Again resourcing may be a key issue. The researchers in Example 2.2 had access to funding and were able to employ an opinion research agency which had already identified a representative sampling frame to carry out the interviews. If your resources were more limited and you had to do the interviews yourself, you would probably have to compromise and select something less than a fully representative national sample. You might, for example, have to draw your sample within easy travelling distance of your own base of operations. This, however, changes the population which can be represented – from 'women in Britain', for example, to 'women in the Middlesbrough area'. You would then need to construct your sampling pattern in such a way as to maximize the chances of your sample reflecting trends in the country as a whole – by making sure you have a mix of urban and rural areas and a mix of affluent and deprived respondents, by ensuring you cover a range of different occupations, by ensuring that you sample both women in paid employment and women who stay at home, and so on. You might want to add a sample from some other part of the country (Liverpool? London?) as a form of control for alternative explanation; if the results from the second sample paralleled those of the first, then you probably have a description of 'women drinkers', not just 'women drinkers in Middlesbrough'. Alternatively, you might be able to draw on someone else's survey results as a check on at least some portion of your own.

Note that specification of the population, properly a 'problem definition' task, is affected reflexively by how you do your sampling. For some research problems, for example, you will probably have to rely on volunteer samples; research on loneliness, for example, might be done by putting an advertisement in a magazine and analysing the replies. Your population is then 'lonely people who are prepared to fill in questionnaires voluntarily', however, and you would have to acknowledge that your research had no bearing on the sort of depressive person who has withdrawn from contact altogether. The drinking research in Example 2.2, we noted, actually explores *domestic* drinking – the drinking of women who live in households. It therefore has little or nothing to say about homeless women or those confined to penal or psychiatric institutions.

At this stage you will also be asking yourself about the *range* of samples needed, and in doing so you will again be exploring the nature and boundaries of your problem. In Example 2.1, for instance, the obvious informants on domestic services for older people are those who receive them or those who deliver them; they can provide different kinds of information, and Abbott sampled both. If we want to know about *policy* as well as *practice*, however, we need to talk to those who make the allocation decisions, and so Abbott added a sample of organizers and team leaders to her research. In the process she extended the nature of the 'problem', from 'Who does what?' to 'Why and in what cases are certain services allocated?'.

Alternatively, you might have started the research with a notion of what sample you want to explore. You are a teacher or a nurse, for example, so an obvious and very relevant research population is schoolchildren or patients, or other teachers or nurses. In that case you will be looking at the sample you have available, deciding what populations it can fairly be said to represent, and using these deliberations as the basis on which to decide what your research problem is going to be. Or, more often, you will be seizing a passing opportunity to obtain information in an area in which

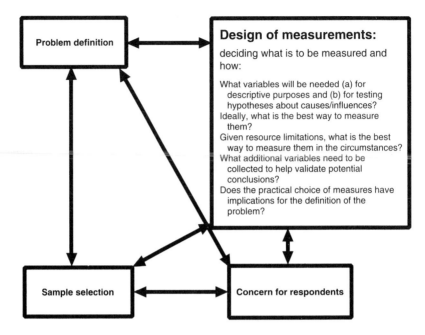

FIGURE 2.4 *Design of a survey project: measurement*

you have prior interest. Example 2.1 above is an example of this, in a sense; Abbott had questions to answer for the commissioning agencies, but she also took the opportunity to explore the nature of the home help job, as a form of women's labour which she had not previously examined.

Deciding on what is to be measured also involves a whole list of questions (Figure 2.4).

List your own questions before reading on.

Some of my questions are the obvious ones. In hypothesis-testing research, what are the dependent and independent variables, and what other factors need to be taken into account at analysis and therefore measured during fieldwork? (See Box 2.3 if you do not understand these terms.) In more exploratory research, what kinds of information do I want, how am I likely to want to interpret it, what alternative explanations may be possible, what data do I need to exclude these? Problem definition and listing variables to be measured are part of one and the same process.

Sometimes what is possible or convenient to measure may reflect back on the definition of the problem by trivializing it. We are interested, say, in pathologically deviant sexuality in the general population, but the questions we can legitimately and safely ask in a questionnaire to get sensible answers will have to be about the range of normal (common) sexual behaviours and preferences; this alters the nature of the research. Or our

---

Box 2.3: Variables

A *variable* is a *measured quantity*. Conventionally we distinguish between:

- *descriptive variables* – those which are just to be reported on, with no conclusions drawn about influence or causality;
- *dependent variables* – those we want to say are caused or influenced by others;
- *independent variables* – those we want to say are doing the causing or influencing;
- *extraneous variables* – those which, it might be argued, could provide an alternative causal explanation and so cast doubt on the one we are advancing.

For example, in a survey we might measure people's place of birth, their social class, their physical strength and their diet. 'Place of birth' is a descriptive variable: we just thought it was something interesting to put in the report. 'Physical strength' is the dependent variable, and we want to argue that 'social class', as independent variable, is a cause of physical strength: being of a higher social class means you will be physically weaker. However, diet varies with social class, so an alternative explanation of differences in physical strength might be differences in diet.

---

theoretical interest is in social class in the Marxist sense – the ownership or control of the means of production – but the Marxist class of capitalists is so small and so well defended against social researchers that we finish up exploring attitude gradients in what is essentially a middle class of managers, professionals and small proprietors – differing social images and perceptions of class interest *within* the middle class.

Doing acceptable research

Questions about how to measure variables and whom to survey slide imperceptibly into questions of concern for respondents (Figure 2.5). Again some of the questions are superficially obvious. You would not want to ask a question which caused all or some of your sample distress or psychological harm – for example, asking the recently bereaved about their feelings for their partners. You might, indeed, feel that bereavement was not a proper subject for survey research, if the recently bereaved were the target population; something more intimate, less 'objective' and more sensitive to counselling needs might be called for, if the research *had* to be carried out. This principle, of not harming the respondents, seems obvious in the abstract, but it is surprisingly often breached in practice. People ask children about their fathers or mothers, for example, without thought that some of them may recently have lost one or both by death or divorce or,

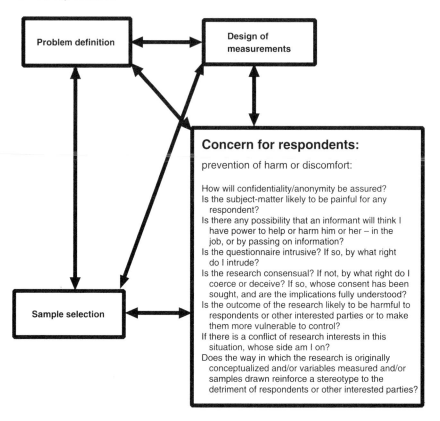

FIGURE 2.5 *Design of a survey project: concern for respondents*

worse, feel deviant and stigmatized because they lack one or the other. In courses with a research project component it is normal practice for tutors or external examiners to have to steer students away from 'sexy' topics which they think would be fun to explore, such as the experience of those who have a relative dying of AIDS or current ideation among women who were sexually abused as children. Some kinds of research are to be undertaken only when there is legitimate reason for them; otherwise, interesting as they may be, they are best left alone.

What might be accepted as legitimate grounds for research into the experience of AIDS?

One legitimation for such research might be that you are already working in the area – you are a nurse or a social worker who counsels relatives of AIDS patients, for example. It must always be legitimate to do research on your own practice, with the aim of improving the service you offer. We should note, however, that research into professional practice has its own ethical, political and practical problems.

What problems would you anticipate when conducting research into your own professional practice?

1 It is difficult to separate yourself from your professional presuppositions and socialization; research into practice can all too easily confirm one's current habits rather than subject them to test. On the other hand, if you succeed in problematizing your practice for the purpose of the research, it may remain a problem, and you may have destroyed the conceptual and emotional basis on which you carry out the job.

2 If the research involves the practice of others as well as yourself – the running of a ward or school or police station, for example – then difficult moral and practical decisions have to be made. Morally the most acceptable way to carry out the research is to make what you are doing public, and this also opens the way to substantive collaboration by colleagues. On the other hand, it is very likely indeed to change normal practice and it may lead some colleagues to feel spied upon. If you conceal the research you cause less immediate harm and disruption, but eventually your colleagues will learn what you have been doing and may not like it. (You may also, in some occupations, find yourself in formal or informal trouble with management!)

3 Many practice situations involve relationships of power which make it doubtful that respondents' consent can be given *freely*. If you are a schoolchild seeking good marks for essays, or a prisoner seeking release, or a patient dependent on doctors and nurses for treatment, it is difficult to believe that you will not damage your chances if you decline to take part in their research. There are, indeed, some situations where research into your own practice can give rise to serious ethical conflicts. A prison officer doing research on prisoners, for example, may want to promise confidentiality and that nothing said in interview will affect the prisoner's chances of release. On another occasion, however, the same researcher will be the officer reporting on fitness for release, and general ethics and professional responsibility may have to take precedence over research ethics.

A second legitimation of research which might otherwise be considered 'tacky' would be that it does some service for respondents, individually or as a class. Conventionally, researchers have tended to treat their respondents in the same way as physical scientists treat inanimate matter – as something to be *worked on* for the *researcher's* purposes. The conventional research process has been likened by the feminist scholar Shulamit Reinharz (1979: 95) to the process of rape:

> the researchers take, hit and run. They intrude into their subjects' privacy, disrupt their perceptions, utilise false pretences, manipulate the relationship and give little or nothing in return. When the needs of the researchers are satisfied, they break off contact with the subject.

This kind of use of people as objects to satisfy the needs of the research and secure the promotion or reward of the researcher is becoming less and less acceptable to the research community. We need to think carefully at the planning stage about whether this charge is true of our own projected research.

What might defend a piece of research against charges such as these?

A minimum justification might be that the future pay-off for the respondents – or people like them – would be substantial. This is a very paternalistic claim, however, that 'I, the researcher, know what you need and so I am justified in acting behind your back as long as it is for your own good'. A stronger move towards treating respondents as people rather than objects is embodied in the notion of informed consent, and most ethical codes of professional and learned bodies now embody the requirement that consent be gained before research is undertaken. Three points need to be made, however:

1 Explaining the purpose of the research could change the nature of the answers. Many researchers compromise by explaining who they work for and giving just a vague idea of what the research is about, but this does not amount to treating others fully as people.
2 It is arguable that the consent of respondents can never be fully informed, because they do not have the researcher's background in theory, scholarship and research technique – in the same way as you can seldom give fully informed consent to a garage mechanic's proposed repairs to your car, because you do not know as much about engines as the mechanic. To say this, however, is not to excuse oneself from providing *any* sort of explanation.
3 Most of us would agree that there are circumstances under which concealment and even downright deceit can be justified. If the research involved investigating corruption, for example, few of us would argue that the corrupt are entitled to be treated with full respect. There is a general feeling that the powerful can look after themselves and that it is those *without* power who need protection from researchers.

The requirement to be concerned for respondents goes beyond the immediate conduct of interviews and the procurement of consent. The last three questions in Figure 2.5 raise concerns of a different sort. The researcher is providing knowledge, and knowledge is power in the sense that research results will be used as evidence for and against this or that policy or practice. There is also the more fundamental notion that research conclusions become woven into the 'common sense' of the culture – or of that part of it that has the power to affect the lives of others – and so the researcher has some power to define who or what people shall be and to set up the agenda of what is expected of people. We have to ask ourselves, therefore, what harm can come from our results. (In Example 2.1, for instance, an outcome could be that people lose their jobs as personal care work is transferred away from district nursing teams.) If there is a conflict of interests (for example, between district nursing teams and home helps, in the case of Example 2.1), the researcher has to determine whose side he or she is on, or indeed whether it is proper to take sides at all. (Received wisdom is that research should be neutral. This seems to me desirable, but it can be achieved only to the extent that we start off the process aware of our own preferences and prejudices.) Finally, we need to be aware when planning research of the extent to which we cast powerless groups into a deviant or 'underclass' role and reinforce stereotypes about them. We shall discuss this further in Chapter 8.

Using the library and initial exploration

One thing which ought to have emerged from the three examples we have explored is the importance of library work in the early stages of survey research. We use the library to look for previous research and for national figures which establish a context for our own work. Earlier research shows us how the topic area has been theorized and understood and gives us clues about methods which might be used. We can also pick up other kinds of knowledge which we will need when planning the research: the numerical context, the formal and informal rules by which the area of study operates, and material on the experiences of people in the situation and the language they use to describe objects and events. Finally, the library may provide sampling frames and checks on validity and may enable us to build an element of replication into our design.

Other people's results are very useful. They may provide a comparison base, as in Example 2.2, where figures from earlier surveys permit comparisons over time. (Note, however, that for comparison to be possible you have to design your measurements and sampling pattern in such a way that they are identical to those of the earlier survey or at least contain the information for reproducing the pattern of the earlier sample – in other words, you need to be able to compare like with like.) Other people's results can act as part of the validation of your own argument: if you replicate their results in respects in which your research overlaps theirs, this may give you more confidence in the validity of the remainder of the research. National figures help to set your problem in context, showing how common or rare it is and who generally experiences it. You may need national or regional figures to plan your sampling so that the sample is divided up in the same proportions as the population on key variables (see Chapter 3) or to test, after the event, how representative a sample you managed to achieve. You may even find that you do not need to do the research at all, because usable figures already exist (see Chapter 12).

You will also need the theoretical, methodological, practical and experiential insights which the library can provide. Past work in the same or related topic areas will give you ideas about how to theorize the topic – what conceptual framework is to underlie the research – and how people have done such research in the past may give you ideas for use in your own research. It may even provide you with fully developed tests or sampling patterns. In practical terms, the library tells you what the 'ground rules' of the area are – what law or regulation underlies practice, what history precedes it, what images are presented of it in the media or by practitioners. Finally, qualitative research – and autobiography, and even works of fiction – in the same area may extend your grasp of what the problem or question *means* for those to whom it is important and for whom it forms part of their daily lives.

In practical terms, then, you will need access to libraries – physically, by visiting them, or electronically by using the Internet. (If you are not already a practised Internet user, however, you may want to limit your use of it to what is essential; now is probably *not* the time to become engaged in another long learning process.) In any library you will find:

- books, generally classified according to subject-based 'shelfmarks';
- the catalogue, which lists what the library stocks by author/name, title and, probably, subject area. The best catalogues are computerized and will allow you to search the library stock by different combinations of subject keywords until you find a relevant set which is small enough to handle.

Academic libraries and the better/bigger public libraries will probably also have:

- a stock of journals, generally arranged alphabetically;
- abstracts and other bibliographical aids – reference sources listing or even summarizing works such as books, journal articles, theses/dissertations, or other kinds of text.

Many of the abstracts and other lists can be consulted on computer – either from disk or CD-ROM, or via a telephone connection to a remote computer. Remote links on the Internet that you can access may include the catalogues of other libraries, which are another useful source of references. Where something is not held in stock, there is generally some way of borrowing the work or obtaining a photocopy of the relevant article – for example, via the British Lending Library in the United Kingdom. A fifth invaluable resource is volumes of published statistics (or material on fiche or film, or computerized access to official statistics).

It is true that most research reports start with some kind of review of the literature, and a 'literature review' which covers *all* the key works on your topic will probably be required of you if you are writing a doctoral dissertation; even student projects are generally expected to cover the key works in an area and to show some awareness of current research and theory. Good research uses libraries early in the planning stage. However, 'doing a literature review' is not where you start when you are planning your research. I usually start with something I have read in the past that seems relevant and useful to me, or with a subject search of the library catalogue to get out a fairly small list of books on the topic area, or by thumbing through current issues of relevant journals to see what people have published recently on the subject. Thinking about this small core of material gives you your starting point.

Having identified a starting point, you can scan backwards and forwards in time to make sure you have covered the important past work and to bring yourself up to date on current thinking and research. Scanning the past is done by looking to see what authors your starting point has drawn on and following up the references to them at the back of the book or article. Forward scanning involves (a) looking in catalogues and abstracts to see what more recent work these authors have published, and (b) going through current and recent journals – physically or by use of abstracts – to see what is being done currently (not forgetting the book review sections of the relevant journals, which will act as a guide to recent books). I also make a practice of noting the shelf-mark of books which I have found useful and going to that point on the library shelves to see what else is catalogued there. At this stage I would also dip into published statistics, having formed some idea of the problem and the likely sample.

Finally – but very much as a late stage of the process – I might do a subject search of the abstracts to see what I have missed. This would include a little serendipitous dipping into related categories, to broaden my vision and overcome newly formed preconceptions. This kind of formal review of literature used to be very time-consuming, but electronic means of searching have made it much easier to manage. Do not be afraid to ask for help, however; librarians are very helpful people and highly trained.

At the same time as you are exploring the library you will probably also want to explore the research setting and make your first approaches to informants. This is a good time for 'casing' the setting, if that is appropriate. You will remember that a quite extensive exploration preceded the questionnaire research in Example 2.1, trying to build up a complete list of the different facilities – statutory, voluntary and commercial – which were available to older people in the three GP practices selected for the research. This made it possible to offer a more or less complete precoded list of them on the questionnaires when asking about which services were used, rather than relying on what happened to be recalled in answer to a vague open-ended question. The researchers also talked to practitioners and policy-makers in the area. In the heart disease research discussed above, this was the stage at which views of interested parties such as the cardiac unit sister were obtained. The aim at this stage is to try to get as rounded a picture as possible of what different 'stakeholders' think is going on. The questionnaire can then be designed to show the extent to which their descriptions are accurate and can include key questions to cast light on any disagreements between them. Perhaps more important, if you have a prior idea of what their different concerns are you can ensure that your research is likely to yield information which will be useful to all of them.

Many researchers carry out informal or group interviews at this stage, as in the heart disease research. Again the aim is to give potential informants and other 'stakeholders' a chance to have their views represented and to talk about what is important to *them*, before being confronted by a structured questionnaire which is more likely to reflect what has become important to the researcher. A secondary aim is to obtain lists of items about which questions might need to be asked – kinds of problems, varieties of activity – and to get the 'flavour' of the language in which respondents talk about them, in order to construct questions which are easy for the respondent to understand and ask precisely and unambiguously what the researcher wants to know.

The research proposal

Obviously research proposals differ according to the purpose for which they are being drawn up. They all cover the same ground, however.

An *introduction*, or *rationale*, will say why the research is of interest – what the problem or question is and why anyone would want to do research on it. The justification may be in terms of public interest, or contribution to theory and knowledge, or evaluation of policy, or evaluation and improvement of practice. It will also contain at least the rudiments of a literature review. It may also be necessary to discuss ethical and/or political issues at this point, depending on the nature of the topic area, at least to demonstrate that the author is aware of them. The purpose overall is to explain why the research is worth doing and to show that the author understands key debates and results in the area.

Next will come a section on proposed *methods* (or more than one, depending on the scope and complexity of the proposal). This will outline what you are proposing to do and who your respondents will be (or what the settings are which are to be investigated, if this is not an 'asking questions' study but requires counts of objects or events).

- It will say what population is the target of the study and how it is to be sampled, justifying the method in terms of precision and representation and/or as a 'best compromise' adopted because of limits on resources or difficulty of access, and considering what the limitations of the sample are likely to be.
- It will justify the use of survey methods, given that surveys are good at asking researchers' questions but less good at getting at respondents' own understandings of their world because of the degree of artificiality involved in standardized measurement.

Box 2.4: Questionnaires and schedules

A *questionnaire* is a list of questions which informants answer themselves – a 'self-completion' instrument. These may be handed out by an interviewer (as is the case in the British Census), but most often they are posted to potential respondents. A *schedule* is a list of questions asked by an interviewer, face to face or over the telephone.

Postal work is easier and reaches a larger sample for the same money, but non-cooperation rates are higher and some topics (such as sexuality) are not generally considered apt for questionnaires which arrive without warning in the post. Interviewer-administered schedules have a lower refusal rate if the interviewer is competent, can be administered in a more structured and standardized way, can overcome differences of literacy or attention span (which is why they were used in Example 2.1), can be longer and more complex than postal questionnaires and can be used to broach more difficult and sensitive topics without causing distress. However, interviewing in this way is quite expensive in terms of the time required.

- It may have to justify collecting people's answers to questions and using them as an index of behaviour or intention, rather than counting observed incidents or outcomes (which is also a valid kind of survey if carried out systematically). A survey of criminal intentions which asked 'Do you intend to steal in the next six months?' would not generally be expected to produce useful data.
- If attitudes/opinions/reports are to be collected, it will have to justify the use of postal questionnaires or interviewer-administered schedules (see Box 2.4).
- You ought to give an idea of how you will get over or around technical problems such as rates of refusal and non-cooperation.
- You will need to outline what is to be measured or collected and how, justifying the measurements as valid.
- Finally, if there are questions which need to be discussed under the heading of 'concern for informants', this may be the place for them. Those whose approval or funding is solicited will want to see that you have a proper ethical appreciation of the duty to protect informants (and possibly others) from harm, and they may be alert to political consequences of your sort of research.

In essence, the whole of a survey project is contained in its proposal and the definition of the problem to be tackled, so this chapter has given an overview of what you will encounter in more detail in the rest of this book. Chapters 3 and 4 deal with sampling in theory and in practice. Chapters 5–8 deal with measurement, the interpretation of results and obtaining results which *can* be interpreted. Chapters 9–11 look at statistical analysis – a return to sampling problems in that statistical techniques are about distinguishing between real population differences and apparent differences which arise merely by the vagaries of sampling. Chapter 12 looks briefly at published statistics and their uses and problems. Finally, Chapter 13 brings the main points together and discusses how to structure and prepare reports of your survey research.

Further reading

Chapter 1 of Sapsford and Jupp (1996) gives a comprehensive overview of design issues in surveys and other kinds of research. The first three chapters of Gilbert (1993b) are also worth reading as an introduction to the research process and its relation to sociological theory, as is the first chapter of de Vaus (1991).

PART B

THE SIZE OF THE PROBLEM

---

3   The theory of sampling

This chapter focuses on sampling as it *should* be in order that:

- the sample is representative of its population within calculable margins of error;
- groups can validly be compared; and
- the size of differences or correlations between them in the population can be assessed.

The next chapter looks at how we *actually* draw samples in circumstances where, for one reason or another, these pure theoretical guidelines cannot be applied or it is not efficient to apply them in full, trying nonetheless to apply the same principles in unpromising circumstances.

Because the theory of sampling is based on a branch of mathematics (the theory of probability), we have to start with a short discussion of the mathematical description of samples. However, the mathematics will be kept to a minimum; you need to understand the principles and be able to apply them, but you will seldom if ever be required to do the calculations yourself. (If you have some facility with formulae, you will find some in boxes throughout the chapter.) I have provided some simple exercises; I presume you will probably do these on a computer or calculator, if at all.

Having established how samples are described statistically, we can go on to look at how the margin of error in estimating population figures from what is observed in the sample can be calculated. At this point we will also look at different ways in which random samples can be drawn and their advantages and pitfalls. We then move on to comparing groups. The importance of comparing like with like is discussed, along with how we obtain groups which can validly be compared when random sampling is *not* the appropriate method.

Some statistical techniques

Simple descriptive statistics: tables and averages

Sampling is about finding a group to survey which is enough like the population under investigation that valid generalizations can be made from the population on the basis of the sample. A first stage, then, is to *describe* the sample. The simplest and most interpretable descriptions are in the form of *tables*, showing the distribution of the sample on a variable or variables. Table 3.1 is an example of a *one-way table* or *frequency distribution*, showing the distribution in a wholly mythical sample of the ownership of cars, from one per household to four or more. Tables 3.2 and 3.3 are *two-way tables* or *crosstabulations*, showing car ownership separately by categories of a rough measure of affluence. Table 3.2 and the first column of Table 3.1 show 'raw figures' – the actual number of households. Table 3.3 and the second column of Table 3.1 show *percentages*, for easier comparison.

TABLE 3.1 *Distribution of car ownership in a mythical sample*

Number of cars	Number of households	%
Total	850	100.0
0	526	61.9
1	274	32.2
2	40	4.7
3	8	0.9
4+	2	0.2

TABLE 3.2 *Car ownership and affluence in a mythical sample: raw figures*

Number of cars	Number of households	Degree of affluence				
		No income	Little income	Low income	Medium income	High income
Total	850	200	300	200	100	50
0	526	200	270	50	5	1
1	274	–	30	145	79	20
2	40	–	–	5	15	20
3	8	–	–	–	1	7
4+	2	–	–	–	–	2

TABLE 3.3 · *Car ownership and affluence in a mythical sample: percentages*

Number of cars	Number of households	Degree of affluence				
		No income	Little income	Low income	Medium income	High income
Total	850	200	300	200	100	50
	(%)	(%)	(%)	(%)	(%)	(%)
0	61.9	100.0	90.0	25.0	5.0	2.0
1	32.2	–	10.0	72.5	79.0	40.0
2	4.7	–	–	2.5	15.0	40.0
3	0.9	–	–	–	1.0	14.0
4+	0.2	–	–	–	–	4.0

If you are not already familiar with the notion of percentaging, or expressing as proportions, see Box 3.1. This is an absolutely essential technique of survey research.

Tables are the easiest and most informative way of describing a sample or illustrating a particular point, and we shall be seeing just how much can be done with them in Chapter 9. Quite often, however, what we need is not a descriptive distribution of figures but an 'average' value, and there are three ways of expressing averages, depending on the level of measurement which is being employed. (If you are not familiar with the concept of level of measurement, see Box 3.2.)

One kind of average value is the *mode*, or largest category. In Figure 3.1, for example, which shows the income distribution in a mythical commercial company, the *modal value* for income is £300–349 per week; more people earn this amount than any other (see also Table 3.4). This does not tell us very much, but it is better than no information. For nominal variables this is the only kind of average that can be offered.

Some distributions have more than one mode – more than one obvious peak. Figure 3.2, for example, which shows the weekly earnings of white-collar workers in our mythical company, displays two distinct 'high points'. Often when this happens we shall suspect that what we have is two dissimilar groups added together. In this case we might suspect that 'white collar' comprises highly paid managers and poorly paid clerks and secretaries, and Figure 3.3 shows that this is indeed the case; when we show the two distributions separately, they barely overlap. Techniques for testing the significance of such differences will be discussed in a later section of this chapter.

For ordinal variables, where the rank order of values is known, we can quote the *median* – the middle case – as the average value.

Where a variable is measured on an integer or ratio scale, an arithmetic *mean* can be calculated as the sum of values divided by the number of cases. (If you do not know how to calculate means and medians, see Box 3.3.)

Box 3.1: Rates, percentages, proportions and probabilities

As you can see in Table 3.2, raw figures are not always easy to interpret when you are comparing groups of different sizes. Many more people in the low-income category have cars than in the high-income category, but this is misleading, because it is also true that many more people in the low category than in the high one have *no* car; the low group is just much larger than the high one in terms of total numbers, and we are not comparing like with like. What we need, therefore, is a way of controlling for size of group in order to make valid comparisons.

One common way is to express the figures as *rates* per something or other. Deaths are often expressed as 'per thousand of population'; speeds are expressed as 'miles per hour'. A very common rate to use for purposes of comparison, because it makes for easy arithmetic, is the rate per hundred cases, or *percentage* (Latin *centum* = 'hundred'):

$$\text{percentage} = \frac{\text{raw figure}}{\text{raw total}} \times 100.$$

In Table 3.3 the percentages are column percentages – the columns add up to 100 – and show the distribution of car ownership for a given category of affluence. An alternative form of presentation would be row percentages, adding up to 100 across the page, which would show the distribution of affluence for a given category of car ownership.

Another method of presentation which is sometimes used is just to divide the raw figure by the total, without multiplying by a hundred afterwards, and this yields a *proportion*. While percentages add up to 100, proportions add up to 1, and can be thought of as shares of a total of 1.0. So the share or proportion of the total sample that have no cars is 0.619 (instead of 61.9%):

$$\text{proportion} = \frac{\text{raw figure}}{\text{raw total}}.$$

Exercise 3.1

To practice these two techniques, express the following figures as percentages and as proportions: (Answers are at the end of the chapter.)

	Income				
	None	Little	Low	Medium	High
Total					
850	200	300	200	100	50
Percentage					
Proportion					

Another way of thinking about proportions is to consider them as probabilities, with 1.0 meaning 'certainty' and 0.0 meaning 'impossibility'. So a proportion of 0.50 owning cars would mean that any individual in the category had a 50% probability of owning one, and a proportion of 0.75 would mean that he or she had a 75% probability – that three out of four people in the category owned cars.

Box 3.2: Levels of measurement

We distinguish four *levels of measurement*. *Nominal* scales, as the name suggests (Latin *nomen* = 'name') may be made up of numbers, but these numbers do not stand in any particular relationship to each other and cannot be used to perform arithmetic. In fact, they might just as well be a list of names, and indeed they often are. We might have a scale made up of three values – 'belonging to John', 'belonging to Mary' and 'belonging to someone else' – and we could give these three possible points on the scale the numerical values 1, 2 and 3. It is evident, however, that we cannot use the commonly accepted properties of the numbers; 'belonging to Mary' is in no sense twice as large as 'belonging to John', for example.

Ordinal scales are made up of numbers which are in a designated order, so there *are* some relationships which can be deduced from them. However, you cannot do the full range of arithmetical operations on them because it is not certain that the distance between a given pair is the same as the (numerically similar) difference between another pair, and there is no true zero in the scale. An example would be the variable 'being North of London', with Watford coded as 1, Birmingham as 2, Derby as 3, York as 4, Middlesbrough as 5 and Aberdeen as 6.

To call something an *integer* scale guarantees that the distances between adjacent numbers are the same, but you cannot multiply or divide with the scale because it has no true zero. A commonly used example would be scales of temperature. On the Fahrenheit scale, water freezes at 32°F, and 90°F would be the temperature of a very hot summer. A ten-degree rise in temperature will require the addition of the same amount of heat wherever on the scale (within reason!) we are working; it takes the same heat to raise the temperature of water from 50°F to 60°F as it does to raise it from 60°F to 70°F. However, 90°F is *not* three times as much heat as 30°F. The same is true of the Celsius scale: the freezing point of water is set at 0 degrees, but this is in no sense a true zero – the temperature can drop much lower than zero!

Ratio scales are made up of numbers with which arithmetic can be done: not only is the difference between 1 and 2 the same as the difference between 3 and 4, but 4 is twice 2 because the zero on the scale is a true zero.

The mean is the most useful average figure for purposes of analysis, as we shall see, but it is not always the most readily interpretable. In a symmetrical distribution the mean and median are identical. The mean and median are fairly close together in the distribution curve provided by the incomes in our mythical company (see Figure 3.4), where the mean salary for the staff as a whole is about £290 per week and the median value is £305.75. If we look at clerical and secretarial salaries (Figure 3.5), however, we can see that most people are bunched fairly low down on the earnings

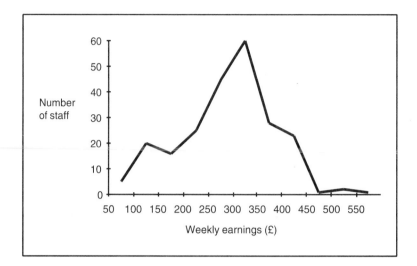

FIGURE 3.1 *Weekly earnings in a mythical company*

TABLE 3.4 *Salary levels in a mythical company*

Weekly earnings (£)	Number of staff	Managerial grades	Secretarial and clerical	Total 'white collar'	Manual workers
Total	226	19	38	57	169
50–99	5	–	4	4	1
100–149	20	–	15	15	5
150–199	16	–	6	6	10
200–249	25	–	5	5	20
250–299	45	–	5	5	40
300–349	60	1	1	2	58
350–399	28	2	1	3	25
400–449	23	12	1	13	10
450–499	1	1	–	1	–
500–549	2	2	–	2	–
550+	1	1	–	1	–

scale, with just a few earning substantially more. Under these circumstances the mean is consistently higher than the median; in this case the median value is £150 per week and the mean is over £180, a full 20% higher. With this distribution we should probably prefer to talk about the median rather than the mean, because it does not make much sense to talk about £180 as the 'average' wage when a large majority of the workers in this category earn less than it.

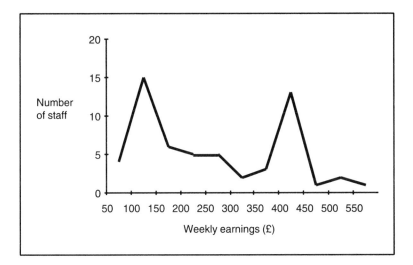

FIGURE 3.2   *Weekly earnings in a mythical company: white-collar workers*

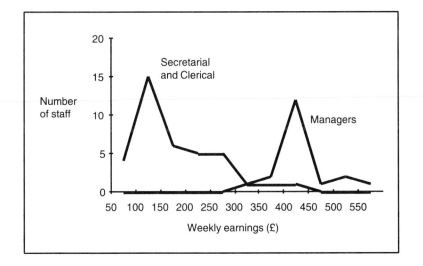

FIGURE 3.3   *Weekly earnings in a mythical company: managers compared with secretarial and clerical staff*

Box 3.3: Calculating means and medians

The median is the middle value of a distribution (or half-way between the two middle values if there is an even number of values), and the mean is the sum of values divided by the number of cases:

$$\text{mean} = \sum x/N.$$

So in the number sequence 1, 2, 4 the median value is 2 and the mean is 2.33 (2⅓).

Exercise 3.2

(a) What are the mean and median of the sequence 1,2,3,4,5?
(b) What are the median and mean of the sequence 1,3,4,5,6,7?

Answers are at the end of the chapter.

When working with data *grouped in tables*, the mean is calculated as follows:

1 Count every case as lying at the mid-point of the band of values in which it falls.
2 Multiply each mid-point by the number of cases that lie at it.
3 Add up these sums.
4 Divide by the number of cases.

See the worked example below.

The median is calculated on grouped data by assuming that the cases in a given band of values are evenly distributed throughout it. The simplest procedure is to start from a frequency table which shows cumulative percentages (that is, each percentage figure shows the percentage of the sample in that band or any lower one). Locate the highest band with a cumulative percentage less than 50; call this percentage *x*. Note the next cumulative percentage (*y*) – which will be higher than (or equal to) 50 – and the bottom value of this band (*z*). The range of scores in (or width of) this band we will call *w*. Then the median is given by

$$\text{median} = z + [(50 - x)/(y - x)] \times w$$

This sounds complicated but is quite easy in practice, as the following worked example will show.

For example, suppose we have the following grouped data, for which we wish to work out the mean and median.

Values	No. of cases n	Cum. %	Mid-point m	$n \times m$
< 5	10	20	2.5	25.0
5–9	5	30	7.5	37.5
10–14	20	70	12.5	250.0
15–19	15	100	17.5	262.5
$i = 5$	$N = 50$			$\sum nm = 575.0$

The mean is simply

$$\text{mean} = (\textstyle\sum nm)/N = 575/50 = 11.5.$$

For the median, we have $z = 10$, $x = 30\%$, $y = 70\%$ and $w = 5$. Applying the formula given above, we obtain

$$\text{median} = 10 + \frac{50 - 30}{70 - 30} \times 5$$

$$= 10 + \frac{20}{40} \times 5$$

$$= 12.5.$$

More complicated statistics: measures of dispersal

To describe a sample we need more than just the average or central value, however. Two samples could have the same average but be very different in terms of how the sample is distributed around that average. There are several ways of reporting on how cases are dispersed or distributed around the mean, but we shall concentrate here on the most important one for survey analysis and sampling theory, the *standard deviation*. To calculate this, you go through the following steps:

1 Express each data value as a deviation from the mean (that is, subtract the mean from it).
2 Square all these deviation scores.
3 Add up the squared values.
4 Divide by the number of cases.
5 Take the square root of the result.

The reasoning behind this apparently esoteric procedure is as follows:

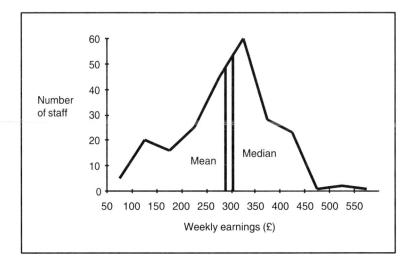

FIGURE 3.4 *Weekly earnings in a mythical company, showing mean and median*

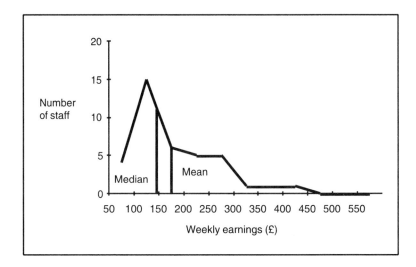

FIGURE 3.5 *Clerical and secretarial earnings in a mythical company, showing mean and median*

1   What we want to assess is the extent to which the mean is a good predictor of what any given value will be, so we need a measure of how far any given point deviates from the mean.
2   We want to give more weight to deviations further from the mean, which is what squaring them achieves – a deviation of 1 becomes 1 when squared, but a deviation of 2 becomes 4, and 3 becomes 9.
3   Then we add these up to get the total deviation score for the sample; but,
4   the size of this will obviously depend in part on the number of cases, so we express it as a rate per case by dividing by N (the number of cases).
5   We usually require a measure of dispersal which is in the same units as the average value; this is why we take the square root.

The figure resulting from steps 1–4 is known in statistical parlance as the *variance*. It is measured in squared units; for the worked example in Box 3.3, if we calculated the variance it would be in 'square pounds'. Taking the square root in step 5 gives us a measure of dispersal in pounds; this is the *standard deviation*.

You will probably never have to calculate one of these by hand – mostly nowadays we use computers, and many electronic calculators also have standard deviation buttons (usually labelled with the Greek letter σ). In case you ever have to do so, however, a worked example of a short-cut procedure for tables is illustrated in Box 3.4.

Calculating error

Having covered these preliminaries, we are now ready to proceed with a bit of sampling theory and consider how to pick samples so that population means can validly be estimated from sample means and the likely extent of error in the sampling can be assessed.

Random sampling

Statistics and sampling theory are based on the mathematics of probabilities, which shows us how to calculate the likelihood of any given event when its occurrence is *random*. To use the traditional example, if you toss a coin, you are equally as likely to get a head as a tail; the probability of getting a head is 0.5 and the probability of getting a tail is 0.5. (If you don't remember this idea of probabilities as proportions adding up to 1, look back to the end of Box 3.1.) If you toss it twice, each time you toss it there is an equal chance of obtaining a head or a tail. This makes the probability of getting two heads 0.25 (1 in 4) – *probabilities multiply*. This is because there are four ways in which the coins could fall, over two tosses, and only one of them yields two heads:

Box 3.4: Calculating standard deviations

The general formula for the standard deviation is

$$s = \sqrt{\sum d^2/N},$$

where d is the deviation of a given value from the mean and N is the sample size. However, it would be very tedious to subtract every one of, say, a thousand cases from the mean. It is easier to work from grouped data in tables and to use an arbitrary origin and values scaled in the same way as the real values, instead of the real ones. The formula to use then, as a short-cut, is

$$s = \frac{\sqrt{N\sum fd^2 - \left(\sum fd\right)^2}}{N} \times i,$$

where d is now the deviation of a row value from the arbitrary origin (the scaled value), f is the number of cases in the row and i is the 'band-width' – the range of values clustered in each row. This will become clearer if you go through the following worked example.

Values	No. of cases (f)	Arbitrary value (d)	d^2	fd^2	fd
<5	10	0	0	0	0
5–9	5	1	1	5	5
10–14	20	2	4	80	40
15–19	15	3	9	135	45
	N = 50			$\sum fd^2 = 220$	$\sum fd = 90$

$$s = \frac{\sqrt{N\sum fd^2 - \left(\sum fd\right)^2}}{N} \times i$$

$$= \frac{\sqrt{(50 \times 220) - 90^2}}{50} \times 5$$

$$= \frac{\sqrt{11,000 - 8100}}{50} \times 5$$

$$= \frac{\sqrt{2900}}{50} \times 5$$

$$= \frac{53.852}{50} \times 5$$

$$= 5.39.$$

1   H   H
2   H   T
3   T   H
4   T   T

In other words, if you can list all the probabilities of a series of random events you can count up the probability (the odds) of a given outcome occurring, and if you know the probability of a single random event you can work out the probability of combinations of events. This is good news for gamblers! For example, we can calculate the probability, when throwing three dice, of getting three sixes. The probability of a six on any individual die is 1 in 6 (or one-sixth), so the probability of doing it with all three is $(1/6)^3 = 1/6 \times 1/6 \times 1/6$ – which is about 0.00463. Translating this back into English, it should happen about once every 216 throws of three dice, so you would want odds of at least 215 : 1 before you would bet on it happening. (By comparison, when throwing two dice, two sixes should occur about once every 36 throws – the probability is given by $1/6 \times 1/6$.)

What we have been covering here is the probability of two or more events happening in sequence. The probability of two or more events happening when either or both is possible is calculated by *adding* probabilities. The probability of throwing *one* head with *two* coins can be read off from the list of outcomes above – one head is produced by outcomes 2 or 3, so the probability is $1/4 + 1/4 = 1/2$. The probability of throwing *at least one* head is greater, because we must include outcome 1, where both throws produce a head, so the probability becomes 3/4.

This illustrates a difficulty with the addition of probabilities – that you have to consider *very* carefully what you are adding, for fear of counting some outcomes twice. (Indeed, a colleague had to point out, kindly and politely, that I got this example wrong in the first draft of the book!) If we had just added the probability of getting a head on the first throw (1/2) to the probability of getting a head on the second throw, we should be saying that there is a probability of 1.0 of getting at least one head on two throws – in other words, certainty – which is absurd. This is because we would be counting outcome 1 twice. What we generally do – particularly where it is tedious or difficult to list all the possible outcomes – is to think about the probability of *not* getting the desired result, which often turns it from an addition problem to a multiplication problem. For example, the probability of *not* getting a head on two throws is $1/2 \times 1/2 = 1/4$, so the probability of getting at least one head is $1 - 1/4 = 3/4$.

Exercise 3.3

(a) What are the odds, with two dice, of getting two fives when you toss them?

(b) What are the chances of getting at least one five with two dice? (Try this two different ways – by enumerating all the possible outcomes, and by working out the chances of *not* getting a five.)
(c) The British National Lottery requires you to pick six numbers out of 49. What are the odds of winning the first prize by picking all six correctly?

Answers are at the end of the chapter.

Now, the point of all this is that if our *sampling* is random, then we can apply this kind of mathematics to it. A random sample is defined as one in which every member has an equal, non-zero chance of being selected. If we sample from a pack of cards at random, every card has 1 chance in 52 of being selected (and so the probability of the sample card being the King of Hearts is 1/52). With very large numbers, such as those we are typically sampling from when we draw survey samples, the calculation of sample probabilities would become extremely complex. Fortunately, however, there are short-cuts we can use based on the properties of the *normal curve*. (Indeed, even with these we do not have to do the work ourselves; obliging statisticians have done it for us and constructed useful tables and procedures which we can use without understanding the mathematics or having to do the arithmetic.)

The normal curve (Figure 3.6) is the distribution of items randomly scattered around a mean. Think of the shape as being a cross-section of a heap of sand and you'll be able to imagine why this is so. If you pour sand or salt through a funnel onto a flat surface you'll get a heap whose highest point is just under the funnel, and most of the sand will finish up close to the point just under the funnel, but a small amount will spread out in all directions – the amount getting smaller and smaller the further you travel from the point under the funnel. In the same way, the highest frequency in a normal curve is the mean (see Figure 3.6), and the majority of cases lie quite close to the mean, while a very few cases lie out in the 'tails', a substantial distance from the mean. Examples of distributions like this are height, weight, intelligence – most people are average or somewhere near the average, but some are notably below or above the average, and in the tails of the distribution, you get a very small number of people taller than 6 ft 6 in or shorter than 4 ft.

It is a property of this distribution that one standard deviation marks off a fixed proportion of the cases, whatever the nature of the items being counted and whatever the units of measurement. This is what we mean by calling it the *standard* deviation – it has been *standardized* to eliminate the effects of sample size and units of measurement. One standard deviation marks off about a third of the normal distribution (see the lines on Figure 3.6), and about two-thirds of the cases will lie within plus or minus one standard deviation of the mean. Ninety-five per cent of cases lie within a range of about four standard deviations around the mean (from $+1.96$

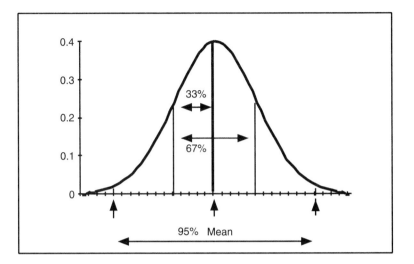

FIGURE 3.6   *The normal curve: percentages of sample*

standard deviations to –1.96), and 99 per cent lie within a range of about five standard deviations (from +2.58 to –2.58).

Estimating and minimizing error

Standard errors and confidence limits

The likelihood of random samples representing their parent population, if they are randomly drawn from it, also follows a normal distribution. If a year's intake at a school consists of 100 pupils – 50 boys and 50 girls – and you repeatedly pick samples of 10, a common result ought to be a sample of five boys and five girls, exactly representing the population with respect to gender. Almost as common will be a sample of either six boys and four girls, or six girls and four boys, so the chances of getting either of these – six of one gender and four of the other – in your sample are actually greater than the chance of getting a perfectly representative sample. Very occasionally you will manage to pick a sample with nine of one gender and only one of the other, or even a sample containing only girls or only boys, but this should *very* rarely happen.

Exercise 3.4

How rarely?

The answer is at the end of the chapter.

Box 3.5: The standard error

The standard error is a measure of the distribution of sample means about a population mean, in random sampling – it is, if you like, a standard deviation of possible sample means. It may be estimated from the standard deviation of the sample and the sample size; the formula is

$$s_m = s_x/\sqrt{N},$$

where s_m is the standard error of the mean, s_x is the sample standard deviation and N is the sample size. So, in the example in Box 3.4 the standard deviation was 5.39 and the sample size was 50. The standard error of the mean, as estimated from this sample, is therefore given by

$$s_m = 5.39/\sqrt{50}$$

$$= 0.762.$$

If the sample size had been 100, the standard error would have worked out as 0.539 – a smaller figure, but doubling the sample size does not halve the standard error, because the *square root* of the sample size is what is involved. You would have to increase the sample size to 200 to halve the standard error to 0.381.

Try this calculation for yourself.

What we are asking about here is how well the *mean* of the sample matches the mean of the population. (Dichotomies are unique among nominal distributions in that they behave like integer or ratio scales (see Box 3.2) – it makes sense to talk about them having a *mean*. If gender is coded 1 (female) or 0 (male), then a sample with a mean of 0.5 has half of each gender. A sample with a mean of 0.6 has six girls for every four boys, and a sample with a mean of 0.4 has four girls to six boys. If the samples are randomly drawn, their means will follow a random distribution with its own 'standard deviation', which is called the *standard error* or *sampling error* (see Box 3.5). Figure 3.7 illustrates the distribution of means in 100 simulated random samples, with the distribution of cases in one sample also shown for purposes of comparison.

With these tools we are now in a position, provided our sampling was random, to estimate the population mean from the sampling mean and to specify how likely the result is to be accurate.

The best estimate of the population mean is the sample mean. The majority of samples drawn at random from a population will have a mean which equals or comes very close to the population value. Some will have a

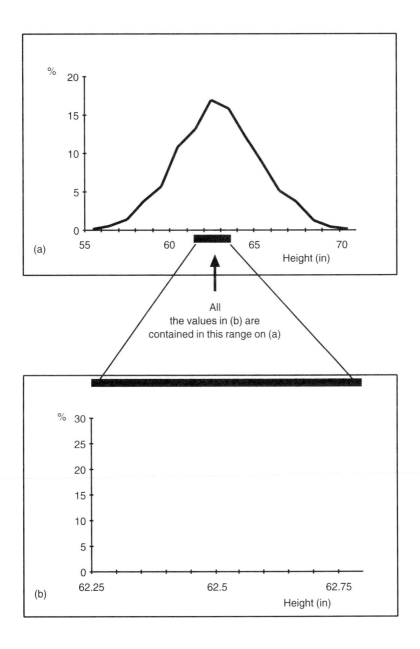

FIGURE 3.7 *Mothers' heights: (a) distribution of a single simulated sample; (b) distribution of means in 100 simulated samples*

Source: derived and adapted from Schofield (1996: Figures 2.4–2.6).

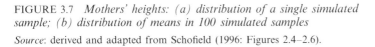

mean rather different from the population one, however, and a few will be very different indeed. So how do we know whether we have a 'good' or a 'bad' sample?

The standard error, as we have seen, is a measure of location of sample means: about two-thirds of the sample means will lie within plus or minus one standard error of the population mean, 95 per cent will lie within plus or minus 1.96 standard errors, and 99 per cent will lie within ±2.58 standard errors. We do not know the population mean, but we estimate it from the sample.

We do not know the standard error of the population, but again we use the sample figure as a best estimate. Now what we are saying is that the true mean probably lies near the sample mean, and we can put a figure to that 'probably' by using the standard error.

This is the time to take a gamble. Two-thirds of the sample means will lie within one standard error of the population mean, but 2 : 1 is not very good odds: to be wrong one time out of three, is not an adequate performance. Conventionally, we set ourselves stricter criteria than this and specify the range within which 95 per cent or even 99 per cent of sample means ought to lie – a probability of only 1 in 20 or even 1 in 100 of being badly wrong.

This range within which the sample mean lies with known probability is called the *confidence interval*. Using the standard error, we can specify lower and upper limits (called *confidence limits*) within which we should expect the mean of 95 (or 99) per cent of the possible samples to lie, by taking the sample mean and adding or subtracting 1.96 (or 2.58) times the standard error.

So, in the case of the example that was used in Boxes 3.3 and 3.4, the mean was 11.5 and the standard error was 0.762. It is 95 per cent likely, therefore, that the population mean lies between 10.01 and 12.99 – these are the 95% confidence limits – and 99 per cent likely that it lies between 9.53 and 13.47.

Run through these calculations for yourself, to make sure you follow what is being done.

System and stratification

Random samples may be selected manually or by computer.

- The first requirement is a complete and accurate list of the population to be sampled – known as the *sampling frame*. (Ways round this requirement, when such a list is not available, are discussed in the next chapter.)
- Every member of the population should be assigned a unique number.

- By far the best way to proceed thereafter is to use a computer to generate a suitable list of random numbers to enable you to select an appropriate sample by picking the cases corresponding to these numbers.
- Failing this, a printed set of random numbers may be used – as found in a set of statistical tables or at the back of a statistics textbook.
- First you look at the size of the population and decide what numbers you can use to give every case an equal chance of being selected. For example, if your population consists of 1000 cases you would need three digits from the tables to represent the cases – from 000 to 999, with 000 standing for the thousandth case. If you had a population of 100, you could use two digits – from 00 to 99. With a population of 500 you would need three digits, but each case could be represented by two possible numbers; case 1 would be selected by 001 and 501, case 2 by 002 and 502, and so on. With a population of 800 you would need three digits, but the numbers from 801 to 999 and 000 would have to be discarded – when they cropped up you would pass on to the next number without selecting a case.
- Then you pick a starting point on the table at random – with a pin, for example – and take the next two or three digits (however many you are using) as the first case number, the next two or three as the second, and so on.

With samples from small finite populations you can proceed by putting all the numbers on pieces of paper in a hat and drawing out as many as you require. If what you want is a one in two sample or one in six or one in 37 you could use a mechanical device such as a coin or die or roulette wheel to decide, for each case, whether it was in or out of the sample. It really does not matter what means you use, provided every case has an equal, non-zero chance of being selected.

Picking random samples by most of these methods is laborious or requires resources such as computers or random number tables. For many purposes a *systematic* sample is an adequate substitute for a true random one. This is a sample selected by taking every nth case, where $1/n$ is the *sampling fraction* – the population size divided by the sample size. So if you had a population of a 1000 and wanted a sample of a 100, the sampling fraction would be $100/1000 = 1/10$ and you would pick every tenth case – from a randomly selected starting point in your sampling frame.

This will work adequately provided there is no *system* in your sampling frame – provided, in other words, that the cases are not listed in some systematic order. As an example of what can go wrong when the sampling frame is in some systematic order and you use systematic sampling methods, consider the case of a 'social' housing estate I once encountered on the outskirts of Manchester. Flats were arranged in blocks of eight. On the ground floor the two outside flats were adapted for people with physical disabilities, and the two inside ones were occupied by older people

5 Two-parent	6 One-parent	7 One-parent	8 Two-parent
1 Disabled	2 Elderly	3 Elderly	4 Disabled

FIGURE 3.8 *Arrangement of flats in a social housing estate*

TABLE 3.5 *Systematic samples on a social housing estate (%)**

	Sampling fraction					
Category	All flats	One in two	One in three	One in four	One in five	One in six
Disabled	25.0	25.0	25.0	50.0	25.0	25.0
Elderly	25.0	25.0	25.0	–	25.0	25.0
One-parent	25.0	25.0	25.0	–	25.0	25.0
Two-parent	25.0	25.0	25.0	50.0	25.0	25.0

* It is assumed that sampling starts from case 1.

for whom climbing stairs would be a problem. The upper floor had two-parent families in the outside (larger) flats and one-parent families in the middle ones; the two-parent families tended on the whole to have more children and therefore needed the larger accommodation. The pattern is illustrated in Figure 3.8, and the results of a number of different sampling fractions are shown in Table 3.5. The first column gives the census – the true percentages. Most of the other columns provide representative samples, surprisingly, despite the extreme degree of system in the sampling frame. You can see in the '1 in 4' column, however, that badly distorted samples can be produced when the system in the sampling coincides with the system in the sampling frame. This kind of distortion can be avoided, sometimes, by taking a random case from within each interval defined by a sampling fraction, rather than always taking the first case. The problem will remain, however, if the research needs to sample some pairs of cases lying next to each other in the sampling frame, because the systematic method of selection will fail to pick any such pairs. When sampling from the electoral roll, for example, there is little chance for both of a pair of spouses to appear in a sample, because co-resident people are listed next to each other in the list.

The failures of systematic sampling illustrate what we mean by the term 'random'. I have refrained from defining it so far because it has little meaning in itself; it is what the philosopher J.L. Austin used to call 'a trouser word', where the negative wears the trousers. You cannot demonstrate that a sample or set of figures *is* random until you have defined what you mean on this occasion by *non*-random, and whether figures are acceptable as random numbers depends on the use to which they are to be put. A random sample is one which does *not* exhibit systematic effects which we would want to avoid (as in the 'one in four' column of Table 3.5), and a systematic sample which can be guaranteed not to exhibit such patterns is an acceptable one. However, we cannot know beforehand all the patterns which might be buried in the sampling frame, so it is probably better to use true random sampling wherever possible.

Thus we have seen that system in sampling can lead to grossly unrepresentative samples. However, it is also possible to take advantage of system in the underlying data to *increase* the precision of measurement by reducing the standard error, by employing techniques of *stratified sampling*. Where you know beyond doubt that some variable will be related to the attitude or characteristic you are trying to estimate in the population, you can reduce the error of estimation by using this variable as a basis of sampling. You split the sample into groups or *strata* by the values of this variable and sample randomly within each group, setting the number to be sampled in a group proportional to the size of stratum in the population. For example, suppose you wanted to assess people's attitudes to the erection of a new supermarket, and previous surveys had shown that attitudes varied very much with social class: the richer inhabitants of the area were keener to have its rural charm unsullied by building, the poorer ones were sick of having to take a bus into town to do the shopping, and those in the middle were more mixed in their response. If you drew a simple random sample there would always be *some* chance that these three groups would not be represented in the sample in the same proportion as the population. You can eliminate this risk by drawing samples from the three groups separately, in proportion to their numbers in the population, and combining the answers to estimate the overall average attitude. Box 3.6 illustrates how to calculate the standard error from such a sample.

Box 3.6 allows us to note one final point about stratification in sampling: the gains are not always as large as advertised! Stratification always improves the estimate of population means, provided the strata are fairly distinct from each other and that each stratum is reasonably homogeneous. However, we can see in this example, where the strata are evidently distinct but there is some degree of internal variation, such as would be expected in real life that the improvement in standard error is in the right direction but not very large. The gain would be larger, however, with bigger samples and measurement scales with more points on them; there is not much space for groups to be distinct on a three-point scale. Thus it is probably worth stratifying your sample where it is important that it is representative on a given variable and the effort of doing so is not very large. However, the major use of stratification in normal practice is to ensure that important

Box 3.6: Standard errors with stratified samples

Stratification is a design principle for samples which aims to reduce the standard error by controlling a proportion of the variance. If you know your composition with respect to some variable, you can 'take out' the variance due to that variable by deliberately structuring your sample so that it is exactly representative of the population in this respect. You pick groups (*strata*) in proportion to the incidence of a given value of the variable in the population, so there is no error in this respect. The only variation left is the variation *within* groups. If you can pick groups which are very distinct with respect to the dependent variable but fairly homogeneous within the groups, the standard error will be reduced compared with the standard error of a similar-sized simple random sample, and the standard error of a stratified sample can never be *greater* than that of a simple random sample of the same size – at worst it will be the same.

For example, the figures below are from a fictional sample of Christians and lions, asked about their attitudes to gladiatorial combat; the scores range from 1 (strongly against) to 3 (strongly in favour). The Christians are against the arena on the whole, but some are resigned to their fate and some actively welcome martyrdom. The lions tend overwhelmingly to favour the arena or at least to think it no worse than any other way of ordering mealtimes – except for one, who is a vegetarian. The mean scale values for the sample are 2.14 for the sample as a whole, 2.78 for the lions and 1.5 for the Christians.

Now, we can work out standard deviations (SDs) for the Christians and lions separately, and these lead to sampling errors (SEs) which can be used, with the group means, to give a much more accurate estimate of Christian and lion opinion than the estimates derived from the overall sample.

Value	Christians f_c	Lions f_l	Total f
1	30	1	31
2	15	9	24
3	5	40	45
N =	50	50	100
mean =	1.50	2.78	2.14
Group SD	0.671	0.429	0.860
SE	0.0949	0.0607	0.086

Now, finally, the *variance* of a group is the mean sum of squared deviations from the mean ($\sum fd^2/N$), and it is a property of variances that the variance of samples added together is equal to the sum of the variances calculated from the samples independently (Hansen et al., 1953: 187). So we can calculate a revised (and, we hope, smaller) standard error for the sample as a whole by making use of this:

---

sum of squared deviations within groups = 33.08,

estimated SD $= \sqrt{\sum fd^2/N}$,   = 0.5752,

estimated SE $= SD/\sqrt{N}$,   = 0.058,

compared with a 'simple random sample' estimate of 0.086.
    Note that if we had used disproportionate stratification, in order to over-sample some rare but important group, it would have been necessary to use the *weighted* sum of variances. (It would not be necessary to weight the figures themselves as well, however.)

---

groups are adequately covered, with sufficient numbers to allow us to explore the relationship of variables within them; stratified sampling can be used to make sure that groups which are very rare in the population are sampled in sufficient numbers for conclusions to be drawn about them. In this case you would be sampling disproportionately, but you could get back to a true estimate of the population average by weighting the figures (see Box 2.2).

Now re-read Example 1.2 above, on the British General Household Survey, for another example of stratified sampling in use.

Comparing groups

Hypothesis testing and comparison

Some surveys require estimation of population parameters – surveys for planning purposes, for example, where what is crucial is to estimate the numbers who are in need of a given social provision such as school places or sheltered housing or transport, or the numbers who would pay for such a service if it were provided. Most, however, are carried out in order to facilitate comparisons – to say how different a given group is from the general population, or to compare two groups. This is a key element in a lot of 'theoretical' research, testing for differences between groups which ought to occur if a given theory is adequate to describe them. It is also a key element of all evaluative research which looks at the effects or treatment or provision or character or circumstance and wants to say that people living in some circumstances are different in some way from those who live in others (for example, average health of the affluent and the deprived) or that people have changed as a result of some treatment. It is also a powerful tool for the *ad hoc* analysis of survey data, characterizing a population by looking for differences: do men and women have the same attitudes to something, do the young differ from the old, do the affluent differ from the deprived?

The model for all comparison of groups is the *experiment*, where a change is made to one group but not to another which is otherwise identical and the dependent variable is measured before and after the experimenter makes some change to the independent variable. (For example, two groups are formed by random allocation of a pool of patients to one or the other, a new drug is administered to one but not the other, and their state of health is measured before the administration and at the end of the experiment.) If the basic conditions can be met – that the two groups are identical except for the treatment and that they have identical experiences during the course of the experiment except for the administration of the treatment – then such studies offer very sound evidence for causal effects.

Survey research is generally called into play to look at cases where experiments cannot be carried out or are unsuitable for the purpose. This may be because it is necessary to obtain measurements from a much larger number than an experiment could handle, in order to have reasonable faith in the results. It may be because it is unethical to use experimental techniques. (You cannot, for example, cause one group of people to smoke and withhold tobacco from the other with the intent of measuring incidence of lung cancer many years later.) It may be, indeed, because an experiment is literally impossible: you cannot, for example, assign a gender at random to subjects and then test for consequent differences in attitude. In all these cases we would either capitalize on natural events or explore naturally occurring variation.

- We might look for a 'natural experiment' – an event in the real world which could be seen as constituting a 'treatment' – and compare a relevant dependent variable before and after the event and between those to whom the event occurred and those who did not experience it. One example of this would be the Connecticut Crackdown research (Campbell, 1969; Campbell and Ross, 1968), comparing traffic fatalities between a US state in which draconian traffic laws were introduced to try to prevent accidents and other surrounding states where this did not occur. Another would be Hilde Himmelweit's comparison of two English regions in the early days of British television, one of which could receive the television programmes while broadcasting stations had not yet been built in the other (Himmelweit et al., 1958).
- Alternatively we might survey a population and look for differences between one group and another. An example would be the research carried out by Richard Doll and Bradford Hill (1950; 1954; 1956; 1964) into cancer among medical practitioners who were current smokers, had given up smoking or had never taken up the habit. Another would be the community care research described in Example 2.1 above, comparing attitudes and practices of home helps and district nurses.

Yet another would be the study of voting behaviour carried out by Himmelweit et al. (1985), trying to predict political allegiance from background, socialization and character.

Such comparisons will never carry quite the conviction of experimental studies, because we can never be quite sure that the groups being compared were identical in the first place and the 'treatment' will never be quite as precisely defined and measured, but if carried out with rigour and from a sound basis of sampling they may be very revealing. Indeed, some survey studies are superior to experimental studies by reason of their representative sampling of the relevant population.

The problem comes when you think you have found a difference. We have noted that some samples represent the population but that a few, even if selected by random methods, can be very different from it. When you obtain a difference between two groups, is it big enough to take seriously, or just a freak of sampling? Is it possible that what you have is a population in which the two groups do not differ, but a somewhat variant sample in which they appear to do so? Can we treat our figures as indicating that the population splits into two relatively independent groups with respect to the variable of interest – as is the case in Figure 3.4 – or have we succeeded merely in obtaining differing samples, with the two apparently different groups selected, by chance, from different ranges of the underlying single distribution? In statistical parlance, is our difference *statistically significant*?

When comparing means we can use some of the same tricks that we used for determining confidence limits, based on the same kind of theory. What we do is to test the *null hypothesis* that there is no real difference between the two groups in the population – that the data are best fitted by positing a single continuous distribution. Then we set a probability for how unlikely this assumption has to be – how poor a fit the model is – before we feel justified in rejecting it. If our result could be explained away as sampling error two times out of three, or one time in four, or even one in eight, we would not feel justified in asserting it as representing a difference in the population. We begin to feel confidence at one chance in 20 (a probability of error of 0.05, described as *significant at the 5 per cent level*), and confidence increases when a mistake is likely to have been made only one time in a hundred (a probability of error of 0.01, described as *significant at the 1 per cent level*). We can estimate these probabilities from the size of the difference and its standard error. How to do so is discussed in Chapters 8 and 9.

Matched samples

Random sampling has been advanced in this chapter as the effective way to obtain figures from samples which will be representative of populations and to find differences or relationships between groups which are demonstrably not just the product of chance. There are circumstances under which it is not effective, however, even if a complete sampling frame is available, and other means have to be employed.

Imagine that you have a population to sample in which some kind of system is inherent in the structure, and you want to make valid comparisons between groups which are identified by the variables which differ systematically or by other variables which correlate with them. For example, think about:

1   looking at people serving indeterminate sentences in prison, or confined for an indefinite term to a hospital or sanatorium, where the people who 'get out early' are different in important respects from those who stay longer, and comparing early releases with longer-stay prisoners/ patients;
2   looking at a remote village which has been losing those of its younger population who have saleable skills to jobs in the towns, and comparing younger and older people;
3   looking at a firm with a gender-discriminatory history of hiring, so that different qualifications have been required of the men hired than the women, and comparing current male and female employees.

Take notes on how you might tackle these problems, then turn to Example 3.1 to see how I tackled the first of them.

Example 3.1: Life-sentence prisoners: design of the study

This is a study I carried out in the 1970s, while working at the Home Office Research Unit. It was a firm item of belief among prisoners and prison staff that men deteriorated mentally in prison (see Cohen and Taylor, 1972; Advisory Council on the Penal System, 1968), but research then currently in progress at Durham University (see Smith et al., 1977) indicated that whatever deterioration might be occurring, intellect itself remained unimpaired or even improved during long-term incarceration. My study was designed to see whether what deteriorated was not intellect itself but the motivational and attributional framework out of which intellect operates – the view of oneself as competent and in control. United States psychological research of the 1960s and 1970s – see, for example, Seligman (1975) – suggested that inescapable, uncontrollable aversive circumstances sometimes led to a state of 'learned helplessness' in which animals (and people) gave up attempting to escape aversive stimulation and appeared to believe that nothing they did had any effect on events. It seemed to me that this framework would explain deterioration in long-term prisoners, and particularly in life-sentence prisoners, who had little or no ability to determine or even to predict when they would see the outside world again.

My study involved interviews and questionnaires administered to British male life-sentence prisoners in one large prison which took prisoners from about a year into sentence to some men who had been there for over 15 years. At this time British lifers typically served 7–10 years before release, but some categories of crime (those involving robbery or sexual molestation of children, or where a degree of psychiatric disturbance was suspected) could attract much longer terms. The first review process for consideration for release on licence began, generally, during the prisoner's seventh year (the papers having been inspected in the fourth year but probably without involving the prisoner himself in any way). If no release date had been given by about the twelfth year, the prisoner would know that he was no longer 'serving an average term' and have little basis for predicting which of the next (roughly annual) reviews might bring him a date.

The study used a range of data sources and methods:

1   Prison and prison medical files were inspected for information from regular quarterly and annual reports written by prison officers, governor-grade staff, medical and social work staff, and note was taken of numbers of letters sent and received, visits and disciplinary infractions. This information was used to provide a 'history' of each man in prison and to construct indices of changes over time in mental state, sociability of behaviour, motivation and dependence, extent of interest in the outside world and conformity to prison rules and norms.
2   Each prisoner who was interviewed completed sets of 'paper and pencil' inventories and tasks measuring personality or psychological state, at strategic points in the interview.
3   The prisoners who filled out these tests were also interviewed about their experiences of prison, what they did with their time and what was important to them. Interviews lasted typically for an hour and a half, and I was invited back for a further conversation in about a quarter of cases. Transcripts yielded quantitative information on some of the variables outlined above and were also used qualitatively to 'tell the story' of the prisoner's life inside.

There are obvious ethical problems in interviewing prisoners on indeterminate sentences, particularly when working for the Home Office. Tentative pilot interviews in another prison suggested that the questions and tests I intended to use would not cause harm or unsettle the prisoners; indeed, they appeared to enjoy telling their story to an unknown person, and this was also my experience during the main study. Each prisoner was interviewed alone, no one had access to my interview notes except me, and each prisoner was promised confidentiality and warned that I had no contact with or influence over the release process. Whether they believed me I cannot say, but they appeared to do so.

The sample was complex, because of the complex nature of the prison population. Numbers had to be fairly small, because I was proposing to carry out long interviews, single-handed, in not much more than a year, and also to work through bulky files. I wanted samples of recently received men, men in the 'main run' of sentence (before the first review for release) and men who had served more than the average term. However, release is a selective process, with men whose psychiatric record is 'clean' and who have committed certain kinds of offence being much more likely to gain release on licence at any given stage of the sentence than other kinds of prisoner (Sapsford and Banks, 1979). In addition, a few men with florid psychiatric symptoms might be transferred out to secure mental hospital accommodation quite early in sentence. The samples had therefore to be drawn in two stages.

1   Random groups were drawn from the most recently received men, from men who had served 5–7 years, and from men who had served 12 years or more. There were 20 in the 'reception' and 'mid-sentence' groups, but only 10 in the 'long-stay' group because of limited numbers available. Because the prison held a substantial proportion of English lifers at that time, these samples should be reasonably representative of lifers as a whole.
2   However, they were not fully comparable with each other because of the selectivity of the release process: the 'long-stay' group were very different from the two groups earlier in sentence, in terms of psychiatric state and in terms of the type of offence committed. Two further groups of 10 were therefore drawn who matched the long-stay group in terms of these characteristics. (These overlapped the existing samples: some men fell in both kinds of sample, but it was necessary to go outside the random samples to find satisfactory matches for the long-stay men.) This yielded groups which could validly be compared, but at the cost of representation; the matched 'early' and 'mid-sentence' groups were not much like their parent populations.

A total of 60 men were interviewed and tested.

The results were as follows. First, differences between the 'reception' and 'mid-sentence' groups were not large. There was a tendency for prisoners early in sentence to exhibit a *greater* degree of hopelessness and disturbance (suggesting a period of settling in and coming to terms) but to score lower on measures of introversion. Long-stay prisoners were, of course, older on average than those early in sentence, and they showed greater orientation towards the prison rather than the outside world, greater identification with staff, received fewer visits and received and sent fewer letters. They were more likely to be described as 'institutionalized' by staff than the random samples from earlier in sentence but *not* more likely than the matched samples.

Second, the test of the 'learned helplessness' thesis was inconclusive because it was not possible, even using the whole range of information (the quantitative data, the 'histories' built up from the men's own words or reports on the prison files) to identify men who had deteriorated in and as a result of prison. Some men exhibited signs of deterioration, but they appear to have shown these signs even before being charged with their current offences.

Finally, the qualitative data were used to build up a picture of *why* men did not deteriorate, in terms of reactance and the attempt to take some control over their lives even in the drab, demeaning, deprived and unpromising context of prison life.

Further reading

For more details, see Sapsford (1978; 1983).

In principle, these problems can be tackled by random sampling. If some characteristic is very much rarer in one of the groups than in the other to which it is to be compared, we might take a very large simple random sample – to be sure of having enough of the rarer cases for analysis – and tackle the problem of the differences by statistical means (see Chapter 9). If the sampling frame listed details of the 'system' variables, a disproportionate stratified sample would be a more economical way of achieving the same effect.

The limitation, however, is available numbers. Mostly when this kind of problem occurs we are sampling from limited populations, and there are just not the numbers available for large samples to be drawn. In Example 3.1, for example, the random 'mid-sentence' sample contained virtually every man in the prison who had served 6–7 years, so there was little scope for extending the sample size. Also, the characteristics which made for very long stay were sufficiently rare in the rest of the population that a very large sample indeed would have been needed for adequate coverage.

Under these circumstances what we often do is to draw *matched* samples. Taking one of the groups – the long-stay prisoners, for example – you try to find someone qualified to be in another of the groups (the 'mid-sentence' group, say) who matches each case in terms of key variables (here type of crime, reported mental disorder and age on admission, the last of these to avoid comparing groups who entered prison at very different ages). Where there is a choice of candidates for the match you will be able to choose among them at random, to minimize selection bias. The variables used for the matching have then been eliminated from the analysis (*controlled*) and you can have reasonable confidence that you are comparing like with like.

There are three problems with matching, however:

1 Matched samples are not representative of their parent populations, so you cannot generalize from them to the population as a whole. (This is why I also drew random samples in the study described as Example 3.1, to be able to talk about the whole population of lifers rather than just certain kinds of lifer.)
2 Matching is quite difficult to carry out. With each variable you use for the matching process, you eliminate a large part of the potential sample, so it becomes increasingly difficult to obtain matched samples of adequate size. With three variables as criteria, I was not able to find matched groups of 10 men from random samples of 20 but had to bring in additional cases. With five or six variables I would have been lucky to find matched samples of 10 in the entire prison population, and with ten or twelve variables it might be difficult to match 10 cases in the entire population of the UK.
3 We know that the samples are controlled for those variables which we use as criteria, but we have no idea what other variables are correlated with them and therefore constrained – including variables which have not occurred to us and which we have therefore not collected. The strength of random sampling, with reasonably large samples, is that the groups to be compared stand a reasonable (and calculable) chance of matching on *any* characteristic, whether or not we have measured it. This cannot be guaranteed for matched samples; indeed, the opposite is to be expected.

Random sampling remains the method of choice for survey research, therefore, but there are circumstances under which other strategies will have to be adopted. The next chapter looks at sampling in real-life (i.e. awkward) situations and how we can do the best available to us when random sampling is not an option.

Further reading

If you have found this chapter difficult and would like to take a different 'cut' at the problems that have been discussed, any of the following may prove helpful: Arber (1993); O'Connell Davidson and Layder (1994); de Vaus (1991); and Schofield (1996).

Answers to exercises

Exercise 3.1

Total sample	Income				
	None	Little	Low	Medium	High
850	200	300	200	100	50
Percentage	23.5	35.3	23.5	11.8	5.9
Proportion	0.24	0.35	0.24	0.12	0.06

Exercise 3.2

(a) Median: 3   Mean: 3
(b) Median: 4.5   Mean: 4.33

Exercise 3.3

(a) The chances of two fives with two dice are precisely the same as the chances of two sixes – $1/6 \times 1/6 = 1/36$. $p = 0.028$
(b) The possible outcomes with two dice are as follows:

1, 1	2, 1	3, 1	4, 1	5, 1	6, 1
1, 2	2, 2	3, 2	4, 2	5, 2	6, 2
1, 3	2, 3	3, 3	4, 3	5, 3	6, 3
1, 4	2, 4	3, 4	4, 4	5, 4	6, 4
1, 5	2, 5	3, 5	4, 5	5, 5	6, 5
1, 6	2, 6	3, 6	4, 6	5, 6	6, 6

There are 36 possible outcomes, and the ones that yield at least one 5 are in the fifth column and the fifth row: they add up to 11 chances out of the 36. The probability of at least one 5 is therefore $11/36 = 0.306$.

Using the other method, the probability of *not* throwing a 5 on each throw is 5/6, so the probability of not throwing one on both throws is 25/36. Taking this away from 1 gives 11/36 again as the probability of throwing at least one 5.

(c) There are 49 numbers to choose from, and the winning combination consists of just six of them. Your first number could be any of the six, so the chances of your first number being a winner are 6/49. There are now 48 numbers left, and 5 winning ones, so the chances of your second number being a winner are 5/48; and so on. The probability of picking the correct six from 49 is

$$\frac{6}{49} \times \frac{5}{48} \times \frac{4}{47} \times \frac{3}{46} \times \frac{2}{45} \times \frac{1}{44}.$$

This works out at roughly seven chances in a hundred million!

Exercise 3.4

The probability of getting a sample consisting entirely of girls is

$$\frac{50}{100} \times \frac{49}{99} \times \frac{48}{98} \times \ldots \times \frac{41}{91},$$

because the first person picked could be any of 50 girls out of the sample of 100, when picking the second there are 49 girls left to choose out of the remaining 99 people, and so on. If you work out this sequence you will get a probability of 0.00059, so you should get an all-girl sample about six times in every 10,000 samples you draw. We have to double this figure, however, to allow for the equally likely (or unlikely!) event of drawing an all-boy sample, so the final answer is about 12 in 10,000 or rather more than one in a thousand.

4 Making do: Sampling in the real world

In Chapter 3 we looked at simple, systematic and stratified random sampling for the 'one-shot' survey – the survey which has a single phase of data collection and may be considered as 'taking a snapshot of the world' at a particular point. In this chapter we elaborate on how samples are drawn in surveys which do not necessarily have the privilege of a complete and accurate sampling frame (a list of the population from which the sample is to be drawn). Its topic area is some of the problems and pitfalls of making do with the kind of sample which is actually available, as opposed to the sample we might wish to have drawn.

First we look at sampling where the sampling frame exists in principle but is not available in practice. (At this point we shall look also at longitudinal survey design – how surveys are designed to follow up results and take repeated samples over time.) Next we look at approximations to the random sample which are in common use, and their disadvantages. We go on to consider what to do about non-response, refusal and losing touch with informants on longitudinal surveys. The final section revises the contents of this chapter and the previous one and offers some practical suggestions on how to take sampling decisions.

Sampling over time

There is one kind of study which regularly does not have a sampling frame but still manages to apply the principles of random sampling, and this is where the sample is drawn from a series of events occurring, one at a time, over an extended period. Examples would be admissions to a hospital ward, or customers in a shop, or cars passing a particular location on the road, or patients visiting a general practitioner or therapist. (However, to generalize beyond the particular location to patients or cars or customers in general would require a demonstration that the ward or the clinic or the shop or the road and its traffic were typical or representative of these classes.) We would probably have some prior idea – perhaps from pilot observation – of how many cases we were likely to get (the population) in a given time period, and so we could sample from the stream of patients or customers at random. We might use a systematic sampling method (every tenth car, say, if we were expecting a thousand cars to pass in a week and we wanted a sample of about a hundred). If we suspected any kind of 'system' in the order in which cars or patients or customers presented themselves, a more sophisticated true random system of sampling might be preferred, and we would construct a sequence of random numbers, centring around a sampling fraction of one-tenth, to determine our choice of cases. We might stratify by size of car or type of patient, proportionately to the population (if known) or disproportionately by collecting cases systematically or randomly until a preset number had been reached and counting the total number of each type over time to determine the proportions in the population. Any of these methods would give us true random samples of the relevant population, providing certain conditions were met.

The conditions to be met concern the possibility of system in the population. Suppose, for example, we were sampling a hospital's accident and emergency department – something with a fairly fast and large throughput of cases. We sample for a week, and the numerator of our sampling fraction is fairly large – we sample only a small percentage of the cases that pass through, because over the course of a week this gives us a sufficiently large sample for our purposes. But the size of the sample is not the only consideration.

- We have to make sure that all times of the day are represented in our sample, because different kinds of case come in at different times – drunks when the pubs are closed, industrial injuries mostly during the day, women about to give birth disproportionately (it often seems) around 2 a.m., and so on.
- Is a week long enough? Are there seasonal patterns? The answer is probably 'yes'; you are unlikely, for example, to get many rugby or football injuries, or many hypothermia cases among the elderly population, in the middle of summer.
- Did our week contain a vanishingly rare event which is distorting the figures? For example, was it the week when the first multiple car pile-up for a decade took place, or the first ever major fire in a block of flats, or the week when the football stands collapsed and killed spectators? If so, the figures will be unrepresentative of the 'normal run of business'.
- Did it fail to contain some periodic event which ought to be taken into account? (For example, if the local football team plays at home once a fortnight, did we pick the week of the home game, when injured spectators are likely to come to our hospital, or the week of the away match, when they are likely to finish up in someone else's?)

When what you want to do is a study over time to measure change – to compare child development at age 1 and age 5, for example, or criminal behaviour at age 12 and age 22, or attitudes to political parties just after one general election and just before the next one – then sampling becomes an important design issue. There are four basic ways of obtaining data with which to make comparisons over time, and each has strengths and weaknesses.

The weakest is the one-shot *retrospective* survey carried out at the end of the time period, using people's recollections to measure the past. This is weak because recollection can be faulty and because we tend to 'recon-struct' and make sense of the past in terms of what has happened to us since, so that what we think now that we felt (or even did) then is likely to be at least in part a current rather than a contemporaneous product.

A better design also involves a one-shot survey but surveys *multiple groups*, comparing groups of different ages within the current population – current 11-year-olds with current 70-year-olds. If we can assume that the older group, when younger, were like the current younger group, then we can assess the difference made by growing 59 years older. The weakness, however, is that this assumption must always be open to question. The two groups have not had the same history; the 11-year-olds experienced at 11 the historical events which the 70-year-olds experienced at 70, not those they experienced at 11.

The third way of tackling this problem is the *time-series design*, where a series of one-shot surveys are taken over time and the resultant 'snapshots' compared. This has the merit of comparing two or more sets of contem-poraneous responses rather than comparing current events with recollected ones. Each survey can also be made as representative as possible of the population at the time. However, because it is not the same informants in the different surveys, we can look only at changes in group averages, not changes in individual response.

The fourth method, generally considered the best, is the *longitudinal survey* or *cohort study*. Here we pick a group or cohort – people of a given age – and follow them through, administering questionnaires at intervals, for as long as interest and funding will permit. Thus in one classic British study (West, 1969; 1982; West and Farrington, 1973; 1977) a group of boys were interviewed at age 8 and thereafter periodically into their twenties, noting also what trouble they had been in with the law, to explore the effects of character, parenting, school and peer group on criminal behav-iour. This is the preferred method for this kind of enquiry, which depends on using information about people at an early age to explain the sub-sequent behaviour of the *same* people. Such studies are costly and difficult, however, the original sample may prove unrepresentative of the population in later years, and problems are caused by *sample attrition* – the loss of members from the sample over time (discussed below).

Cluster sampling

Another set of circumstances under which random sampling is possible despite the absence of a sampling frame of individuals is when their geo-graphical location and distribution are known, even though their identities are concealed. It is then possible to sample geographical units, and sub-units within them (and so on, for as many levels of complexity as may be desirable and practical), and finally to sample a randomly determined number of individuals within the smallest unit as so determined, its size now being known.

For example, a simple random sample of British schoolchildren would require a complete list of every child in every school, which would in itself require a research project for its compilation. However, we can make use of the fact that these are *school*children to construct such a sample without the need for such a list.

- First, we might sample randomly among education authorities (assigning private schools, for this purpose, to the authority in whose geographical area they lie). An alternative approach might be to pick commercial telephone directories, in which every school is listed, at random.
- From the authority lists, or the telephone directories, we would then pick schools at random.
- Within schools, we could pick classes at random.
- Within classes – whose rolls could now be used as a sampling frame, because there would be relatively few of them – we could pick a pre-selected number of children at random, and these would be the target of the survey.

At every stage it would be necessary to weight the selection so that account was taken of the size of the authority, telephone directory, school, class or whatever; otherwise children from smaller authorities or schools or classes would have a greater chance of being selected. Provided the selection is done with probability proportional to size, however, what we would finish up with would be a true random sample – every child would start off with an equal, non-zero chance of being selected for the sample. Similarly, it would be possible to pick a sample of the general population by selecting geographical areas at random, and then households, and then people within households – in Britain, perhaps, by using the Register of Postcodes.

The problem with random samples of the general population, from the practical researcher's point of view, is that the population is very widely spread. Even if your sample is confined to one town, a random sample of 100 could involve visiting 100 streets or every school in the neighbourhood; a national sample, even if much bigger, could involve a very great deal of travelling in order to pick up one or two cases at each stop. For this reason it is very common to use a procedure called *cluster sampling* to rationalize the spread of the sample and make the travelling more manageable and more economic. Instead of sampling randomly, even where a complete frame is available, the researchers select sampling units. So, for example, instead of sampling children across a county, they sample schools and concentrate their resources in particular schools. From the point of view of practicality, obviously, the maximum gain is obtained by selecting a small number of clusters. Compared with the cost of travelling to 100 schools to interview 100 pupils, it is clearly a lot cheaper to go to a single school and interview 100 pupils there. Even within the school, it may be cheaper and more practical to sample whole classes and have your questionnaire administered *en bloc* by the teacher than to pick out children at random and approach, say, five or ten from each class. Similarly, if you were sampling the general population by door-to-door interviewing, there are obvious practical advantages to selecting whole streets rather than odd houses scattered across the town.

What are the disadvantages of this form of sampling? Look again at the sampling in Example 2.2, the study of women's drinking, and consider what problems might be encountered in the interpretation of results.

The problem with cluster sampling is that it is not a random sampling method – people located close to a given respondent are more likely to be sampled than those further away. This means that any 'local oddity' in distribution will be exaggerated. If all the Irish people with red hair happened to live in one street, for example, and you sample whole streets, then such people will be either grossly over-represented in your sample or absent altogether. Even apart from such oddities of distribution, there is a tendency for people who live close to each other or go to the same place of work or the same school to have similar attitudes and behaviours. Housing and work are substantially segregated by social class and material affluence, and schools follow housing areas in their characteristics. People who live in the same area will tend to have similar attitudes because they have similar backgrounds and lifestyles: they are mostly 'locals' coming from local families, or they are mostly affluent, or they are a transient population working (or not working) in similar kinds of jobs. In other words, there is a strong tendency for cluster sampling to exaggerate the homogeneity of the population.

This fault will be worse, the smaller the number of clusters sampled. The study of women's drinking is quite good in this respect – it sampled about 100 clusters from a population previously selected by random means, and these clusters were themselves randomly selected. Even 100 is not a large number of locations across the whole of the United States, however, so some of the variation of the population may have been missed. Further, the number of cases per cluster is small – about 40, to yield an overall sample of about 4000 – and we are not told how they themselves were picked within clusters. It could be that clusters were small enough that they yielded around 40 cases; alternatively, they could have been relatively large, with the 40 or so cases picked by random means within them. The former would lead to more exaggeration of homogeneity than the latter. (The sample was also stratified disproportionately by level of drinking, but that does not affect the argument here.)

To summarize, cluster sampling is a widely used means of picking samples, and it has very substantial advantages in terms of cost and convenience, as well as being usable in cases where a sampling frame is not available. It can be combined with a degree of stratification to improve precision, either by selecting cases on the basis of their answers to a screening questionnaire (as in Example 2.2) or by selecting areas in terms of their known characteristics ('posh', 'ordinary' or 'rough' schools, middle-class or working-class areas, and so on). Its fault is that it is *not* in itself a random sampling method: it exaggerates the homogeneity of attitudes and behaviours and may also represent rare characteristics disproportionately. It can be used to *simulate* random sampling, however, and the simulation becomes better, the more clusters are taken.

Non-probability sampling

As we have seen, non-probability methods can also yield acceptable approximations to random samples – in the case of the more elaborate forms of cluster sampling, for example. Many other sampling forms exist which share far less with random sampling even than cluster methods, however, and yet they are in common use as research tools. This section looks at the two major forms – *quota sampling* and *haphazard sampling* – and the extent to which they may be used despite their obvious shortcomings.

Quota and haphazard samples

One very common way of sampling in, for example, market research studies is to leave the choice of respondents up to the interviewers but set constraints on their choice so that the sample matches the population in terms of variables which are known to be important for the question under investigation. You might determine, for example, that your sample of 1000 respondents shall be split equally between men and women and divided by age bands and by social class in the same proportions as the general population (using census data to obtain the information on the population). You would then send each of your interviewers out to obtain so many middle-class male respondents in the youngest age band, so many middle-class female respondents in the youngest age band, so many middle-class male respondents in the second age band, so many middle-class female respondents in the second age band, and so on. The interviewers are then free to find the informants to fit these *quotas* as best they can – possibly with additional instructions such as that they shall choose a street at random to start their search, pick not more than four households in that street and then skip three streets before starting again, or with interviewers assigned to particular areas of the city known to differ in important ways.

This kind of sample is necessarily representative of the population with respect to the variables which have been used to set the quotas, and it is claimed to give consistently representative results in some areas of research – political opinion polls, for example. It is a great deal cheaper than random sampling for 'general population' studies, because with a random sample it is necessary to call back, perhaps several times, if the designated respondent is not available at the first call, while if a respondent is out when a quota-sampling interviewer calls, he or she simply goes on to find another respondent. However, the method can have very serious drawbacks.

What do you think are the potential drawbacks of quota sampling? Look at the sampling method in Example 4.1, a national survey of class attitudes, before reading on, and think what might have gone wrong with the sampling.

Example 4.1: Women and social class: the People in Society survey (1)

The People in Society survey was a national student survey carried out annually from 1968 to 1981 by undergraduate and graduate research methods students of the Open University. Its topic areas were social class position, class attitudes and class-related behaviours. The students received some training from distance-learning texts, a television programme and, in some cases, locally provided tutorial sessions.

There were about 200–250 students each year. These were all mature students, typically in their early thirties or older and many of them employed in teaching, nursing, social work or a range of mostly white-collar jobs, and they were distributed throughout Great Britain. Students who were currently prisoners, hospital inmates, etc. were told not to collect data, for fear of biasing the sample unduly. The remainder each collected information from four respondents. The sample was picked by quota means, so designed that every eight respondents were evenly divided between men and women, middle and working class and older or younger respondents; students made a random choice (based on the last digit of their student serial numbers) of one half of the eight-cell quota design or the other. They were advised to put an element of randomness into their selection – not using just friends and neighbours but picking streets at random in which to locate respondents – but we cannot be sure that they did so. Each set of four cases was coded and sent in for inclusion in a central computer file which all students analysed as part of their assessment work.

The interview schedule covered, firstly, basic demographic information – current and previous jobs of self and spouse, income of self, spouse and 'head of household' (principle wage earner), age, education and father's employment. Secondly, it asked for views on the nature of social class, and thirdly, it used semantic differential scales to collect data for a 'profile of self', 'working class' and 'middle class' on scales of 'position in life' (scoring on items such as 'successful/not successful', 'rich/poor') and 'conservatism' (scoring on items such as 'spends/saves', 'careful/reckless', 'law-abiding/criminal').

Although the data were not of high quality, the survey was unique in its period for collecting information about women's education, employment and income on the same basis as for men, and it was therefore worth analysing the data to explore questions about women's class position. The headline results of this analysis were as follows.

- Women's social mobility did not closely match that of men, being more strongly modal (with a strong concentration in class C1 – secretarial, clerical and other routine non-manual work), more constrained (with women less likely to appear in the highest positions) and more bounded by class C1 as a barrier or ceiling which women had difficulty passing intergenerationally in either direction. Britain was therefore a less open and meritocratic society for women than for men.
- Women's class and political sentiments were broadly similar to those of men, and their commitment to the labour market certainly no less strong.
- For married women, the husband's class was a good predictor of self-assessed class, giving some credence to the argument that women's class position is derived from that of their husbands' or fathers', but a combination of education, father's class and (where available) own current or most recent employment was almost as good a predictor. Husband's class was a poor predictor of a woman's perceived class where the woman's job was or had been of higher social class than that of her husband, and the predictive effect may have been at least in part a result of the fact that the majority of marriages involved two people in the same social class, or else a C2 man married to a C1 woman.

The overall conclusion was that the tendency in British mobility studies of the 1950s to 1980s to sample only men, and of British class theory to treat women as having no social class position except one derived from the family, led to serious distortions of our understanding of the structure of British society.

Further reading

Results of this research may be found in Abbott (1987) and Abbott and Sapsford (1986; 1987).

Quota samples match the population well – if correctly drawn – on the variables which form the basis of the quotas. They may well not match it at all well on other variables, however, leading to large distortions. In market research, for example, there is a tendency for interviewers to over-represent people who have no paid employment outside the home, if they are sampling door to door, or people in paid employment or shopping in the town if they are sampling in the street. As the purchasing behaviour (and the purchasing power) of full-time housewives is different from that of women in paid employment, this can lead to false conclusions about the population of purchasers. In the People in Society survey we know that a substantial proportion of the 'interviewers' ignored the instruction to approach strangers on a random basis and used people they knew and/or people who were readily available in the locality. We know this because of two notable biases in the data.

First, the sample grossly over-represents people with degrees or higher education, and also women in full-time paid employment. We suspect that the friends of Open University students – who are socially mobile, often in paid employment and seeking education – may have similar characteristics.

A second, more subtle misrepresentation, but one which is potentially interpretable, is that the middle-class women (and to a lesser extent men) in the sample consistently, year on year, showed a greater affinity to the Labour than the Conservative Party when asked how they usually voted. Now we know from other sources that there is a middle-class bias towards the Conservative Party in Britain, but that this is partially reversed for people in public sector employment. Thinking about 'filling the quota', we imagine people looking for middle-class women in a given age band and filling that part of the quota by the easiest means available – by turning to their female colleagues at work (and many of our students were teachers, nurses or social workers) or approaching a teacher at their children's schools.

In general, a random sample controls for sources of variation which we have not even considered, let alone measured; all characteristics of the population should 'even out' if the sample is sufficiently large. With a quota sample this cannot be guaranteed. Indeed, we *can* more or less guarantee that there will be biases in the sampling arising from the manner in which interviewers choose to fill their quotas. Worse, this would not matter as much if the biases were random among interviewers, but they are likely to be more or less constant within a given interview force working under a given set of circumstances.

The worst samples of all, from the point of view of representing the population, are *haphazard samples* and *samples of opportunity*. When the market research report says that interviewers stopped people 'at random' in the street, it is very unlikely that they achieved a random sample of the population by doing this; what they are most likely to have done is to have picked a biased sample by haphazard means:

- Without some independent form of selection, such as a list of random numbers, the interviewers will not have picked at random but followed their unconscious biases. (If asked for a random number between 1 and 10, far more people pick 3 or 7 than any other digit. If asked to pick someone at random out of a crowd most people will pick the one who is smiling at them or someone who attracts their attention by moving.)
- They will certainly have avoided, consciously or unconsciously, those whom they felt would refuse to co-operate or whom they found threatening, and the co-operative do not necessarily have the same attitudes as those perceived to be unco-operative.
- Most important of all, they can only have selected from those who are there at the time to be selected. They will miss those who stayed at home or went somewhere else. During working hours they are more likely to find shoppers than workers. In the evening they are more likely to find drinkers than schoolchildren. On a Sunday, if there is no reliable bus service, they are more likely to find those with cars. On the day of the away match they will not find many dedicated football players.

The sample of opportunity – the class or team or people at a conference that just happen to be available when you want to do research – is clearly even more likely to be unrepresentative of the population as a whole. (One commentator once characterized the psychology of the time as the study of white rats and students and the sociology as the study of the working class and other sociologists, to indicate that neither could claim much knowledge of the human race as a whole, given the usual subject of their research.) In this context we should also mention the *volunteer sample*, obtained by putting up a notice or running an advertisement in a magazine. There is clearly no good reason to suppose that those who choose to volunteer are a random subset of the population which includes volunteers, non-volunteers and those who did not even see the notice or advertisement.

Using statistics with non-probability samples

You cannot use statistical means of estimating errors with non-probability samples in the same way that you can with random sampling. Quite simply, statistical estimates are valid only for samples where every member of the population had an equal chance of selection, and this can be virtually guaranteed *not* to be the case if the sampling design was not a random one or a good simulation of a random sample (such as a cluster sampling design which uses a large number of clusters and selects both the clusters at each level and the informants within the clusters by random means).

However, this having been said, we mostly still use estimates of sampling error on, for example, quota samples as if they were random ones. While they do not yield accurate estimates of error, they are better than nothing, and a statistical test of the significance of differences between the groups is better as a decision principle than merely asserting that the differences look large enough to be interesting. Providing the nature of the sampling is made clear, the reader can make his or her own judgement of the extent to which the statistics are appropriate and useful as a guide to the nature of the population. Schofield (1993: 99–100) suggests that

> In presenting standard errors in circumstances such as this, researchers are in effect saying:
>
> > OK, I know I haven't got a random sample and so can't estimate sampling error. But this is the best I could do. It could be the case that it hasn't mattered very much, and thus I have calculated the standard errors and have used them in further tests. My finding has support from the literature and looks useful. It's up to you, dear reader, to decide how much reliance you will place on it. Perhaps you'll think that the result is important and will be able to replicate it without the sampling difficulties which I have had *and have reported.*

Schofield also points out that replication – running a study twice, on independent samples – is worth a great deal, particularly where the sampling design is less than ideal. The probability of getting a significant result twice, on independent samples, is obtained by *multiplying* the probabilities together and is generally very small. So if sampling is difficult it may be worth building a replication into the design rather than spending vast resources trying for the perfect sample; the 'pay-off' could be greater, in terms of justified confidence in the results. We should note, however, that this holds only for samples that are independent. Any source of bias which they have in common will just be repeated in the second sample. So the biases in two quota samples which are interviewed during the day at home do not cancel each other out, and the results do not become more certain; on the contrary, precisely the same kinds of individual will be missed by the second study as by the first.

Improving performance in sampling

Sample size and non-sampling error

As we have seen, the sampling error of a simple random sample is dependent on the size of the sample. It decreases, in fact, as the square root of the sample size: with the same amount of variation in the sample, multiplying the sample size by *four* will have the effect of *halving* the

---

Box 4.1: Calculating required sample size

We have already seen how to estimate the necessary size of sample for a given size of confidence interval (Box 3.5). If you remember, a standard deviation (SD) of 5.39, with a sample size of 50, gave us a standard error (SE) of 0.762. With a sample size of 100 it would have given us a standard error of 0.539, and with 200 we would have had a standard error of 0.381.

With our sample of 50 and standard error of 0.762, we can set confidence limits to the likely range of the population mean. If we took a very large number of samples from the same population, they would vary around their mean (estimated here by the mean of the sample we did take). As the standard error functions as a standard deviation of these possible means, we can say that 95 per cent of them should lie within plus or minus 1.96 × the SE around the mean – plus or minus 1.49 in this case, to two decimal places. If we want to get the confidence limits down to the range from +0.2 to −0.2, we can do the calculation in reverse. The size of confidence limit can be expressed as

$$1.96 \times SE = 1.96 \times SD/\sqrt{N}.$$

So, given that we want confidence limits of 0.2, and our standard deviation is 5.39,

$$0.2 = 1.96 \times 5.39/\sqrt{N}$$

$$\frac{5.39}{\sqrt{N}} = \frac{0.2}{1.96}$$

$$\sqrt{N} = \frac{5.39}{0.2/1.96}$$

$$N = \left(\frac{5.39}{0.2/1.96}\right)^2$$

$$= 2748.9.$$

So the required sample size is about 2750.

---

sampling error, and multiplying it by *nine* will have the effect of reducing it to *a third*. Box 4.1 shows how to calculate the sample size required for an effect of a given size to register as statistically significant, in the (relatively rare) case where you have an idea of the size of difference to be expected before you carry out the research.

There is a trade-off here, obviously, between precision and cost. Where it is necessary to be very precise in one's estimates, or it is very important not to rule out a difference as a chance product of sampling when it might really exist in the population but not be very large, the larger the sample the better. However, if the cost of the study (in money or time) is directly related to the size of the sample, then it will cost not twice as much but four times as much if the sampling error is to be halved. Putting this another way, to halve my standard error I might have to interview 400 respondents instead of just 100, and to halve it again I would have to increase my sample to 1600.

We should also remember that there is an important difference between *statistical* significance and *substantive* significance. With a large enough sample, very small differences will be statistically significant – they are likely to be characteristic of the underlying population rather than chance products of sample selection. In a census, a count of 100 per cent of the population, all differences are by definition characteristic of the population and no calculation of sampling error is necessary. If we find that 51 per cent of males give a certain kind of answer and only 50 per cent of females, however, this real difference is not likely to be of the slightest interest to us. As McNemar (1962: 69) put it: 'A statistically significant difference doesn't necessarily mean a difference either of practical significance or of scientific import. Sometimes a "What of it?" is not an impertinence.'

One use of this calculation, however, is an adaptation of the principles of *sequential sampling* which are used in industrial quality control. When inspecting the quality of a product – light bulbs, say – one common procedure would be to test a small sample from each batch. If none were faulty, the batch would pass. If more than the predetermined acceptable rate of rejects were damaged, the batch would be scrapped. In between, if the number of faults rose over a given level a further sample would be taken, and another, until the underlying trend became clear and the batch – the population – was classed either as acceptable (the rate of damaged bulbs in the sample being taken as a product of sampling error) or as probably containing too many damaged items to pass inspection. In the same way, you might want to start with a relatively small sample and carry out statistical tests on the variables in which you are interested, setting a lower than usual level of 'significance' for the results – perhaps the 0.1 level, one chance in ten of being mistaken. If the results produced a higher probability of error than this, the null hypothesis would not be rejected and you would say there was no significant difference. If they produced an acceptably low probability of error – 0.05 or 0.01, depending on your chosen level – the null hypothesis would be rejected and you would declare the results significant. If the result lay between these two limits you might take a further sample to see whether the result came out as significant or non-significant with the larger sample. The size of sample you needed to take could be calculated using the methods of Box 4.1.

As with stratification in sampling (see Box 3.6), the decision about sampling size is generally taken on grounds other than the size of the standard error, although we would always keep in mind that sampling error is reduced by increasing the sample size. A useful rule of thumb for sampling in surveys is that you will want at least 40 cases – and 100 would be better – for each independent variable that you intend to enter into the analysis, if you want to be able to present meaningful tables. Comparing the heights of men and women, for example, you would want a sample of at least 40 of each gender if you wanted to be reasonably sure of having 20 of each gender in each of two height categories. The minimum would be higher if the independent variable had more categories; comparing arts students, mathematics students and psychology students, for example, the rule of '20 of each' gives a minimum sample of 60 (and more would be highly desirable). If you will want to split up the men and women, or the students, by social class of origin (middle versus working), to get 20 in each 'cell' of the design you would need a minimum sample of $40 \times 2 = 80$ for the study of height and gender and a minimum of $60 \times 2 = 120$ for the student study. Each new variable adds another multiplier. Comparing the students by class *and* gender requires a minimum sample size of $60 \times 2 \times 2 = 240$.

The foregoing assumes that the sample is split up equally between the categories of the variables. If the split is disproportionate, larger numbers will be required. If you wanted to look at height by ethnic group (say, just 'white' versus 'non-white'), and non-white people made up only 5 per cent of your population, you would have to draw a sample of at least 400 to be reasonably sure of getting 20 non-white people (and 800 if you wanted to analyse it by, say, gender). If you wanted to look at country of origin (or origin of parents) in more detail rather than conflating all 'non-white' people together, you would need much larger numbers still. An alternative stratagem would be to sample disproportionately in order to get a large enough sample of the groups which are rarer in the population and then use weighting to restore the figures to an accurate description of the overall population.

This brings us to the final point about sample size and sampling error in this chapter: that there are some faults which just increasing the sample size will not correct. *Sampling* error – the error of measurement due to the predictable variation between samples when drawn randomly from the same population – is dependent on the size of the sample. However, there is also *non-sampling* error – error built into the design or the mode of collection of data. If your sampling method is biased in itself, taking more cases will just confirm rather than eliminate the bias: for example, a bent penny will not come up heads on 50 per cent of the throws, and you will become the more certain that it is biased the more often you toss it. To take a real-life social science example, a notorious (and erroneous) opinion poll before a US presidential election in the 1930s used the telephone directory as a sampling frame and thereby failed to include large numbers of working-class and unemployed people who could not afford a telephone. If the sample size had been increased to a full census of the telephone directory these people would still have been excluded from the sample, and their voting intentions were not the same, on average, as those of telephone owners.

Indeed, the position may sometimes be worse than this suggests. Non-sampling error includes errors of measurement, errors of coding and analysis, mistakes on the part of the interviewers, mistakes on the part of informants (due often to bad questionnaire design) and so on. When these sources of error are taken into account, we may sometimes feel that a small-scale survey well designed and well conducted may be preferable to a larger sample more sloppily investigated.

Non-response and lost cases

Even a sample which perfectly fitted the criteria of random selection at the time when it was drawn may not be random by the time the data have been collected. A proportion of the sample will not be traceable. Another proportion will refuse to take part in the survey. Yet another proportion will yield unusable questionnaires, through their own fault or the interviewer's. There will also be mistakes at the coding and data-manipulation stages. The problem is often at its most acute with cohort studies, where a substantial part of the sample may move away and lose touch with the researchers between the waves of data collection, or people may lose patience with the survey after being approached in several data collection waves. (This is called *sample attrition.*)

None of this would particularly matter if the people lost from the original sample in these ways were themselves a random subset of the sample, but this is very unlikely to be the case. Those who cannot be traced will contain a disproportionate number of the socially mobile or rootless and/or the very ill (who might have transferred to a hospital). Those who fail to provide acceptable answers may well include a disproportionate number of the poorly educated, the elderly and the frail, and/or of people for whom English is not a first language, and/or of people unfamiliar with filling in forms. Those who decline to take part may well have different attitudes and behaviours from those who do co-operate.

Loss of cases through errors of the questionnaire, the interviewers and the coders is minimized in any competent survey by careful attention at the design and planning stage. Where a 'completed' questionnaire is in fact incomplete, or garbled in some way, it is still sometimes possible to salvage some part of it, either ignoring the rest or seeing what can be done to recode it into analysable sense; data preparation is discussed in Chapter 6. In any event, the case should be entered into the data file, with whatever demographic information we do have, in order to assess the distribution of 'lost cases' and the consequent bias in the sample of usable ones (see below).

The usual solutions to untraceable members of the sample are either to omit them and settle for a smaller sample or to replace them from a randomly drawn 'reserve list' of extra sample members (after making several attempts to contact them, at different times of the day and week). Neither solves the problem – omitting the cases biases the sample, as they are likely not to be randomly distributed, and replacing them also biases it, because the replacements are likely not to match those whom they are replacing. The important thing is probably to try to keep *some* kind of record of anything known about the missing people – anything about them in the source which was used as a sampling frame (which will probably have at least their gender and possibly other information about them), and perhaps 'visible' details such as type of house and nature of area as pointers to affluence and social class. Then we can at least report on the kinds of people we have *not* managed to interview and so have a basis for guessing the probable direction of bias.

The only real solution to refusals or non-cooperation is to keep trying, preferably by a variety of means. With interviewer studies this is more difficult, but some research teams have tried a follow-up by another (more senior) interviewer or by letter. With postal questionnaires it is routine to send out a reminder – a second copy of the questionnaire, with a letter apologizing for the fact that the first one 'evidently' got lost – and this retrieves a proportion of cases. If the questionnaire is anonymous this is difficult because you do not know who has already replied. Generally the second mailing is sent to everyone, explaining that anonymity means that the people who have already replied cannot be identified. (Some researchers place a surreptitious code on the questionnaire so that they *can* identify the respondents and so do the second mailing only to those who have not responded. This saves annoying those who have co-operated by sending them a redundant questionnaire, but it is, of course, unethical.)

The important thing, again, is to try to find out as much as possible about those who have not responded, in order to be able to estimate the likely biases in the sampling. Where respondents are identified on the questionnaire this is relatively easy – we can cross them off the list, and the remainder can be coded for available information. This is not possible where the questionnaire is anonymous. However, we would normally compare the achieved sample with anything known about the target population (for example, from census figures); the absence of discrepancies on known variables gives us some confidence in the accuracy of the rest of the data. This is also *very* good practice with quota and cluster samples.

Practicalities: selecting samples

Figure 4.1 illustrates most of the practical decisions that have to be taken when you are selecting your sample. It looks complex – a bit like a maze for one of the psychologists' white rats – but the questions it poses are relatively simple.

The first question is whether you have a sampling frame – a complete list of the population. If so, straightforward random sampling is possible. You need to check, however, that the list is complete. Voting lists are generally out of date; directories list only those who subscribe to the service and

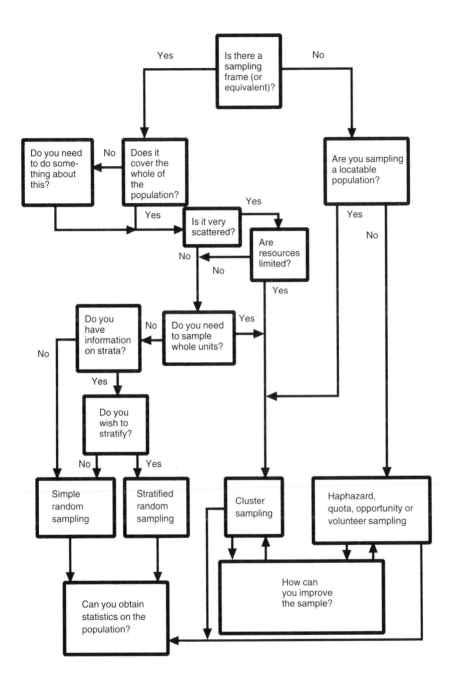

FIGURE 4.1 *Selecting a sample*

choose to be listed. You may wish to do some preliminary research to extend the list, or at least think what kinds of people could be missing from it and consider whether to draw some kind of supplementary sample to obtain at least partial coverage of them. You need to consider also what your *sampling units* are. We have proceeded in this chapter as though all surveys sampled individuals, but you might be sampling households or schools or neighbourhoods or shops. You need also to think about the kinds of unit that are listed on your sampling frame. If you are sampling individuals, for example, and your list is one of addresses of households, you will need to think what to do about (a) picking an individual, or individuals, *within* households, and about (b) the problem that households differ in size, so that picking one individual per household (for example) favours individuals in small households.

If you do not have a sampling frame, then random sampling is likely to be impossible except under certain specific circumstances. It *will* be possible to sample randomly if you can take random slices from a series of events – random patients from the stream of patients admitted to hospital, for example – or where the individuals occupy named slots – random beds within a hospital, for example. Here there *is* something equivalent to a sampling frame – the individuals occupy designated 'slots', and it is possible to sample these slots. You will need to be careful, however, that there is no 'system' in the presence of certain kinds of individuals and not others at certain times.

We are now on track for random sampling, which is the best method for overcoming the random errors of sampling and rendering them susceptible to estimation. If our population is very scattered, however, and if the interview is interviewer-administered rather than delivered by post, this may not be feasible. If you are drawing a sample of 200, for example, you will not want to interview two people in each of 100 widely separated towns. Under these circumstances cluster sampling is undoubtedly the most appropriate – you would sample towns at random and within your randomly sampled towns you would select at random a reasonable number of people for interview. If the number of clusters is reasonably large you should obtain a reasonable approximation to a random sample, though with some tendency towards exaggerated homogeneity. So if picking a sample of 200 you might go for 10 sampling areas, each yielding 20 interviews – one or two days' work in each location, depending on the length of the interview. The ten sampling areas might either be randomly selected from an entire list of possibles or else randomly selected from sub-lists classified by type of area (urban versus rural, affluent versus deprived, racially mixed versus segregated, and so on). The latter would amount to a crude form of stratification and might improve representation. The principle of selection in proportion to size is important to remember here: unless the sampling areas are exactly equal in size, it will be necessary either to pick your cases so that the number in the sample reflects the number in the population or to apply some sort of weighting after the event.

Another reason for cluster sampling would be where you need to sample whole units for ethical or practical reasons. You may feel that it is invidious – liable to misinterpretation and prone to provoke anxiety – to interview or test some people on a ward and pass over others. You may feel it rude to talk to one member of a couple and ignore the other. You may feel that it is impractical to pick out some members of a school class to fill in a questionnaire and deny the experience to others. Under these circumstances you would sample whole classes, whole wards, whole marriages. Provided there are a reasonably large number of them and randomly chosen, you should obtain a reasonable approximation to a random sample, but with some tendency towards homogeneity of response.

The next question, if you are working towards random sampling, is whether you want a simple or a stratified sample. Stratification does improve the representation of the population with respect to the variables which are the basis for stratifying, and it may improve it overall by reducing the sampling error. As we have seen, the reduction is often not as large as one might have hoped – even where distributions differ markedly at the mean, their variability means they often overlap substantially at the margins, and stratification works best when the groups are maximally distinct *between* groups and maximally homogeneous *within* groups – but stratification is probably worth the effort if it does not cost too much in terms of time and labour. Disproportionate stratification is the only way, other than drawing massive samples, of being sure of obtaining adequate numbers of rare categories of people. However, stratification depends on having reliable information about the sampling frame with respect to the variables by which you wish to stratify.

If you do not have a sampling frame (or some equivalent, as discussed above), then you cannot draw a straightforward random sample. However, if your sample can be located geographically – in streets in towns or in classes in schools or in wards in hospitals – then cluster sampling can be used. In principle this is not a random sampling method, but it can be made a very good approximation to one. If you were sampling the general population in a town, for example, you would divide the town up into areas (maximally distinct, for preference, in terms of social characteristics) and sample areas at random. (The areas should be small and numerous, to optimize the approximation to a random sample.) Within the areas you would sample streets at random, and within the streets, houses at random. Finally, you might identify households within the houses and sample individuals within them at random. The more numerous the clusters at each stage, the closer the approximation to a true random sample. The principle of stratification can be used at one or more stages to improve the representation of the sample – stratifying your initial choice by affluent areas versus deprived ones, established areas versus new ones, settled areas versus transient ones and so on. A point to keep in mind, however, is that the clusters will differ in terms of their size, and where possible it is desirable to build in a mechanism for selecting cases in proportion to the size of the cluster (or to collect information on cluster size to be used in subsequent analysis).

If cluster sampling is not appropriate, quota sampling would be the next choice – picking cases to match the characteristics of the population on known variables. The more you can impose a degree of randomness on the selection of cases and control the places and times of their collection to give a fair representation of the geographical and temporal spread of availability, the better the representative quality of the sample. If even quota sampling is not feasible then you will have to fall back on haphazard sampling – just stopping people in the street, for instance – or volunteer sampling, or samples of opportunity (the class you happen to be teaching, the conference you happen to be attending). These are better than nothing but probably not much better. The results will be more plausible if you at least *try* to improve the quality of the representation by, for example, taking more than one class, in different schools, or varying the time and place at which you stop passers-by, or making sure that your magazine advertisement appears in a representative range of periodicals.

A final point is that it is always a good idea to compare your sample with any available population statistics – census or government figures, local authority figures or whatever may be available – or with other surveys of the same population. If the sample can be shown to be reasonably representative on known variables, this gives us more confidence in it when it comes to unknown variables.

Further reading

The reading suggested at the end of the previous chapter is also appropriate for this one.

PART C

OPINIONS AND FACTS

---

5 Measurement: Principles

This part of the book looks at what is measured by survey research and how it should be measured. Chapter 5 starts the examination by looking briefly at the two major branches of survey research – surveys which use direct observation and surveys which rely on asking people questions. We shall be concerned with the twin problems of *operationalization* – getting from our concept of a characteristic worth measuring to something which can actually be measured – and *validation* – showing that the measures we have taken are indeed appropriate for the concept under discussion. The chapter acts as an introduction to the next two, in which some of the principles and practices discussed will be explored in more detail.

Systematic observation

We tend to talk as if all surveys involved asking people questions, but a lot of survey work uses more direct observational methods. Monitoring traffic involves counting and classifying vehicles passing a given point over a period of time. Monitoring TV viewing involves, as a first step, noting when the television is on and what channel is showing; this can be (and is) observed by a mechanical recorder. The first step of the British decennial Census, from the point of view of the enumerator, is going round his or her area noting what has been built or pulled down since the last Census and what dwellings have been converted to multiple occupancy or to commercial use – surveying the domestic housing stock of the area.

Observational survey reports are taken as factual: they count observable objects or incidents and do not require complex interpretation. However, all research involves *some* degree of interpretation, and some research topics require it more obviously and to a greater extent than others. If I want to survey the number of children in school playgrounds at break time, I can go round and count them. Issues to consider will include not only my accuracy – do I miss any children who are lurking in corners, and am I able to make accurate counts of large, milling crowds? – but also my interpretation of things to be counted. The interpretative issue in this simple survey would be whether each 'object' is a child or not a child. Some of the people there may be teachers, or other adults. Some may be children who do not belong to the school – visiting siblings, potential new pupils – and whether these are to be counted will depend on what my research is about. (If I am just looking at numbers – as a control problem, for instance – then I want a count of all children; if I am looking at the proportion of the school's child population that chooses to spend its break time in the playground, extraneous children must be excluded from the count.) Nonetheless, the count of children in playgrounds is a comparatively simple conceptual problem.

Suppose, however, that my research was about child violence in playgrounds (comparing, perhaps, an area where a particular television programme had been shown with another area where it had not, and looking for effects). Now my apparently factual count is bedevilled by a large element of interpretation. What counts as violence? Do I mean physical assault, and if so how serious does a piece of fighting have to be before I count it as an assault? How do I distinguish play from real violence? Do I wish to exclude behaviour which may be purely gestural – taps on the shoulder? Or do I want to count every incidence of physical contact, reducing the amount of interpretation of behaviour that I have to make but knowing that a proportion of what is being counted is irrelevant to my research question? Is it right to exclude 'verbal violence' – abuse, teasing and the like which do not involve physical contact (unless the victim retaliates) but might be counted as a form of bullying conceptually continuous with physical violence? If I am interested in the effects of a television programme, do I want to count particular *kinds* of violence, to identify 'copying from the television'? Could I define them with sufficient precision to permit accurate counting and to identify behaviour which is uniquely due to the programme's influence and could not have occurred for other reasons?

This process of translation, from the concept of 'violence' to instructions for what to count in the observed behaviour of children in playgrounds, is called *operationalization*. It requires the substitution, for something whose measurement a theory or hypothesis demands, of something which can actually be counted without ambiguity. It is part of the process of scientific measurement which requires that what is presented as evidence should be available to all who wish to repeat the procedures. This is a serious enough problem with something in principle visible though susceptible to definition, like violence, but it becomes more serious still when the existence of the phenomenon is in part *deduced* from the measures used, as in the case of intelligence or personality traits. It is also a problem in surveys of opinion, attitude, belief and intention, where the supposed (and theorized) nature of these phenomena is crucial to the interpretation of the data. These problems will be discussed below and throughout this part of the book.

Given an operationalized measure, the other logical necessity if it is to be used as evidence is *validation* – demonstrating that it does indeed measure what it purports to measure and has some claims to consistency and accuracy (see Box 1.3). This is a topic around which a considerable technology has grown up, and it is discussed in more detail below.

Asking questions

Facts and attitudes

Many things cannot be observed directly, and most surveys have at least some element of questioning informants and obtaining verbal answers (whether these are recorded by interviewers, written by respondents or precoded as a choice of responses offered by the researcher). Obtaining television viewing figures involves a mechanical count of what channel is switched on and when, but generally also a diary of who is in the room at the time, which is filled in by respondents. The two are similarly 'factual', however. The presence of family members could in principle be recorded by a machine rather than the respondents – we could have a continuous video record of the room, or family members could wear electronic 'tags' whose presence was recorded by a machine. Such measures do not require a great deal of interpretative thought, only checks on accuracy – whether they constitute a complete and accurate record of who was present at the time.

Note, however, that what is measured in this kind of research is not quite what it purports to be. The presence of someone in a room does not guarantee that they are watching the television. Market research companies are well aware of this, but they settle for the less valid measure in their operationalization precisely in order to have one whose factual accuracy can be demonstrated. If they asked 'Who was watching the programme?', the answers would be open to the interpretation of the respondents and to the vagaries of their memories. Do you remember whether you were actually *watching* the programme which was on at 7.30, as opposed to reading a book or talking to someone else or daydreaming? Were you *really* watching or just sitting there while it was on? Did you watch all of it, or did only some of it grab your attention? How much of it do you have to watch, and how closely do you need to be paying attention, in order for the occasion to count as one of 'watching a television programme'? These questions can be settled to a large extent by your instructions to the respondents, but they are complex and involve the discretion of the respondent, so they can potentially mean different things to different sorts of informant. This means that when differences appear between the answers of different informants we cannot guarantee that they are due to genuine differences in behaviour; they could be due at least in part to how the question was interpreted by different kinds of people.

Further, there are certain kinds of well-known systematic effects that might be expected to occur. 'Did you watch the Queen's Christmas message on TV?', we ask older women. 'Yes, of course', they say, meaning quite genuinely that they always have the programme on, as a mark of respect for tradition. That they were asleep in front of it, having drunk too much brandy after Christmas lunch, is not information that they are likely to volunteer to a young and well-presented interviewer. This is called the *social desirability effect* – the effect on answers of wishing to be seen as behaving in socially approved ways. Other aspects of it would be the wish not to appear silly to the interviewer – 'What? Me watch children's cartoons?' – or the wish not to stand out from the crowd – 'Yes, I watched the big match', 'No, I don't watch opera when there's football on television'.

This kind of effect will be even more marked when we ask about attitudes or opinions. You may feel that homosexuality is something to be encouraged, or on the other hand that all homosexuals should be flogged, but you are unlikely to admit to either belief to an interviewer or on a questionnaire. Similarly, we are all in favour of honour and virtue and feel that more should be spent on the poor and on health. (When the research asks about increasing taxes to pay for this, however, the answers tend to be less uniform.)

There are two other problems with attitude data, stemming from our uncertainty about what kind of 'thing' an attitude is and what the nature is of the person who 'has' or 'holds' one. Being part of meaning systems, attitude/belief/opinion statements partake of the nature of such systems, and one property of such systems is a tendency to autonomy or closure. That is, a statement can reflect a belief or opinion which is firmly and genuinely held and still have no connection with everyday behaviour. Beliefs tend to form themselves, as coherent sets, into *rhetorics* or *ideologies*: they tend to become mutually supportive and to evoke each other in a consistent way. At this level, however, they may be a purely verbal/conceptual form of behaviour; holding the belief is not predictive of what one will *do* in a given circumstance but only of what one will *say*.

On the other hand, some belief statements are not so much reports of feeling as expressions of determination to act: to say 'I believe . . .' in church is an act of affirmation, not a report of an internal state. As such it may be that they are evoked by the question which the research asks – that the questionnaire or interview is itself an instrument for changing people's behaviour (by focusing their mind on problems, for example) and so not competent to predict the attitudes of a population which has not been exposed to it. The problem is, most often, that we cannot tell in a given case whether the answer constitutes a valid report of feeling or belief, or is evoked as part of a rhetoric, or is influenced by the social desirability of the answer and/or the light in which it casts the respondent, or constitutes a *change* of attitude following focused thought about the topic. This kind of ambiguity is even more marked when we ask about intentions, because an intention can be a determination to act, expressed by the person making that determination, but alternatively it may be a prediction on the part of the respondent. 'How do you think you will vote at the next election?' could evoke the answer 'I *intend* to vote for the Green Party!', but it could equally evoke 'I *expect* I'll vote for the Green Party'. It may not be possible to distinguish the one response from the other.

Direct and indirect questions

'Factual' material may safely be collected by direct questioning. It is no particular problem for the respondent to say what his or her address is, or how many children he or she has, or how much he or she earns, or what his or her age is. Even here, however, some caution is needed in how questions are phrased and in how the researcher interprets the answers.

- As we saw, even direct observation involves interpretation rather than just recording events – we can count blows administered in playgrounds, but we need to decide whether these are to include play-fighting, demonstration of boxing moves, over-heavy 'friendly' slaps on the back, etc. When asking people how many children they have, we – and they – need to know whether stepchildren are to be included, and at what age someone ceases to be 'a child'. All questions include some ambiguity, which it is our job to minimise. Bram Oppenheim (1979) points out, for example, that as simple a question as 'Do you have a television?' is open to misunderstanding: it confuses personal ownership with collective (household) ownership, and both with access via renting agreements. (The British Census question about cars is 'Does your household *have access to* a car or cars?') Similarly, questions about income need to state whether it is gross or net income which is to be given and whether benefit payments, dividends, investment interest and so on are to be included.
- Informants may not wish to give precise answers about some variables. We usually ask not 'What is your age?', but 'When were you born?' or 'In which of the following age bands do you fall?', because these have turned out to attract a lower refusal rate. Indeed, informants may not *know* the precise answer to some questions at the time when the question is asked. They may know that last year's (gross) income fell between £20,000 and £25,000 but be unable to be more precise without excavating tax returns.
- Social desirability factors and other similar influences can bear on the answers to factual questions. Asking 'How many children do you have?' of someone who is not married may not elicit a factually honest answer. As we noted when looking at Example 2.2, asking people how much they drank last week does not always provide answers in whose veracity we can have confidence.

When asking about attitudes or opinions or intentions, all of these factors, and more, may come into play. The precise meaning of the question may be much influenced by its precise wording. 'How will you vote in the next general election?' is not quite the same question as 'How do you *think* you will vote in the next general election?'; the one invites a 'don't know' answer – 'I haven't yet made up my mind' – while the latter may be interpreted by the researcher as a firmer prediction than was in fact meant by the respondent.

Most often when asking for opinions/attitudes/beliefs we take a less direct approach. A straightforward question can all too easily evoke a rhetorical or ideological response, and this is often not what the research requires. If you ask people to affirm or deny the proposition that children's interests must come first, for example, they will affirm it, and their doing so tells us very little except that they know the culturally acceptable answer to this question. At the very least we would ask them a range of questions which presented the negation of the proposition as an equally acceptable answer – perhaps 'Women have the same rights to a career as men' or 'Women should not have to sacrifice themselves for their husbands and children'. If possible we might try to 'sneak up on the question' by a still more indirect route – perhaps embedding statements such as these in a battery of attitude items on a range of subjects, so that it becomes less evident what kind of an answer the researcher is seeking.

This illustrates a very basic point about survey research into attitudes and beliefs – that it is based fundamentally on deception. To the extent that we are open about what we are doing, we tell the respondents what sort of answers we are seeking and, often, what answers are acceptable. Being helpful people, they will generally try to help us by giving the 'right' answers, which may defeat the purpose of the research. The purpose is therefore often concealed or obscured in order to get a little nearer to what the respondents might have said in their ordinary lives, as opposed to the very artificial context of the survey interview or questionnaire.

Even less do we reveal the purpose of the questions when trying to measure traits of personality or diagnostic states. When measuring depression, for example, we seldom ask 'Are you depressed?'. There are two reasons for this: first, it invites the 'public answer', denying depression, which would probably be given whatever the state of the person; and second, by suggesting that we think the respondent the kind of person who can relevantly be asked about depression we cast doubts on his or her mental fitness. Instead we are likely to ask a series of questions about symptoms of depression – 'Do you have difficulty sleeping?', 'Do you find yourself worrying about nothing?', 'Do you sometimes cry without a reason?' and so on – and from this we construct a rating of the respondent's degree of depression. When measuring traits of personality the direct question would probably be inappropriate in any case, because there is no good reason to suppose that the respondents themselves are able to place themselves in terms of the researcher's theoretical constructs. The construction and rationale of personality inventories and diagnostic batteries is discussed in more detail below and in Chapter 7.

A final class of measures, even more indirect in their approach, are called *projective* measures. Here the idea is that we do not ask for respondents' attitudes or beliefs at all. Instead we ask them to tell a story or describe a scene, in the hope that they will project some of their own feelings into the answers. Classic measures of this kind include the *Rorschach test*, which uses people's descriptions of ambiguous shapes to form clues about their inner mental condition, or the *thematic apperception test*, which asks people to tell a story about ambiguous pictures and analyses it, for example, for images of achievement, on the principle that the respondent's own achievement motivation will be projected as the motivation of the characters in the pictures. Simpler variants would include standard ways of measuring *future time perspective*, by getting people to complete a story and seeing how far into the future they project the lives of the characters, reasoning that those who themselves have a long future perspective will also attribute one to their fictional characters.

The validation of measures

By 'measure' or 'measuring instrument', I mean here any procedure in a survey for the gathering of data. The scope of the term embraces not just the 'scientific' instruments devised to measure intelligence or personality or attitudes, but any question asked of respondents or any procedure for gathering observation data. All of these 'measure' the world.

The first and preliminary requirement of a measuring instrument is *standardization*. We expect a measure to be applied in a standardized way, so that every informant is asked precisely the same question in the same way, or every observation is regulated by the same set of definitions as to what is to count. If measures are not standardized they are of no value in surveys: differences between sections of the sample could be due to variation in procedures rather than underlying population differences. This seems a simple and obvious requirement, but it is very difficult to achieve in practice. Ways of doing so are discussed in more detail in the next chapter.

The need for standardization of our procedures is part of what we mean by *reliability* (Box 2.1). What is required of a measuring instrument is that it should produce consistent measurements of the same thing. The traditional simile here is the contrast between the rubber tape-measure and the yardstick; if the latter measures something as a foot long on one occasion it will do so on the next, while the measurements produced by the former will vary according to how much it is stretched. In the same way, we expect questions to produce consistent answers and observation procedures to produce consistent counts. We should, of course, remember the definition of 'reliability' put forward by the psychologist George Kelly, as 'that characteristic of a test which measures its insensitivity to change'. If our tape-measure shows no change when we measure someone's height at age 6 and at age 12, it is probably at fault. We expect it to show no change, however, if we take two measures of someone's height separated by only five minutes.

The reliability of measures is checked literally by asking the same questions twice in the course of a survey, or by repeating them later. Generally this is not practical in the body of the survey questionnaire (but see Chapter 7, on the measurement of complex constructs); however, pilot work should strive to assure us that the measures produce consistent results. In the case of observation or observer rating a common technique is *inter-rater reliability* – comparing the observations of two or more judges, on the principle that variation between them is due to individual idiosyncrasy.

Your measures may be standardized and of demonstrable reliability, but clearly there is more that you need to show: that they actually *do* measure what you *say* they measure (*validity*). When asking about factual matters, validity is increased mostly by careful attention to question phrasing and ordering, to minimize the likelihood that the answer is affected by factors other than those which we are trying to measure. We do our best to avoid annoying the respondents or making them feel threatened, and we certainly avoid indicating what kind of answer we would like to be given. In pilot work, before the questionnaire is widely distributed or the interviews carried out, we would try out different ways of asking questions, and talk to respondents afterwards about what they thought about when they were answering, to try to obtain the most useful answers. It may also be possible to apply some kind of cross-validation or check – by comparing the answers to different questions, or by comparing the responses of different informants – for example, husbands' and wives' accounts of the same events, or children's accounts compared with teachers'. More formally, when constructing the more elaborate kind of measuring instrument, we can validate it *concurrently* (by comparison with scores on another kind of measure whose validity we already know) or *predictively* (by using the measure to predict scores on some future event – for example, tests of mathematical reasoning can be validated against mathematics examination results). The validation of tests and inventories is discussed in Chapter 7.

Further reading

For alternative accounts of measurement in surveys, see de Vaus (1991) Chapter 4; Rosemarie Newell's chapter in Gilbert (1993); Oppenheim (1992) Chapter 6; Sapsford and Abbott (1996) Chapter 2; Smith (1975) Chapter 4; or Michael Wilson's chapter in Sapsford and Jupp (1996).

6 Putting it into practice

Varieties of data-collection method

In this chapter we look more practically at the design and administration of questionnaires and interview schedules, as well as observation schedules and the use of computers for the administration of questions. The principles discussed briefly in the previous chapter will inform the discussion, and the next two chapters in their turn will expand on them.

The first decision is whether to use an interviewer-administered schedule or a questionnaire which respondents complete themselves. The decision may effectively be made for you by the nature of the questions you wish to ask. If they are complex – difficult to understand in themselves, or numerous and exacting – then it will be necessary to use an interviewer. If you want to ask questions in an indirect way and lead up from generalities to more specific questions, or if you want to follow up on some aspects of attitude or behaviour without necessarily alerting the informant to your interest in them, then again an interviewer presentation will be needed. This may also be necessary because of the nature of the respondents: interviewers will be needed if respondents are very young or frail or ill, or if they are illiterate or do not have as first language the language in which the questionnaire is written, or if it is important that there be no bias in responses due to working-class people's lower fluency in writing.

The biggest advantages of self-completion questionnaires over structured interviews are their cheapness and the saving of the researcher's time, allowing much larger samples. Even if you post out your questionnaires with a reply-paid return envelope, twice – in order to minimize refusal/non-completion – you can still afford five postal questionnaires for every interviewer-administered schedule (assuming you have to pay the interviewers and cover their travel costs). If you can get the questionnaires delivered by some cheaper means – putting them through letter-boxes yourself, or persuading teachers to hand them out in class – then the multiplier is very much larger. Researcher time is even more important; a single hard-working interviewer is unlikely to manage more than 40 half-hour interviews in a week, and fewer would be reasonable, but you can mail out as many questionnaires as you like for the relatively trivial labour of stuffing them into envelopes.

Another advantage of self-completion questionnaires is that they are necessarily an entirely standardized measuring instrument – the questions are always phrased exactly in the same way, for all respondents. Where interviewers are involved there is always an element of personal reaction in the interaction, and it is very difficult to use *exactly* the same phrasing and intonation in every single case. One major disadvantage of questionnaires, the converse of this, is that there is no one to explain what questions mean and help the respondent to understand what is required, so there will be more 'spoiled' responses with postal questionnaires and an unknown amount of wrong information due to misunderstanding. (However, explanation is not without its problems for survey research – a topic discussed at greater length below.) You will also have higher non-response rates with postal questionnaires; it is much more difficult to refuse an interviewer face to face than to fail to complete and post a questionnaire.

The next decision, if you have decided on interviews, is to determine whether they are to be carried out face-to-face or by telephone. Normally face-to-face interviewing is preferred, because the rapport which it generates allows respondents to relax and become maximally co-operative; telephone interviews are always more remote and generally more formal. Strangely, telephone interviews can also be more startling and intrusive for the respondent, because they 'arrive out of the blue' with no chance to look the interviewer over and decide to co-operate, and because a great deal of 'cold canvas' sales work is done over the telephone, so the refusal rate is generally substantially higher if you use this method. However, they are quicker and cheaper than face-to-face interviewing, because they save on the costs and time of travel.

What do you think the other major problems with telephone interviewing are?

As you will remember from earlier chapters, refusal is a problem for representative sampling, so the greater the refusal rate, the more likely the achieved sample is not to be representative of its target population. The problem is compounded, for telephone survey work, by the fact that those who have access to a telephone are still an unrepresentative subset of the general population, and by the lack of interviewer control over who answers the telephone.

Finally, for completeness' sake, we should note the increasing use of computers at the interviewing stage of survey work. Some large-scale, well-funded surveys run the survey questionnaire as a program on the interviewer's laptop computer, thereby ensuring standardized presentation and perhaps giving the respondent some illusion of privacy but retaining the advantages of interviewer-administered surveys. Alternatively, a computer version of a 'postal' questionnaire could be installed on a network in school or at work, with the co-operation of the network managers and computer department, so that a message inviting people to take part appeared when people sign on and an interactive questionnaire program was available for them. Presumably the same could be done on the Internet at large, but at the time of writing I do not know anyone who has tried this.

Whatever the form of presentation, three things are necessary, in a successful questionnaire:

1 clear, unambiguous questions – see the earlier discussion of TV 'ownership' – or, more generally, when taking an indicator of a more complex concept, valid and reliable measures, to eliminate errors of measurement which might confuse the results;
2 standardization of presentation, so that everyone is asked precisely the same questions in the same order and as much as possible of the variation due to interviewer 'style' is eliminated; and
3 a trustworthy, efficient and, preferably, cost-effective way of translating (coding) the data for subsequent analysis.

These are the subject areas which we shall be exploring in the rest of this chapter.

A practical example: the People in Society schedule

To put some flesh on the bones of the above discussion, we will start by looking in more detail at the schedule used in the student survey of social class which was described above as Example 4.1. The schedule is selected for discussion not because it is perfect, but because it has some good questions and also some poor ones.

You should look back to Example 4.1 at this point and remind yourself of the broad outlines of the research, and then look through Example 6.1, which shows some of the questions that were included.

Example 6.1: The People in Society survey (2): selected questions

First, I should like to ask you a few questions about society.

Q.1 Do you see yourself as belonging to any particular group in society?
(IF YES) What group?
Yes – mentions 'social class'   1 Go to Q.3
    – mentions other group (specify)

_____   2

No   3

Q.2 Do you think there are different social classes in our society?
Yes – there are classes   1
(IF NO OR DON'T KNOW)
Are there any significant social differences or inequalities in our society?
Yes – there are differences/inequalities   2
No   3 Go to Q.10
Don't know   4 Go to Q.10

. . . .

Q.4 What is the name of the class/group in which you would place yourself?
(DO NOT READ OUT)
Upper   1
Upper middle   2
Middle   3
Lower middle   4

Upper working   5
Working   6
Lower working   7
Lower   8

Other (specify) _____   9
Don't know   10

IF CODE 3 OR 6 IN Q.4, CODE Q.5 BUT DON'T ASK

Q.5 If you had to say you were either middle or working class, which would you say?
Middle class   1
Working class   2
Don't know   3 Go to Q.8

Q.6 What sort of person do you mean when you talk about the middle/working class? (RESPONDENT'S CLASS AT Q.5)

. . . .

Q.8 (SHOW CARD)

    (a) Which of these do you think is the most important in determining a person's class?

    (b) And which is the second most important?

	(a) Most	(b) Second
Occupation	1	1
How people live	2	2
Education	3	3
Wealth and property	4	4
Manner	5	5
Income	6	6
Background	7	7
Power	8	8
Other (specify) _____	9	9
Don't know	10	10

. . . .

Q.10 Which political party do you usually vote for or support at general elections?

Labour	1
Conservative	2
Liberal	3
SDP	4
Other (specify) _____	5
Various	6
None	7
Refused to answer	8

Q.11 Which of these statements comes closest to your own point of view? (SHOW CARD)

(a) In Britain today there are basically two classes, bosses and workers	1
OR Most people in Britain today belong to the same class	2
OR There are several classes in Britain today	3
Don't know	4

And which of these? (SHOW CARD)

(b) A man's working life is like a ladder which he climbs up from rung to rung	1
OR If a man has a steady job and a good wage he should be content	2
Don't know	3

Q.12 Please put a tick in whichever box applies in each line.

THE KIND OF PERSON WHO IS WORKING CLASS IS

	Extremely	Fairly	Slightly	Neither	Slightly	Fairly	Extremely	
Rich	☐	☐	☐	☐	☐	☐	☐	Poor
Hard life	☐	☐	☐	☐	☐	☐	☐	Easy life
Dependent	☐	☐	☐	☐	☐	☐	☐	Independent
Reckless	☐	☐	☐	☐	☐	☐	☐	Cautious

. . . .

Finally, I'd like to ask you a few questions about yourself.

Q.15 Are you married?

Married	1
Single	2
Widowed/divorced/separated	3

. . . .

Q.20 Are you working nowadays?
(IF YES) Is that 30 hours or more?

Yes – 30 hours or more (full-time)	1
Yes – less than 30 hours (part-time)	2
No – retired	3

IF NOT WORKING, OTHER THAN RETIRED
How long is it since you last worked?

Less than two years	4
Two years or more	5

Q.21 IF YES

What is your main occupation?	A	1
(WRITE IN AND CODE)	B	2
_____	C1	3
	C2	4
IF RETIRED OR UNEMPLOYED < 2 YEARS	D	5
What was your last occupation?	E	6
(WRITE IN AND CODE)	Refused	7

_____

. . . .

Q.26 (SHOW CARD)

Taking into account all the money you earn after tax, would you tell me which figure on the card comes closest to your own personal income?

Weekly	*Annual*	
No income	No income	1
Less than £21	Less than £1001	2
£21–40	£1001–2000	3
£41–60	£2001–3000	4
£61–80	£3001–4000	5
£81–100	£4001–5000	6
£101–120	£5001–6000	7
£121–140	£6001–7000	8
£141–160	£7001–8000	9
£161–180	£8001–9000	10
£181–200	£9001–10,000	11
£201–240	£10,001–12,000	12
£241–300	£12,001–15,000	13
£301–400	£15,001–20,000	14
Over £400	Over £20,000	15
Refused		16
Don't know		17

CODE RESPONDENT'S SEX

Male	1
Female	2

Direct measures

A large part of the interview schedule is concerned with strictly factual information – see Questions 10, 15, 20 and 26, as examples, and the coding of gender at the end of the questionnaire. Only one of these measures, the measure of gender, is as straightforward as it seems on the surface, though the 'occupation' question (Question 21) is relatively straightforward once you realize that it is coded from a list which puts occupations into social class categories and that interviewers were told what amount of detail they needed to record to facilitate this.

Question 15 on marital status is straightforward, but it needs a degree of interpretation before it can be filled in, in a small but significant minority of cases, and was somewhat misconceived for the purpose for which it was intended.

What problems do you see with Question 15?

It is essential, if we are to obtain valid information in the same way for all respondents and thus be able to compare across cases and groups, that every question should offer a range of answers which exhaust the possibilities and are mutually exclusive. There must be no possible condition under which you could fail to find an answer to fit your case or have to tick more than one answer. The problem comes with 're-formed families': how do the partners code themselves? Take, for example, a family where the woman has been married and divorced and is now cohabiting with a man not previously in a marital relationship, and suppose the two have been together for 15 or 20 years and have children. Both will hesitate about how to code themselves. Both, or either, might tick 'married', as they are for all intents and purposes in a marriage even if it has not been formalized legally. On the other hand, the woman ought strictly to record herself as 'divorced' and the man as 'single'. A modern survey would have 'cohabiting' as a category.

Similarly, the politics question (Question 10) was carefully phrased but made too little provision for the nationalist parties of Wales and Scotland and for the fact that some of the major parties do not contest Parliamentary seats in Northern Ireland. The failings of these questions will have added 'noise' round the 'signal'; they increase the proportion of unusable or uninformative responses.

Question 26, on income, is deceptively straightforward. It is coded in income bands, because no one remembers annual or even weekly income to the exact dollar or pound sterling without a great deal of research into payslips and the like. (We had to add some bands to the top of the scale during the course of the survey, as inflation moved everyone's salaries and wages up it, and it would be necessary to add more if the questionnaire were to be used today. Survey questionnaires and schedules for use over time are difficult to design with the future in mind.) The question asks about take-home pay – income received from employment, after tax has been deducted. This may in itself be a problem: some monthly-paid people do not have their annual take-home pay in memory but only gross salary. As we wanted total available income, however, the question is flawed. It does not ask for other sources of income – investment interest, profits from sale of property and so on. Worse, it does not collect benefit income and can therefore say little about variation between those at or near the bottom of the scale of deprivation – the unemployed, the permanently sick or disabled, state pensioners and those on such low income that it has to be 'topped up' by a state benefit. (Worst of all, in common with most other such questionnaires, it does not even attempt to assess income from theft, fraud and undeclared and untaxed work.) Again, the validity of the information is reduced by a degree of thoughtlessness in the construction of the question; it is neither as useful, nor as accurate, as it might have been.

On the other hand, the way in which the respondent is led from Question 1 up to Question 5 in the search for an appropriate class label is very much a model of its kind.

Look at Questions 1–5 again and think why they are structured in the way they are.

The problem here is that we would not want to ask respondents directly whether they are middle- or working-class if there is any way of getting the information without doing so. They might not, themselves, naturally use these labels or put the same meaning on them as the researchers do. They might understand the labels and be perfectly prepared to use them but have a different way of classifying people in society which would be more natural to them. Further, for some people 'class' is a fundamental and visible reality, at the forefront of their thoughts, while for others it is an academic notion, usable but not normal or natural for them. The first question, therefore, just asks whether society falls into groups and provides an opportunity for the respondent to show that class is a salient category for him or her by naming it spontaneously. If it is not named in Question 1, Question 2 raises the topic explicitly. Similarly, Question 4 gives respondents considerable scope to use fine gradations, before Question 5 forces those who did so into a simple dichotomy of 'middle' and 'working'.

The same principle is at work in the progress from Question 6 to Question 8. Question 6 asks for a description of the respondent's own class in his or her own words. (Question 7 does the same for the other class.) This maximizes the chance of capitalizing on individual variation and learning about ideas which had not previously occurred to the researcher. Then Question 8 uses a preselected list of categories, to ensure that the same list is considered by all respondents. The aim throughout is to increase the validity of the information by cutting down on the influence which a highly prestructured question can have on the answers which are given.

Indirect measures and attitude/personality scales

Arguably, unless you take the position that attitudes are something simple in the head which can be 'read' and reported on by those who have them, anything which has an attitudinal component has to be measured to some extent indirectly. That is, the attitude is something complex, and one is looking for relatively simple *indicators* of it. Question 11 on the People in Society interview schedule is an item of this sort – straightforward in what it asks but indirect in that the answers are indicators rather than direct measures of what is at stake (see Box 6.1). The statements are typical of models of society which sociologists have put forward and are to be used as indicators of the model that the respondent holds. In themselves, however, the questions are simple and direct. (Note the mistake in Question 11(b), however: because of the mix of 'is' and 'ought', it is just about possible for someone to assent to both propositions – life *is* like a ladder, but people with a steady job *should* be content. Note also the use of 'man', which may make this a different question for female than for male respondents.)

Direct questions such as we considered in the last subsection need little validation, beyond assurance that they are clearly phrased and do ask precisely what the researcher meant to ask and needs for the research. Indirect measures require more in the way of validation, because you need

---

Box 6.1: Indicators and measures

We call something a *measure* when it directly assesses the quantity in which we are interested. An *indicator* is something which is known or believed to correlate with the quantity of interest, and therefore to predict it, but which does not directly measure it.

As an example: we are interested in the temperature outside the house. A thermometer measures this directly. (Actually, what it measures is the height of a column of mercury in a capillary tube, but let us not make matters too complicated at this stage!) If there is no thermometer, we could take several other measurements which would be indicators of the probable temperature. For example, degree of undress of passers-by would be an indicator – to the extent that people are in shirt-sleeves rather than overcoats, the temperature is probably high. Another indicator might be the extent to which people are sweating as they walk by. Another might be the degree to which the ground looks dry and cracked. All of these are consequences of heat (or, in the case of clothing, reactions to it) and thus should vary with it.

---

to demonstrate that the indicator does indeed vary exactly with the quantity which is to be measured. In the case of these attitude statements the claim to validity lies in the derivation of the statements from other people's research; they have successfully been used in the past as indicators of the models we want to explore, so there is no reason to suppose they will not be useful again in this questionnaire.

A more complex form of indirect measurement is provided by Question 12, only part of which is reproduced in Example 6.1. This 'question' consisted of 14 bipolar items on which the respondent was asked to rate 'a person who is working class' on a seven-point scale – from, for example, extremely rich to extremely poor. (Respondents filled in the sheet themselves, after being taken through a sheet of printed instructions by the interviewer.) There were two further sheets with the same adjectives on them, on which respondents described 'a person who is middle class' and 'I am . . .'. These 14 ratings for each of the three 'objects' were added together to make two scales, one of which measures 'position in life' (rich, easy life, independent, powerful, free, high status, successful) and the other 'lack of conservatism' or 'lack of forethought' (lives for the present, spends, radical, dissatisfied, not law-abiding, reckless, friendly). Factor analysis (see Chapter 10) indicated that these two clusters were relatively homogeneous and relatively independent of each other – the items correlated fairly highly within the group and fairly lowly with items outside the group. This is necessary – and a part of the validation process – if the scales are to be consistently interpretable. Looking at data over several years, they appeared to be reasonably reliable – they gave similar distributions year after year – which is another aspect of validation. We shall look at the construction of scales and tests in more detail in Chapter 7.

So every stage of survey design and the conduct of surveys is concerned with the question of validity. At its minimum, this means asking whether the question asks (or the observation records) what it was meant to record and does so with a fair degree of accuracy; every effort is made to minimize error (which can be conceptualized as 'noise around a signal', concealing real differences or relationships in a cloud of imprecision or, worse, bias). Where the nature of what is supposed to be being measured is not itself straightforward but depends on theoretical interpretation, more extended arguments about validity may be necessary. This involves validating the theoretical arguments as well as the measurements which depend on them – the process of *construct validation* which is discussed in Chapters 7 and 8. One key to validity at every stage of survey work, however, is standardization: making sure that the measurements are taken in the same way for every respondent, so that differences between them are not due to differences of measurement technique.

Designing the instrument

Interview schedules and self-administered questionnaires

With a schedule which is to be administered by an interviewer, the most important thing is to guarantee standardized presentation as far as possible; if groups are to be compared, it is imperative that differences between them cannot be ascribed to differences in the questions that were asked or the way in which they were asked. Partly this is ensured by practice and training (discussed below). Partly, however, it is a function of the design of the schedule.

The phrasing of the questions needs to be precise, to ask for exactly the information which is required: it is no good asking 'Do you have a television set?' when what you want to know is whether the informant actually watches television. Questions must be unambiguous; 'Do you have a television set?' might be answered 'Yes, there is one in the house – it belongs to my Dad', or 'No, but my Dad has one', or even 'Yes (or No), (but) our set is rented, not owned'. At the same time they must be as colloquial as possible, to be easily understood and to create some feeling for a natural conversation rather than an esoteric checklist (or else the reactivity of the situation may distort the data). 'Do you own or rent or otherwise have a chance of watching a television in your house?' is accurate but cumbersome. 'Do you have access to a television set?' is precise but rather pedantic and formal. Best might be to ask three separate questions: 'Is there a television in your house?' (explaining a bit further where people live in, say, rented rooms within a house), 'Do you watch it at all?' and, if the answer is 'No', 'Could you watch it if you wanted to?'. The questions should be phrased in such a way that they do not necessarily suggest what answer is to be given: so, not 'Do you ever beat your wife?', but

'Sometimes people lose their temper when things are getting on top of them and strike out at others who happen to be around. Do you ever find yourself doing that?

Have you ever actually hit someone?

What sort of a person was that?

Have you ever actually hit your wife, for example?'.

Question *routeing* is also important – where the interviewer goes next, depending on the answer to the question just asked. In the People in Society example (Example 6.1), Question 1 asks whether people see themselves as belonging to a social class without ever using the word 'class' – informants are left to come up with it for themselves. If they do not, then class is obviously not the most salient form of social structure for them, but they may still have it as part of their 'conceptual armoury', so a more directive question is asked which does contain the word 'class'. If they agree at this point, or still fail to state that Britain has social classes but acknowledge social divisions, then questions about class can be asked. If not, however, we have by this stage done all we can by way of not taking no for an answer, and the interviewer skips the rest of the 'class' questions and goes on to Question 10.

Thus routeing can be used to avoid asking questions repetitively, or in contradiction to what the respondent has just said, and thereby annoying him or her. (It is obviously important that any such routeing instructions are entirely clear, so that there is little chance of the interviewer missing out questions that ought to have been asked.) It can also be used to check up on answers and get people to expand beyond the immediate response – in this case, to try to elicit agreement about the existence of classes from those who have failed to mention them or even explicitly denied their existence.

Now look at Figure 6.1 before reading on.

Figure 6.1 gives another example, of a dance-hall conversation conceived as a survey interview. The first part of the interview here is in fact directed not at eliciting information but at obtaining co-operation, in a situation where it is easier for the respondent to brush the interviewer off. A standard introductory question – 'Do you come here often?' – is used to note whether the respondent is initially co-operative, rejects the approach or just ignores it. If the approach is ignored, a second question is 'Are you deaf?', used just to open up the conversation; any reply whatsoever is taken as denying deafness (with those who continue not to reply after extensive interrogation being written off and dropped from the sample). For those who rejected the initial advance (by means of verbal abuse, for example) and those who initially ignored it but have now made some kind of response, the next question asks 'Can I talk to you?'. Those who say 'yes' (or something not necessarily interpreted as an out and out 'no'!) join those who were co-operative in the first place, and the real interview starts.

```
Q.1 Do you come here often? Code answer:          Co-operative    1 Go to Q.4
                                                  Rejecting       2

If rejecting in words or gestures, go to Q.3
If rejecting by ignoring question, proceed with Q.2

Q.2  Are you deaf?                                Yes             1 See below
                                                  No              2 Go to Q.3

If respondent fails to answer, when asked this question repeatedly, code 2 and
end interview
If respondent says yes, code 1 and go to  Q.3


Q.3 Can I talk to you then?                       Yes             1  Go to Q.4
                                                  No              2 End interview


Q.4 What do you think of the band?
Write in answer. Probe for more detail:
                                 What about their music?
                                 What about their clothes?
                                 Are they sexy?
                                 Is there anything you like about them?
```

FIGURE 6.1   *An interview schedule*

This kind of follow-up questioning is called 'prompting' – asking 'supplementaries' to try to improve the quality of the answer. Often the interviewer is instructed to try to get fairly full responses, and possible 'prompts' are listed on the schedule for use in encouraging a longer response – as in Question 4 of Figure 6.1. Prompting is an important part of survey work – it is what helps to obtain more than the bare immediate responses and gives us more interpretable responses. It embodies an inherent and unavoidable paradox, however. To the extent that we *do not* prompt, the amount of detail in the answer may be a product of the informant's personality rather than of his or her knowledge or system of beliefs – he or she may just be more or less forthcoming. To the extent that we *do* prompt, we are not asking all informants the same questions, and the principle of standardization is breached. The same goes for help provided by the interviewer, where a respondent does not understand the question or some of the words in it. If help is offered, the questions are not the same for all informants; some people were given additional 'feeds' by the interviewer. To the extent that help is not offered, however, people may understand different things by a given question and so in effect be answering different questions. Neither of these is a soluble problem, which is why I call them 'paradoxes'; we just have to keep them in mind and do the best we can.

Turning from interviewer-administered schedules to self-administered questionnaires, we find that much of the discussion stays the same but that in some respects questionnaires raise equal but opposite problems to schedules. Standardization is still the goal, along with precise and unambiguous phrasing within questions and clear and unambiguous routeing between questions. These are all the more necessary because the questionnaire must 'stand up by itself'. There can be no *ad hoc* assistance for people who do not follow the question. There can be no progressive prompting to elicit longer responses and to direct the respondent's attention to areas of interest to the researcher. The questions have to do all the work, so they have to be thought out very carefully. Even the kind of graded and gradual approach which the People in Society survey took to questions about social class is not likely to be effective.

Look back at the first few questions of Example 6.1. Why might these be less effective in a postal questionnaire than when administered by an interviewer?

When interviewer-administered, these questions are presented one at a time. This is not necessarily the case with questionnaires which the respondents fill in themselves. Many people will look through the whole of a questionnaire before starting to fill it in. Even if they look at one question at a time it would be difficult not to notice, when filling in Question 1, that the word 'class' appears in Question 2.

The enormous advantage of self-completion questionnaires is their cheapness: thousands can be sent through the post at very little cost in terms of either time or money. What we pay for this cheapness – unless the questionnaire is completed under controlled conditions (as part of a school class, for example) – is that we cannot guarantee the amount or quality of attention that the respondent will give it. Nor, for that matter, can we be sure who filled it in – whether the target respondent, or someone else, or a committee of a whole family or friendship group collaborating over it. These are matters which might greatly affect the validity of the information we receive. There are also colossal problems of non-response, as discussed in the previous section.

Observation schedules, and counting in text

Constructing observation schedules is much simpler on the face of it than designing questionnaires – largely a matter of common sense and foresight. You need to have worked out precisely what it is you want to count, and then, quite simply, you design a form on which you can record the results of the count with the greatest ease and the least confusion. Figure 6.2, for example, illustrates a schedule put together for a fictional study of behaviour in shops. The design of the study is that a given observer sticks to one kind of customer – young men, say – and positions himself or herself where a clear view can be obtained of a given check-out desk without

Check-out: M / F					Date: 7/5		Start time: 10.30	
Dur- Cust- Gender ation omer			Customer			Check-out operative		
		Friendly	Neutral	Belligerent		Friendly	Neutral	Belligerent
1	M / F							
2	M / F							
3	M / F							
4	M / F							
5	M / F							
6	M / F							
7	M / F							
8	M / F							
9	M / F							
10	M / F							

FIGURE 6.2 *An observation schedule*

giving customers or the cash-till operative the feeling of being observed. (Care would also have to be taken not to appear to be loitering with the intention of stealing, or the research will be disturbed by store detectives!) The top row of the schedule records the date and start time of the period of observation and the gender of the check-out operative. Then each row stands for one complete interaction, between the first item of someone's shopping being picked up and the change being given after the shopping is paid for. For each, the gender of the customer is noted. The individual behaviours (smiles and frowns, verbal interactions, 'body language' such as turning away or not looking up) of both parties in the interaction are then recorded in the body of the form, under the three categories of 'friendly', 'neutral' and 'hostile'. Finally, we record the duration of each encounter, in a column placed well away from the main data-collection area of the form to avoid accidental misuse.

The simplicity of direct observation is in many ways deceptive, however; the collection instrument may be simple, but what is being collected is often very complex. Observation is seldom about observable behaviours, but usually about unobservables for which the observable stands as an operationalized indicator; behaviours are nearly always *interpreted* as signs of the trait or state or process which is to be measured and explained. Thus the quality of the measurement, as an operationalization of a research concept, is crucial to observational research. The concepts must be well operationalized – the variables to be collected must, as far as possible, be true indicators of the concepts under investigation. The schema for classifying them must be consistent and consistently used, rather than dependent on the whim of the individual observer. Thus in the example in

TABLE 6.1 *Flanders' interactional categories*

Teacher talk:			
Response:	1	*Accepts feelings*, clarifies a pupil's feelings, in a non-threatening manner.
	2	*Praises or encourages* pupil action or behaviour, makes tension-releasing jokes (not at another's expense), nods in response.
	3	*Accepts or uses pupils' ideas*, clarifies or develops them.
Initiation:	4	*Asks questions* about content or procedure, for pupil to answer.
	5	*Lectures*, gives fact or opinion, gives own ideas or cites an authority other than the pupil.
	6	*Gives directions*, commands or orders.
	7	*Criticizes* – behaviour expected to change pupils' behaviour from non-acceptable to acceptable.
Pupil talk:		
Response:	8	*Talk in response to teacher* – freedom to express own ideas is limited.
Initiation:	9	*Pupil talk initiated by pupils* – own ideas or opinions, own questions going beyond the existing material of the lesson.
	10	*Silence or confusion*.

TABLE 6.2 *Bales' interactional categories*

Task-related categories:			
Attempted answers:	1	*Gives suggestion*, direction, implying autonomy for others.	(4)
	2	*Gives opinion*, evaluation, analysis, expresses wish or feeling.	(5)
	3	*Gives orientation*, information, clarifies, confirms.	(6)
Questions:	4	*Asks for orientation*, information, repetition, confirmation.	(7)
	5	*Asks for opinion*, evaluation, analysis, expression of feeling.	(8)
	6	*Asks for suggestion*, direction, possible ways of action.	(9)
Socio-emotive work:			
Positive:	7	*Shows solidarity*, raises others' status, gives help, rewards.	(1)
	8	*Shows tension release*, jokes, laughs, shows satisfaction.	(2)
	9	*Agrees*, shows passive acceptance, understands, concurs, complies.	(3)
Negative:	10	*Disagrees*, shows passive rejection, becomes formal, withholds help.	(10)
	11	*Shows tension*, asks for help, withdraws from group.	(11)
	12	*Shows antagonism*, deflates others, defends or asserts self.	(12)

Note: These categories have been reordered. Figures in brackets are Bales' original numbering.

Figure 6.2 we would need precise definitions of what was to count as 'friendly', 'neutral' and 'hostile'. These might be based to a greater or lesser extent on the research literature, but a period of initial 'free' observation might well be needed, to form a picture of the range and frequency of typical behaviours. It would be necessary to practise the use of the categorization (see discussion below) until each observer was fluent in it and consistent with other observers. Even then, it would be a very good idea to have more than one observer and average the results, as a way of controlling for the inevitable bias and carelessness of individuals.

The classification used in Figure 6.2 is one made up 'on the spot' – little better than codified common sense. More complex 'ready-made' schemata are available for categorizing what is going on, based on clear theoretical perspectives on the nature of social interaction. Two such are illustrated in Tables 6.1 and 6.2. Table 6.1 shows Flanders' interactional analysis categories for recording what goes on in classrooms (Flanders, 1970). Table 6.2 summarizes a set of categories devised by the functionalist sociologist R.F. Bales (1950), a colleague of Talcott Parsons, for recording what was being achieved in group interaction, distinguishing between task-oriented contributions and 'socio-emotive' work designed to maintain or dissolve the group's cohesion. These are subtle, rich and sophisticated measuring instruments but would clearly require a great deal of training and practice before they could be used reliably, and it would again be very sensible to use more than one observer in order to 'average out' errors of judgement.

Just the same considerations obtain when we are looking at text in a survey-like manner – observing the differences between newspapers with different target audiences, for example, or comparing the treatment of particular subjects over time. We have to decide *what* to count and *how* to count it.

The former is a question of validity: what concepts are important in our study, and how can we best operationalize them? Typically, three kinds of classificatory system have been used. First, we may characterize the material by its topic area: when analysing newspapers, for example, we may count 'crime stories' separately from 'business stories', 'sports stories' and so on. Second, we may classify items by the stance they adopt or something else internal to their content – for example, whether they support or attack the line taken by the government of the day, or whether they express or attack 'family ideology' propositions such as the notion that a woman's place is in the home with the children. Both of these involve a judgement – the second more than the first – about the category to which the item belongs, and it might, again, be good practice to have this judgement made by more than one 'observer'. The third common way is to look at the words themselves, for what they betray – comparing, for example, the relative incidence of 'woman', 'girl', 'wife'/'mother', 'worker' and 'person' and drawing conclusions about degrees of sexism and the influence of family ideology. Less personal judgement is required here at the stage of data collection, but obviously the results still have to be interpreted.

As to how we are to collect data, if you are using the third approach above, you will be counting words, but for the other two you may wish to use something less tedious to count. A common trick, when comparing text of equal density (for example, two editions of the same newspaper) is to measure column-inches, so that we can say that a given edition has, say, 44 inches of crime stories and only 10 of economic news. When comparing different newspapers this is obviously an inadequate strategy, because the type size and column width will vary, but one can still count inches and express the results as proportions – 55 per cent (44 inches out of a total of 80 inches) in newspaper *A* is devoted to crime reporting. A similar approach has been used for analysing the content of television news broadcasts: what proportion of the news time is given over to government spokesmen, for example?

Having decided what to count and how to count it, all we need is a schedule for recording the results, after the style of Figure 6.2. We must remember, however, to take a count of the total of a given document (in words, or pages, or column-inches, or whatever), so that the categorized items within it can be expressed as proportions of the total. Only in this way is it possible to compare documents of different lengths or print styles.

Training and briefing

The first stage of the survey interview process is the briefing of interviewers to ensure standardized performance within a framework of apparently natural behaviour. Even if you were doing all the interviews yourself, you would take the time to think about how the interview was to be managed, how to introduce yourself and what to say about the survey's purpose, what might 'go wrong' or prove difficult in the presentation and how to handle the sensitive questions and those where certain kinds or amounts of information are required. (This takes place, of course, even with postal questionnaires: it is part of the process of designing them so that they *can* be self-administered.) If several of you were conducting the interviews, you would get together beforehand to co-ordinate your approaches and decide how problems were to be resolved. When using outside interviewers, it is necessary to go through the schedule in detail and answer any questions and problems which the interviewers raise. You need to standardize the way in which they introduce themselves to informants, so that all are 'set up' for the interview in the same kind of way. You also need to tell them enough about the purpose of the survey that they can recognize what is important in the questionnaire. (The advantage of using outside interviewers, however, is that you do *not* have to tell them what results you expect, so one possible source of error is diminished.)

People new to the interviewing business may need to be trained to administer questionnaires in a standardized but sensitive way, to avoid annoying or disturbing respondents and to build rapport. Most commercial organizations give their interviewers at least a one-day course in interviewing, including role-playing of interviews and discussion of their performance. Most of the reputable organizations give more than a day's training.

Where judgemental classifications are concerned – for example, the classification of behaviour into 'friendly', 'neutral' and 'hostile' in Figure 6.2 – training and practice are of paramount importance in ensuring reliability of measurement. It is essential that the person making the judgement does so consistently, and that different judges classify the same occurrences in the same way. Video is very useful here; a recorded scene or sequence of events can be used as stimulus material which can be observed time and time again until judgements about it are reliable. Where a more complex schema is used, such as those shown in Tables 6.1 and 6.2, training in their consistent use is even more important. Often, complex instruments (particularly psychological ones) are licensed for use only on condition that training is undertaken, and training courses are provided by the instrument's designers. These ensure not only that users are consistent in their judgements, but also that judgements are consistent across users – that different interviewers/testers will use the instrument in the same way, allowing their results to be compared validly.

The conduct of interviews

In the field, then, we have trained and briefed interviewers (perhaps ourselves!) to be ready to contact potential respondents and carry out standardized interviews. From the very beginning of the contact every effort is made to keep the procedures as similar as possible for all informants – even introducing the study in the same way and making the same kinds of effort to secure the interview rather than a refusal to co-operate. However, we cannot claim the rigid and rigorous standardization of the laboratory, where precisely the same stimulus is applied to every subject of the experiment. People differ, and what is an appropriate and effective 'stimulus' for one is inappropriate or ineffective for another. To take the very simplest example, English is not everyone's first language, so when we run into a speaker of some other language when selecting the sample we have three choices – to reject the respondent, confining the sample to speakers of English; to translate (thereby altering the schedule of questions); or to collect data which are likely to be useless because the questions were not properly or fully understood. In general, as Oppenheim (1992: 87) points out, we are not seeking a mechanical identity of procedures, but the presentation of questions (in as similar a manner as possible) which are *understood* in the same way by everyone:

> what we are seeking to produce is not 'stimulus equality' but 'stimulus equivalence' . . . that is, that the respondent's understanding of the question or task will be the same as that of every other respondent interviewed by this or any other interviewer . . . This means that interviewers must be trained to use their judgment in departing sometimes . . . from the exact text of their schedules . . . while always trying to remain non-directive and not 'putting the answer in the respondent's mouth'.

The need for equivalence, rather than strict equality, goes beyond the phrasing of the questions and the use of prompts and explanations, to the way in which the situation as a whole is framed and handled. A major problem with the survey interview, as a social situation, is that it *is* a social situation. All situations have rules, and the rules of surveys are really quite well known in popular culture. It is the duty of the interviewer to ask the questions and the respondent to respond to them. Beyond this, the interviewer as researcher (or the researcher who hired him or her) is trying to get certain sorts of answers, and the respondent will oblige by giving them wherever possible, picking up on any accidental or careless hints about what the right answers actually are. The respondent will also want to be seen in a good light by the interviewer, so social desirability factors come into play. The antidote to all this is a reflexive awareness by the interviewer of the nature of the situation and an attempt to make it as much like an informal conversation as is compatible with reasonably standardized presentation and as little as possible like a formal interrogation. One important aspect of this is building a rapport with respondents – establishing a relaxed relationship in which even sensitive and embarrassing topics can be discussed, and establishing the sort of friendly relations in which the truth is more likely than deliberate deception and the respondent will work to give as accurate and useful an answer as possible. Most important of all, it is rapport which allows the interviewer, to some limited extent, to 'see inside the respondent's head' and perhaps know when a question has not been fully understood or fully answered.

Initial impressions are very important. There are no hard and fast rules for who makes the best impression and conducts the most successful interviews; who is most acceptable as an interviewer will vary from person to person and group to group. On the whole we try to match interviewers to respondents to some extent, so that the interviewer is broadly similar in background and expectations to the respondent. Certainly, when interviewing Black or other minority ethnic populations we would try to get interviewers of the same ethnic group, because they would probably be more acceptable than interviewers from other ethnic backgrounds and would probably understand better what was meant by some of the answers. We would not send spiky-haired teenagers to interview business people, or vice versa. On the other hand, sometimes it is thought appropriate to pick interviewers who differ from the target population in particular ways. Old people often give the best interviews to people whom they see as being their children's age or even their grandchildren's. Children often give the best interviews to people who resemble their parents or teachers – though not where 'secrets' are involved that would naturally be kept hidden from such people. The general finding is that middle-class interviewers are often more acceptable than working-class ones and that both genders tend to relax more with a female interviewer than a man.

Beyond these fixed characteristics, the response to the interviewer can be controlled to some extent by the process of *impression management*. The interviewer does not so much express her personality as think what kind of personality she needs to be seen as having in order to make a positive impression on the respondent. Beyond this, she tries to be friendly but as neutral as possible – to give as few clues as possible about what is likely to please her or be acceptable to her as an answer. In this way it may be possible to keep unwanted biases to a minimum.

Impression management and the building of rapport are all the more difficult when the interview takes place on the telephone. Telephone interviewing is cheaper and therefore now sometimes preferred where an adequate sample can be constructed, and one would think that there would be less reaction to ascribed characteristics of the interviewer when only an auditory channel is available for conveying them, so that in principle telephone interviews ought to be easier to deliver in a standardized manner. In practice, however, 'receiving a telephone call' is also a social situation, and the nearest equivalent call is 'cold canvassing' by telephone sales staff, so the telephone interviewer can often meet with considerable hostility, if not immediate refusal. Further, the telephone interview is surprisingly intrusive: it comes right into the home uninvited, rather than being vetted on the doorstep and invited in by the householder. Time of day is an important factor, and where the interview is to be of some length researchers often make a preliminary call to book a convenient time for phoning back. Problems are also encountered with people who are hard of hearing, older people and some ethnic minority groups. The interviewer needs in particular a good 'telephone manner', which is not at all the same set of social skills as those needed for building rapport face to face.

Inevitably some mistakes and inaccuracies will be perpetrated in interviews, and some informants will give deliberately or unwittingly misleading or false answers. Provided the errors are randomly spread throughout the sample they are not especially important; they generate noise around the signal but will not give systematically distorted results. The problem is systematic errors and biases – particular kinds of people that all interviewers find difficult to understand or explain things to, or with whom they have consistent difficulty in forming a rapport. The only protection against systematic error of this kind is the reflexivity of the interviewer – the ability to 'read' the situation and his or her reaction to it and to compensate accordingly.

Coding the answers

The final stage of ensuring data which can be analysed to provide valid evidence is the coding of the answers into numbers (or other labels – some kinds of analysis can cope with alphabetical representation). This can be done by the interviewer at the time of the interview (or the respondent who is filling in the questionnaire), or by someone else after the event. This section looks in turn at both ways of proceeding.

Precoded answers

We try, when designing a questionnaire or interview schedule, to have as many of the answers as possible coded at the stage of the interview or observation. This saves time and expense later on. Obvious necessities, for this to be possible and useful, are that the codes for the questions are laid out in a form which is easy to read and so designed that it is easy to see which code goes with which answer. Example 6.1 shows the kind of thing that can be done.

Look back at Example 6.1 and remind yourself of how codes were attached to questions in the People in Society schedule.

You can see that, for most of the questions, each of the answers we had decided to accept is aligned with a unique number, which will be the respondent's code on the final data file with respect to that variable. In one place (the coding of social class) the code does not simply identify an answer but has to be ascribed by the interviewer on the basis of rules for what jobs count as of which social class. This is easy enough for interviewer-administered schedules but obviously cannot be allowed in self-administered questionnaires. Here we should have needed either to ask for a 'longhand' description of the job to be written in, for later coding, or asked a number of more precise precoded questions from which social class could have been deduced mechanically.

It is important, for each variable whose answers are to be precoded, that the code list is complete, accounting for every possible answer. Where the range of responses cannot be entirely predicted beforehand it is common to add an 'Other (please write in)' category and code this after the event. It is equally important that categories do not overlap, if informants have been told to pick only one code. You will remember that one of the People in Society attitude questions was criticized above for the possibility that a respondent could select *both* of what was supposed to be a pair of mutually exclusive statements.

If, as is now usual, you intend to have the codes directly typed into a computer from the questionnaire (or even optically scanned in) then the layout of the document needs to be such that the typist can read it easily and quickly, or the scanner can make an error-free transcription. Generally we lay out questionnaires and schedules so that the code appears down the right-hand margin, with one box for each variable. (Remember that each question may give rise to more than one variable. Every piece of information needed in the analysis must appear as a separately identifiable variable. So 'place of birth' might give rise to two variables – geographical area and 'metropolis' versus 'other' – or even three if you wanted to distinguish hospital births from home or nursing home deliveries.)

The codes need to be compatible with your computer and the software that will be used for analysis, so you need to know the limitations of the package you will be using. For example, many statistical packages can deal with multi-coded variables – variables which carry more than one code. (An example would be 'mode of travel', where you want the respondent to select the code of *every* means of transport used in a journey – foot, bus, train, underground and taxi, for instance.) However, some packages cannot deal with this, in which case you would need to use some other form of coding – for example, a string of variables for every trip, each coded yes/no for a given mode of transport. You also need to think about whether the package you are using can 'decode' complex information matrices into usable variables. For example, many researchers have coded details about six or more jobs or trips or domiciles or children as separate records, only to find that they cannot work out how to get from this the simpler variables they actually wanted, such as whether *any* domicile was rented from a housing association or *how many* children have had measles or which was the *highest* social class of job.

In other words, you should have the analysis in mind when you plan the questionnaire or schedule and the coding list. This means even knowing roughly what kind of statistics you will want to use. For some kinds of analysis you want nominal variables with quite large clusters of cases in each 'break'. For others you want continuous – integer or ratio – measurement. If in doubt, it is generally better to record at the highest level of measurement, on the principle that it is easy enough to degrade this into a nominal or ordinal scale but impossible to create an integer scale from a true nominal variable.

Office coding

Not all of the questions, as a rule, can be precoded – particularly on self-completion questionnaires. Sometimes, as with social class, it is necessary for someone to be trained to determine the appropriate code, on the basis of information supplied by the respondent. Often the full range of possible responses is not known, so that an 'other' category has to be included, and we generally ask respondents to specify what the 'other' is. If there are few such responses we may be content to leave them in an unexamined 'other' category, but if there are many we generally examine them to see if they can be coded back into the main code list or whether it is worth inventing a new category. For example, the People in Society schedule had a question on 'highest educational qualification' with an 'other' category, and examination of the 'other' answers might well have allowed us to salvage many of the 'other' responses as usable; many listed nursing or other vocational qualifications which have a known equivalence to diploma, degree or postgraduate level. If there had been a large number of professional qualifications which did *not* have an established equivalence to academic qualifications, we might have wanted to set up a special code category to house them.

Beyond this, there are often questions which were never intended to carry previously determined codes. If we do not know what the likely responses are (or their relative frequency) or it is important that respondents give their full and considered opinions in ordinary language, then we ask them just to write in their answers and then we code the responses after the event, 'in the

---

Box 6.2: Coding of responses to open-ended questions

Question: What do you look for when marking essays and theses?
Responses (fictional data):

- Knowledge of the subject and the course
- Knowledge of the subject (6 cases)
- Knowledge of/familiarity with the course (6 cases)
- The ability to answer the question logically (9 cases)
- Arguing logically and cogently
- Logical and cogent argument
- Argument on the basis of evidence (3 cases)
- A valid answer to the question (10 cases)
- Insight, intelligence (12 cases)
- Good writing skills (2 cases)
- 'Graduateness', demonstrating graduate standards (3 cases)
- Skills of reasoning
- The skills needed in the discipline (4 cases)
- The knowledge needed in the discipline (6 cases)
- Whether it 'feels right' as an undergraduate essay
- Progress from the previous year (2 cases)
- 'Value added' – something more than a non-graduate could supply
- The ability to go on to the next stage (5 cases)
- Something that does not bring the university into disrepute
- Something the external examiner will agree is worth the mark

Coding systems:

	Representational	Anchored	Hypothesis-guided
1	Question/essay (20)	Subject/discipline (16)	What (19)
2	Knowledge (19)	Course-related (11)	How (41)
3	Logic, skills (12)	Defensible grade/quality of answer (46)	Other (16)
4	Nature of person (15)	Other (3)*	
5	Progress, etc. (8)		
6	Other (2)		

* Includes one case where both subject and course are mentioned.

---

office'. The same is true of the 'debriefing' page which many good designers include on questionnaires and schedules – the open question at the end asking whether there is anything else that should have been asked or that the researcher needs to know or anything that the respondent wants to say about the topic or about the questionnaire or interview.

Betty Swift (1996) distinguished three ways in which we can approach the coding of such material – the *representational* approach; *anchoring*; and the *hypothesis-guided* approach.

The representational approach The aim here is simply to represent the surface content fairly, so you often go for key words in what has been said as the core concepts in the coding categories. The example in Box 6.2, for instance, is a fictional survey of university-level teachers, and the material to be coded comes from their descriptions of how they go about marking essays in coursework and examinations. I have made up a representational code list (the first column at the bottom) by putting together:

1   all those answers which refer specifically to the nature of the answer or essay ('answering the question', 'a valid answer', 'feels right as an essay');
2   the answers which refer to knowledge (of the subject, of the course, needed for the discipline);
3   answers which refer to skills (writing skills, skills needed in the discipline) or logical argument (including 'arguing on the basis of evidence') – originally I separated these, but the 'logic' category contained only five responses, and the ability to produce logical argument may relevantly be seen as a graduate skill);
4   answers which mention a quality of the person (insight, intelligence, 'graduateness');
5   other answers which indicate that progress has been made;
6   a couple of 'others' which do not fit these categories (both to do with the reputation of the university).

Anchoring This refers to code lists which take into account the context of the question and anchor themselves in the topic under investigation. In the example in Box 6.2 (the second column at the bottom), let us say that other questions were about course content, the nature of the subject/discipline and whether students are learning to be social scientists and researchers or just learning about, say, research methods. Let there have been other questions on what validates marking and whether innovative methods or non-traditional students pose a problem to the validity of the university process. The coding list I have put together to go with this has categories covering:

1   subject/discipline-specific answers (knowledge of subject, knowledge or skills needed for discipline);
2   specifically course-related answers and answers about the degree process seen as a series of progressively higher hurdles (knowledge of the course, progress from the previous year, ability to go to next stage);
3   answers which are explicitly or implicitly concerned with the validity of the marking and demonstrating its validity ('valid answer', 'insight', 'intelligence', 'graduateness', 'feels right', 'does not bring the university into disrepute', etc.);
4   a couple of 'others' ('writing skills', 'argument on the basis of evidence') which seem to me either not to fit this list at all or potentially to fit more than one category.

The logic behind the classification scheme is that some answers express a dichotomy between focusing on the course and the degree process and focusing on the subject/discipline and the student becoming an academic. Some, on the other hand, are purely about the quality of the product (whether seen as the essay or the student) and – at least implicitly, in my view – defending this quality to the outside world.

Hypothesis testing   Behind the questionnaire, let us say, lies the researcher's views about the conventional models of what a graduate is supposed to get out of his or her studies and the question of whether university-level learning is about knowledge or skills. My code list grounded in this set of views is the third column in Box 6.2. Quite simply, it distinguishes *what* the student produces (level of knowledge, familiarity with course) from *how* the student demonstrates it (reasoning, logic, use of evidence, valid answers – assumed to mean logical and based on evidence – demonstrating graduate standards, 'ability'). All the other answers go in an 'other' category as not focusing on this debate or not clearly taking one side or the other within it.

The three approaches are superficially similar but express different principles. The first – the most common – just tries to summarize the manifest content of the replies. The second tries to relate the replies to the general drift of other questions around them and contribute to the theme of the schedule/questionnaire. The third imports theory from outside to devise categories which will test the position respondents take on specific issues. The choice will depend on what is needed in the analysis.

If you have been working through the example in Box 6.2 with me, one thing must have struck you very forcefully by now.

What do I mean here? What would you say, standing back from it, has been the most notable characteristic of this process of constructing code lists?

What strikes me, at any rate, is just how *un*scientific the process is. Constructing a code list more closely resembles art than science – it is a matter of interpreting what is there, systematically but not very rigorously – and a great deal of personal judgement and preference is brought to bear on it. This is another area, therefore, where validity would be best served if we used more than one judge to devise the code list and assign the items to it, so that it does not reflect only the personal preferences of one researcher.

A final note on this topic: irrespective of the mode of coding adopted, you may be able to use a machine to help you: 'qualitative analysis' computer software works by assigning numeric codes to themes or topics, at the instruction of the researcher, and some packages (for example,

NUD.IST) will allow you to copy off the indexing system as a file of numbers which may be merged with your file of precoded variables. This does not in any way lessen the element of personal judgement involved – it is still the researcher, not the machine, who makes the choices – but where large data files are involved it can substantially decrease the amount of time and effort involved in making full use of the 'office-coded' variables and allow you to do a more thorough job of the classification.

Conclusion: the final product

In this chapter and the previous one we have gone from the initial thinking about survey questions to the final product – the set of numbers which encapsulate the data, ready for analysis and presentation. We have looked at questions of accuracy and of validity – whether we are correctly interpreting what we are measuring or collecting and how much error there is in the measurement. In the next chapter we shall continue with the 'technical' consideration of measurement, looking at scales and inventories for measuring complex concepts, and in the process of doing so we shall elaborate our understanding of the concept of validity and how it is ensured in practice. The final chapter in this part of the book stands back from the technicalities and reconsiders the problems and pitfalls – some of them inherent and unavoidable in the survey style – in the interpretation of the figures which we have collected and prepared.

Further reading

Alternative coverage of this chapter's subject-matter may be found in: de Vaus (1991) Chapter 7; O'Connell, Davidson and Layder (1994) Chapter 5; or Oppenheim (1992) Chapter 6. Betty Swift's chapter in Sapsford and Jupp (1996) is very good on the transformations data undergo between collection and analysis.

7   Complex concepts

Attainment and ability

In principle, it should be relatively straightforward to measure *attainment* – achievement of a goal – provided the nature of the goal is reasonably clear. In teaching, for example, it is normal to set tests to see what has been learned during the year and how much of it has been retained. You pick items which have a high *face validity* as measures – they look as if they ought to measure what you think they do. (Indeed, they may well correspond exactly with what you want the pupil to have attained: if what you are teaching is the solution of mathematical problems, then setting the pupils mathematical problems is a very good way of testing their learning.) You make sure that there is a spread of difficulty in the questions, if you want to be able to discriminate between the good and the poor: you need some very easy questions, to discriminate among the poorest learners, some very difficult ones to discriminate among the best, and probably a spread in between to stretch out the class into a rank order. You may be able to validate your test, if its validity is not certain, by comparing it with a test whose validity you already know (*concurrent* validity) or, after the event, by correctly predicting scores in the end-of-term examinations (*predictive* validity). There are no conceptual problems here, however, except the possibility of artefacts due to the mere fact of testing: 'exam nerves' could mean that some children were able to solve problems at home or in class but unable to solve them in the examination. (If you remember, I suggested in Chapter 2 that under these circumstances it might be necessary to redefine what you were looking at – not 'mathematical ability', but 'mathematical ability when under stress'.) If you were going to use the test again and again, with a succession of classes, you would probably check its *reliability* – whether the same children get (more or less) the same score if they retake the test a little while later. (If they do not, we might need to rethink our whole concept of mathematical attainment, because it would obviously be something very unstable.)

When we start to think about *ability* rather than attainment, however – what the child *could* achieve, rather than what the child *has* achieved – the problems of measurement and validation become more complicated. Attainment is in some sense a thing which can be seen and *measured*. Ability is something which has to be *operationalized*. The problem is to devise a test which will show capability independently of culture, background and level of education – 'pure' ability. This was precisely the problem faced by Binet and his colleagues at the turn of the twentieth century: how to measure a child's capability and pick out the ineducable ('feeble-minded') children from those who are just badly taught. The answer – the first intelligence test – was an instrument of high face validity but not much else: a list of questions and 'mental tasks' on which those of high capability were expected to score highly.

Since then, psychologists have worked to refine or replace the original measures with others of more evident validity:

1 They have validated the tests by outcome against a range of criteria, including both examinations and actual problem-solving tasks, and by comparing academically successful and unsuccessful groups.
2 They have demonstrated the relative stability of scores over time – that tests applied at age 12 will tend on the whole to put groups of people in the same rank order as tests administered at 15, for instance.
3 They have examined the patterns of scores, to see the extent to which right answers on one question predicted right answers on others. Given the theoretical postulate of *general* intelligence – intelligence as a *single* quantity – they have thrown out items which scored in the opposite direction to the test as a whole or appeared unrelated to it. (The statistical technique of *factor analysis*, which identifies clusters of variables more highly correlated with each other than with other variables, is regularly used for this task. The technique is discussed in Chapter 10.)
4 Examining scores on tests and comparing them with performance on various kinds of task, they have explored the extent to which there might be two *different* abilities which are measured by the tests ('verbal' and 'visual' or 'performance' intelligence) and devised tests to measure these in more nearly pure form. Alternatively, they have taken the line that intelligence is a superordinate construct, one which expresses the correlation between a range of different but related abilities, and have devised tests such as the Wechsler scales which measure separate abilities and sum the scores to arrive at an overall intelligence rating.
5 They have noted that measured intelligence does grow with education and experience – more difficult test items can be handled by older children – and devised ways for controlling the effects of age. The first and best known was the *intelligence quotient* (IQ), which works by taking the average age of people able to do the items which you are able to do, dividing this by your chronological age and expressing the result as a percentage. (Thus if you are 10 but cannot pass higher than 8-year-old tests, your IQ is 80; if you can pass 12-year-old tests your IQ is 120.) This was unsatisfactory because it gave silly results for adults; once your ability to pass the tests reaches its ceiling, your IQ necessarily declines as your chronological age increases. The more recent way of controlling for age is to express your test score as a position on the normal distribution of scores for people of your age, with mean of 100

and standard deviation of, commonly, 15. (Thus if your score were 115 you would lie one standard deviation above the mean for your age – in the top sixth of the range.)

6   They have made extensive efforts to take out the cultural and education-related components of the tests. The original Binet test had many questions testing vocabulary, arithmetical skills taught in schools and cultural and even moral norms of French culture of the time. Many of these were removed – but by no means all – when the test was revised for use in the United States by Terman and Merrill. Subsequent tests have tried to reduce the cultural and language-dependent component even further, for example by using symbol-matching tasks instead of asking verbal questions.

These are all forms of validation of the measuring instrument; in terms of Box 7.1, (1) covers predictive and criterion-related validity, (2) reliability and (3) unidimensionality; (4), (5) and (6) are more concerned with the wider question of the validity of intelligence as a *construct*: with the number of factors which have to be posited and with the notion that it should in theory be possible to measure ability independently of culture and schooling.

Personality

Much the same kinds of consideration enter into the construction of personality scales and inventories, except that the underlying concepts are even more nebulous than intelligence and in greater need of theoretical justification. Two main methods are used in constructing the measuring instruments.

The first method depends largely on criterion-related validity. Here what you do is compile a huge 'bank' of statements with which people might agree or disagree or on which they could rate themselves and administer them to two groups which differ in a known respect. Your scale then becomes those items which are consistently answered in one direction by one group and in another by the other. For example, the Minnesota Multiphasic Personality Inventory, an instrument widely used to measure aspects of personality and psychiatric state, was originally put together as a large bank of items and tried out on different diagnostic groups – comparing, for example, depressives with other kinds of psychiatric patient (Hathaway and McKinley, 1942) and nominating the items which discriminated between them as a 'scale of depression'. The same has been done for a large number of other traits and states. Validity is demonstrated by replicating the procedures with fresh criterion groups, by retesting groups to establish reliability, and by collecting scores for very large national samples, to obtain scores for the normal population (people who are not diagnosed as depressive but may exhibit some of the same traits to a

Box 7.1: Validating measuring instruments

A number of terms are used for the processes of validating measures. The major ones in common use are as follows:

Face validity: A measure looks, on the face of it, as if it should be a valid one. Sometimes this is a strong and sufficient argument: the test is to measure ability at mathematical problem-solving, and it consists of mathematical problems to solve. More often it is weak.

Concurrent validity: The test correlates well with an already validated measure.

Predictive validity: The test predicts an outcome which demonstrates that it is a correct operationalization – tests of mathematical ability predict success in mathematics examinations, tests of depressive tendency predict subsequent hospitalization for depression.

Criterion-related validity: This is a concept very similar to predictive validity – the test correctly identifies respondents as belonging or not belonging to a relevant group – it correctly picks out mathematics undergraduates from those reading English literature, or correctly separates diagnosed depressives from diagnosed manics.

Unidimensionality: Where the test is supposed to be measuring a single concept, all its items correlate with each other and with the total score.

Reliability: Where the test is supposed to be measuring something relatively unchanging, the scores are stable over short periods of time.

Construct validity: This is a higher-level concept, and is applied to a test which fulfils predictions which would be made given the nature of the construct which it is supposed to operationalize. All of the above may, in some circumstances, be brought into play. Key concepts in construct validation are *convergent validity* and *discriminant validity*. The latter indicates the power of the test to discriminate between persons or situations which theory says should be different. The former is its property of *not* making discriminations where theory says there should not be any. A test of general intelligence should tend to score people as highly intelligent who are good at academic subjects; if it is a test of *general* intelligence it should not make a major discrimination between academic subjects.

Validity is not a yes/no property of evidence but a process of testing which evidence undergoes. No evidence will be valid absolutely, but we aim for as much proof of validity as we can obtain.

varying but lesser degree) and to establish national norms (that is, the expected average score and how wide a spread of scores can be expected).

Items do not have to have high face validity, using this kind of procedure; what matters is *whether* they discriminate between groups, not *why*. The second broad method involves building a bank of items which *do* have high face validity – which appear likely to measure the trait or state in question – and then using factor analysis to identify those which seem to be measuring a single and stable dimension of personality. Eysenck's Personality Inventory, for example, started as a bank of items which might be expected to measure the theorized concepts of extraversion/introversion and stability/neuroticism. (Eysenck later added a 'psychoticism' factor.) Scores are obtained from large samples, and factor analysis is used to show which items 'clump together' into clusters which can be identified as the personality traits to be measured, and to discard items which correlate with none of them or with more than one (so that they are poor *discriminators* between concepts). You would then go on to improve your evidence for validity by checking reliability on retest and by using the test to see if you can distinguish between criterion groups which theory says should differ on it or to predict outcomes which theory would predict.

Other tests have used somewhat different methods. Cattell's 16PF, another widely used personality inventory, took all the words in an American English dictionary which could be used to describe personality, got people to rate others on them, and used factor analysis to establish which are regularly used in the same way about the same people. Inspection of these clusters of words consistently used in the same way gave underlying factors which Cattell could argue represented economically the ways in which we are accustomed to judging and describing people. Janet Taylor's (1953) Manifest Anxiety Scale was intended to duplicate clinical judgement about whether a person was currently displaying anxiety; it was constructed and initially validated by asking a number of clinicians to describe the symptoms of anxiety and using for the scale those items on which the vast majority agreed.

Attitudes

As we have seen, straightforward questions about attitudes, opinions and intentions may be treated as directly factual ones (with substantial reservations, mentioned already and discussed in more detail below). In principle, we ask a direct question – 'What do you think of this?', 'What would you do if . . .?' – and record the answer.

More often, however, in academic and market research, we are seeking to measure 'attitudes' in the more generalized sense of 'feelings about' or 'reaction towards'. Attitudes about AIDS, or even attitudes towards a given brand of coffee, are not matters simply of factual belief; there is an emotional tone attached, and they form part of a whole constellation of working rules about the world and reactions to it, not all of which need be consciously available. Much attitude research seeks to 'sneak up on' people's attitudes by asking questions in an indirect way and deducing overall attitude from the pattern of replies. In the People in Society schedule, for example, we were not concerned with whether people thought the working class rich or poor, dependent or independent, but with their overall 'social maps' – their picture of the social world and how to get around in it. We therefore asked respondents to describe social classes and themselves on a wide range of adjectives and used the technique of factor analysis to see which items typically 'went together' and thus to deduce the important dimensions for classifying them. (A much wider range of adjectives was used on the pilot study; those which finished up in the final questionnaire were those which did tend to distinguish middle from working class in people's attitudes.) This is not unlike the way personality theorists think about the instruments they design – the two People in Society dimensions were constructed in the same sort of way as Eysenck's dimensions of introversion and stability – and the same kind of technology is used in designing this kind of attitude scale.

It is a problem for attitude theory in psychology, however, that the relationship between expressed attitudes and observed behaviour tends to be very low, in a wide range of empirical studies (Wicker, 1969). A lot of the variance in behaviour seems to be attributable to circumstance and history; a lot of the variance in 'attitudes' seems attributable to reactivity – to the circumstances of the research and the way in which the questions are asked. This is at least in part because the relationship between attitudes and behaviours is not necessarily a simple one even if we think of attitudes as something 'residing' in the person. Fishbein and Ajzen (1975; see also Ajzen, 1988) have claimed much better predictive power for a 'theory of rational behaviour' or 'theory of planned behaviour' which takes into account an intermediate stage of 'intentions' intervening between attitudes and behaviours, mediated by 'norms' about the behaviour and the likely reactions of significant others to it, and affected also by the perceived degree of behavioural control the subject has (which in a recent version of the theory is seen as having a direct influence on the likelihood of the behaviour occurring as well as an indirect one). The 1988 version of the model is illustrated in Figure 7.1.

When studying social, educational or psychological practice, or the policy which informs it, it is often necessary to ask specific and explicit questions about what a practitioner or policy-maker would do under a given set of circumstances. This runs us into all the problems of policy statements and statements about practice. Sometimes policy-makers think they have no settled policy but treat each case on its merits – though quite often research can show a core of consistency in the decisions that are made, often predictable from remarkably few variables (see Wilkins and McNaughton-Smith, 1964). Sometimes practitioners think they behave consistently and without bias when their observed behaviour shows

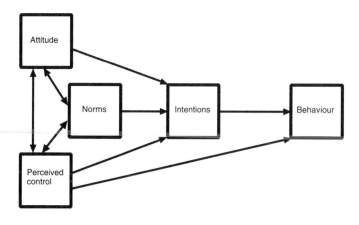

FIGURE 7.1 *Attitudes and actions: a theory of planned behaviour*

otherwise: see, for example, the literature on attention paid to boys and girls in class – for example, Spender (1982). Sometimes there are right answers – the policy is such and such, as laid down by those who determine such things – and this rather than actual practice may inform the answer. Sometimes it is clear what policy is and what practice ought to be, but budgetary or staffing considerations, or considerations of available time, may mean that the practitioner works 'against policy' or 'against practice' in a significant proportion of cases. We need some way of approaching such questions which draws much less on rhetoric and the official 'party line'.

How would you go about doing this?

Direct observation is one obvious way of seeing what is done in practice, and analysis of records is another. The latter is often a very efficient way of proceeding but is limited by the nature of the records – records can be analysed only for what was recorded there in the first place and may not include the practices in which we are interested. They also have their own problems of validity and reliability. Direct observation is an effective way of collecting data, but very time-consuming – it is not generally possible for a given observer to cover very many cases – and it is limited by the cases which happen to be available for observation at a given time. These may not be the most informative for the purposes of the research.

One way round this, employed in Abbott's research into the community care of older people (Example 2.1) is the use of *vignettes*. These are artificially constructed case descriptions, presented for respondents to consider and to report on what they would have done in the circumstances. They have a long history of use in social psychology, where they have often formed the 'stimulus material' for studies of group decision-making and moral reasoning. They have also been widely used in social policy research, to explore how practitioners or policy-makers carry out their decision-making and what affects their judgement. They can be as short or as long as is desired – ranging from one or two key sentences to whole files of information or even (Wasoff and Dobash, 1992) real people acting out the interactions which are to be explored. (Wasoff and Dobash confronted solicitors, with their consent, with a 'simulated client' who purported to be seeking a divorce.) The cases can be real ones (suitably anonymized) or cases artificially constructed with controlled differences on key variables. They are *not* the real situation, and care has to be taken in interpreting the results of their use, but they can come much nearer to the real situation than direct questions about policy or practice in general. See Abbott and Sapsford (1993) for a discussion.

Social factors

This chapter may have suggested, so far, that psychologists have a monopoly on complex measurement, but this is far from being the case. Sociologists and researchers into social policy also use operational constructs of considerable complexity, but to describe social relations and social and material location rather than the nature of the individual.

The most frequently used set of complex constructs in British sociological research revolve around the notion of social class. These are in no sense 'derived from data', but from attempts to give a measurable reality to theoretical ways of understanding how societies work. Social class is a very common variable used to distinguish between people, not only in 'theoretical' research (for example, into class sentiments, class action, or voting behaviour) but also in applied social research into health, education, poverty, social welfare, crime and its 'treatment' and many other areas. Class theories differ substantially in the model of society that underlies them, but they have in common that they locate people within society on the basis of occupation, aggregating groups of occupations into complexes which are thought to have interests in common and show some homogeneity of behaviour. Marxist conceptions of 'relationship to the means of production' underlie much of British class theory, but the class of 'owners' is so small that survey research is seldom concerned with it. Most research is concerned with distinctions to be made, within the 'non-owning' classes, between relatively advantaged managers, entrepreneurs and professionals on the one hand (even if few of them control capital in their own right) and those whose form of occupation and occupational opportunities leave them relatively disadvantaged in the market – a distinction owing less to Marx than to Weber:

broadly speaking, wage labourers have different interests from those of the self-employed or from those of salaried managers and professionals. Their incomes may overlap, but the conditions under which they earn that income differ quite markedly . . . It is the competitive position of different groups in the labour market which provides the basis for their differing values and political principles. (Heath et al., 1985: 14)

The boundary between the middle class (white-collar) and working class (manual and routine service occupations), and whether it is permeable within the lifetime or between generations, has been a common focus of research in the last 30–40 years.

A range of scales has been devised reflecting different theoretical or practical interests. One of the oldest is the Registrar-General's Social Class Scale, which first appeared in the Registrar-General's annual report for 1911, where it was used as a tool for analysing differential infant mortality rates; substantially revised to reflect changes in the labour market over the years, this scale is still much used in government publications and applied research. The classification was never based on formal analysis or research but was devised 'from the armchair' to reflect current thinking about the relative standing of occupations and their lifestyle. Other scales have been devised by academic researchers on the basis of systematic survey research on people's ranking of the social standing and/or social advantage of the various occupations (see Hall and Jones, 1950; Goldthorpe and Hope, 1972; 1974) – but with a heavy admixture of the authors' social theory. In market research another scale, the British Market Research Society's Social Grading of Occupations, has enjoyed wider currency.

On the whole the Hope–Goldthorpe scale and its variants and derivatives have proved the most useful for the analysis of social behaviour such as voting; the Registrar-General's scale tends to overlook useful distinctions between middle-class occupations, and the Social Grading Schema overemphasizes income and lifestyle in its construction at the expense of other factors. All of the scales underrate the differences between women's labour occupations, and scales have been devised which make better sense of these – for example the Surrey Occupational Class Scale (Dale et al., 1983; Arber et al., 1986). The main categories of four different class scales are illustrated in Table 7.1. Another common occupational classification, used where detail is required and overall hierarchical ranking is not at issue, is the Registrar-General's classification of socio-economic groups, illustrated in Table 7.2.

The concern with social class as a measurable characteristic applicable to individuals tends to be a specific focus of research in Britain and countries whose social research tradition is most influenced by Britain. On the continent of Europe there is less concern with specific social location; in Germany, for example, the predominant occupational classification is concerned with sector of employment rather than hierarchical level. In the United States class theory as a whole is less influenced by the Weberian

TABLE 7.1 *Main headings of four British social class scales*

Register-General		Hope–Goldthorpe		Social Grading Schema		Surrey scale	
I	Higher professional and managerial	I	Higher professional and managerial	A	Higher professional and managerial	1	Higher professional
II	Lower professional	II	Lower professional	B	Lower professional	2	Employers and managers
IIIN	Supervisory and lower/ routine non-manual	III	Routine non-manual	C1	Supervisory and lower/routine non-manual	3	Lower professional
		IV	Small proprietors and the self-employed	C2	Foremen and skilled manual workers	4	Secretarial and clerical
IIIM	Skilled manual workers	V	Foremen and technicians	D	Semi- and unskilled manual workers	5	Foremen and self-employed manual workers
IV	Semi-skilled workers	VI	Skilled manual workers	E	Not economically active	6	Shop and personal service workers
V	Unskilled manual workers	VII	Semi- and unskilled manual workers			7	Skilled manual workers
						8	Semi-skilled manual workers
						9	Unskilled manual workers

Notes:

(a) Coincidence of name does not mean that the same occupations appear under the same headings. For example, the Social Grading Schema is more affected by income in its location of occupations.

(b) Only the Social Grading Schema includes the economically inactive in its classification scheme.

(c) The distinctive feature of the Hope–Goldthorpe scale is its separation of the types of employment in the middle of the scale. Classes III–V are seen as distinct but equivalent, and no hierarchy is implied in their numbering.

(d) The distinctive features of the Surrey scale are: (i) the enhanced distinction between employers/managers and lower professionals; (ii) the separation of shop workers from secretarial/clerical workers and sales representatives; and (iii) the separation of personal service workers from semi-skilled factory workers.

model of bounded classes and more inclined to see status and remuneration as linked – so that people who become unemployed may be seen as dropping down the class ladder – and as forming a smooth gradient. This difference reflects the difference between the two countries in terms of commonly held models of the nature of society.

On the whole the major guarantor of validity for these scales is their face validity – that they 'fit the theory' and look as though they ought to measure what the researchers intend them to measure. Academic scales such as the Hope–Goldthorpe are based on research into people's perception of social status, but in some ways this merely confuses the issue; they are to measure social location, not just social status, so the standing of professions and so on in people's eyes is not a central question. Scales such as the Social Grading of Occupations are also informed by relative pay

TABLE 7.2 *The British Registrar-General's socio-economic groups (main headings and significant sub-headings)*

1	Employers and managers in central and local government, industry, commerce, etc.: large establishments.
	1.1 Employers in industry, commerce, etc.
	1.2 Managers in central and local government, industry, commerce, etc.
2	Employers and managers in central and local government, industry, commerce, etc.: small establishments.
	2.1 Employers in industry, commerce, etc.
	2.2 Managers in central and local government, industry, commerce, etc.
3	Professional workers – self-employed.
4	Professional workers – employees.
5	Intermediate non-manual workers.
	5.1 Ancillary workers and artists.
	5.2 Foremen and supervisors – non-manual.
6	Junior non-manual workers.
7	Personal service workers.
8	Foremen and supervisors – manual.
9	Skilled manual workers.
10	Semi-skilled manual workers.
11	Unskilled manual workers.
12	Own-account workers (other than professional).
13	Farmers – employers and managers.
14	Farmers – own account.
15	Agricultural workers.
16	Members of the Armed Forces.
17	Inadequately described/occupation not stated.

levels, but again this does not necessarily improve their validity for purposes of social analysis, though it may increase their usefulness in market research. Scales are compared to each other, and one preferred to another, through the construct validation provided by their utility in predicting expected class-based outcomes such as voting or social attitudes. It was on this basis that scales such as the Surrey one have been preferred to the older scales, as making better sense of the attitudes and behaviour of women while still doing justice to the data from men.

Social class is a strange variable in survey and secondary-source research because it is often used not in its own right but as the available indicator of something which is actually much simpler. In the field of health, for example, the *Black Report* (Townsend and Davidson, 1980) used it as a readily available indicator of poverty and deprivation; data on occupation and therefore social class are collected in the British Census and so are available for analysis, while data on income are not. Subsequent studies of health and deprivation (among them Carstairs, 1981; Townsend et al., 1985; Abbott and Sapsford, 1994) have tended to use a range of more obvious deprivation measures – overcrowded housing, type of housing tenure and the like. Similarly, market researchers have used social class as an indicator of disposable income on the one hand and consumption lifestyle on the other. However, the advent of electronic access to detailed databases has permitted more precise targeting in terms of income, house type, family size, leisure interests or whatever the relevant variables are for the precise commercial question being explored.

Complexity and reality

We have seen how complex indicators are put together – composite indicators which estimate the level of some characteristic of the person. We have seen that they can be tested for their internal consistency and reliability and validated against other measures or against performance of some sort. We have seen that measures to do with the person are generally put through these procedures quite rigorously, to establish them as of no less scientific status, as measuring instruments, than the physical instruments of the physical sciences. (We have seen also that sociological instruments, characterizing people's positions in society and social relations, are typically less rigorously constructed and owe more to 'face validity'; the nature of the subject-matter does not always lend itself to the same techniques of validation as are used for measures of individual's 'internal' characteristics.)

What are we to say about the concepts which these indicators purport to measure, however? Are they 'real things', or just working heuristics useful for prediction purposes? Social research has to be about truth in the first instance (else why would anyone pay attention to it?), and we may fairly ask whether it is *true* that people have intelligence or personality traits or attitudes or, for that matter, a social class. Survey research is set solidly within the ambit and rules of science: it is concerned with theory-testing, and theorized description, on the basis of exact measurement to provide valid evidence which is openly available. What science could there be if these concepts which we measure in our surveys have no objective reality?

These questions go to the heart of a fundamental debate in the philosophy of science, between *realism* and *instrumentalism* – on the one hand the belief that science is about true description of a real world, and on the other the acceptance of it as a set of techniques for prediction and manipulation, judged by the extent to which they work in practice. From the point of view of the research itself the debate probably does not matter much. We would probably do the same surveys and other research studies and use many of the same measuring instruments, whichever stance we adopted. It matters for social practice, however. The belief that our constructs have some absolute reality validates their real-world use in ways which might not be thought acceptable or sound if we had less faith in the scientific basis of the constructs they explore. We shall examine these questions more in the next chapter.

My own position, for what it is worth, lies between the two extremes. I have no doubt in the reality of the external world, and little in the reality of the social world and the world of personal experience. However, I do not suppose that we 'know' that world, and I do not allow much sense to *any* claim to 'knowledge' in a simple and absolute sense. The world is as it is, and there is nothing absolutely true and comprehensive that we can say about it. What we do is to *describe* it, to *tell stories* about it, to *make sense* of it. Everything we say about the world is literally an abstraction and a construction: it latches on to features that we think important and fits them into overall models of what the real world is like, modifying the models as necessary. So the concept of intelligence develops because it is useful – it makes usable sense of the world – to say that people differ in overall mental ability; this explains what they can do, and it guides us in how we behave to them and what we can expect of them. The concept of social class develops because it is useful for understanding social relations, the possibility and actual existence of bonds of solidarity between people who have similar lived experience and stand in similar relationships to the means of production and the ownership of capital and property, and the extent to which (and means by which) some people set the rules and procedures by which other people have to live. However:

1 The choice of what is important comes from previously formed theories about the world and expresses values about it; 'social class' is not a characteristic necessary to take into account, but one we have in a sense 'invented' by selection, which we find offers explanation and under-standing. (Other differences between people – their eye colour, their preferences in music – are not accorded this status but are equally real.)
2 No such abstraction is ever 'the whole story'; in offering understanding, it necessarily simplifies. The understanding we derive from our 'social scientific' concepts is always partial, and what we say on the basis of them is always too simple.
3 Following from this, what we have here are *useful concepts*, not literal and value-free descriptions. They characterize the world rather than encapsulating it, and they give us ways of navigating within it rather than just offering a snapshot. They are validated or refuted by what they predict about the world, but they are not themselves the world; the map is not the territory.

We have also to note both the temporary nature of our constructs and their curious permanence in afterlife. Our constructs are temporary in that they constitute a sort of 'agreement' to see the world in a certain way and see what follows, how far the idea can take us in the way of understanding. They can and will be superseded by other ways of framing the world which offer *better* understanding, and these will sometimes contradict them or just bypass them and render them redundant. The view of the physical world as earth-centred, with planets and stars revolving in their paths, is replaced by a view of the world as sun-centred, with forces impelling the earth and other planets around the sun, which itself is just one of very many stars. This in turn is replaced by a relativistic model in terms of forces, distances and time, with matter no longer the fundamental reality of physics. The last of these, the Einsteinian universe, formally invalidates the physics of Newton, but Newton's physics is still useful for most purposes. However, we hear little now about the earth-centred model, and questions about what keeps the stars in their spheres are no longer even asked. This is how science progresses, by the replacement of dominant paradigms or models – ways of viewing the subject-matter and sets of questions which it makes sense to ask about it. However, each paradigm arises in a world which contained the previous one – Einstein's physics would make little sense in a world which did not have Newton's – and the older paradigm continues to inform our understanding. In the same way, both sociology and social psychology are currently concerned with the ways in which the world of *meaning* is structured by history, but this does not invalidate the 'grand theories' of modernist sociology or the practical and theoretical insights of individual, psychodynamic or humanistic psychology. What it does do is to complicate the ways in which these can be used; it provides a looser but more fruitful understanding.

Further reading

Chapter 15 of de Vaus (1991) and Chapter 11 of Oppenheim (1992) are both good general discussions of composite measurement. Michael Procter's chapter in Gilbert (1993) expands the discussion of attitude measurement; Coxon et al. (1986) talk about social class as a composite measure; and Romney (1979) gives a comprehensive account of the construction and validation of a personality measure.

What does it all mean?

This chapter covers remaining issues in the interpretation and use of survey results, before we go on to look at statistical analysis and how to draw conclusions from figures. It begins by picking up issues from earlier chapters and considering the error margin in results – sampling error and the kinds of non-sampling error which can be built into surveys and distort our interpretation of them. Beyond this, it considers the political use of survey tools and the political/ethical positions we tend to adopt in doing survey research.

Sampling error

We have carried out the survey and are about to try to make sense of the data. Before we do so is a very good time for pausing to think what might have gone wrong. The first thing we must consider is that we took a sample, and so there is the risk of *sampling error*. As we saw in Chapter 3, even true random sampling from a sampling frame can produce unrepresentative samples from time to time. Indeed, it *must* do so, with calculable probability. So when the figures from our sample show a difference between two groups (between the genders, perhaps, or between older and younger people), this may represent a real difference between these groups in the population, but it may be a product merely of sampling error. That is, there is a genuine difference between the groups in the sample, but this does not represent a genuine difference between them in the population. When looking at our figures we must always bear this possibility in mind.

What we do is take a gamble – we compute the probability of getting the result we obtained by chance, or one more extreme still, and reject the likelihood of the result being a product of chance if the probability is small enough. If successive samples are random, then all the statistics that can be computed about them will follow a random (normal) distribution – the mean, the standard error and, most importantly for our current purpose, the size of the difference between subgroups within them. The distribution of possible means has a standard deviation – the *standard error*, which you calculated in Chapter 3. Similarly, the differences between subgroups will have a standard deviation – the *standard error of the difference*. Box 8.1 shows how to calculate this and goes on to outline how we test for the *statistical significance* of the difference – the likelihood of a result as big as

Box 8.1: Comparing means

The general formula for testing any statistical hypothesis using the properties of the normal distribution is $Z = X/s$, where X is some statistic and s is its standard error. If Z is greater than 1.96, then the difference or correlation (or whatever X is) is significant at the 5 per cent level, and if it is greater than 2.58 then it is significant at the 1 per cent level. If it is less than 1.96, then X is not significant – we cannot reject the hypothesis that it is a chance product of sampling.

Comparing two means, the difference D is given by subtracting one mean from the other. The standard error of the difference is given by the formula

$$s_d = \sqrt{s_{m1}^2 + s_{m2}^2},$$

where s_d is the standard error of the difference between means, s_{m1} is the standard error of the mean of the first group and s_{m2} is the standard error of the second group.

The following worked example of scores in a mythical school mathematics test will help to illustrate this.

Score band	Class 1					Class 2				
	f	x	x^2	fx	fx^2	f	x	x^2	fx	fx^2
0–10	2	0	0	0	0	1	0	0	0	0
11–20	4	1	1	4	4	7	1	1	7	7
21–30	8	2	4	16	32	8	2	4	16	32
31–40	3	3	9	9	27	4	3	9	12	36
41–50	3	4	16	12	48	–	4	16	0	0
Sums	20			41	111	20			35	75

In this table the x column contains an arbitrary set of scores, such that when x is 0, the score for the band is 5.5, when x is 1 the score is 15.5, and so on. Scores from here on are given after conversion back to points on the examination by multiplying by the interval width of 10 (and adding 5.5 in the case of the mean).

	Class 1	Class 2	Difference, D
Mean	26.0	23.0	3.0
Standard deviation	15.78	12.25	
Standard error	3.53	2.74	4.46

Then we calculate $Z = 3/4.46 = 0.67$, less than 1.96, so the difference is not significant – these could be random samples from a single population of scores.

Box 8.2: Comparing proportions

The formula for the standard error of a difference between proportions is

$$s_{prop} = \sqrt{p_c q_c \left(\frac{1}{n_1} + \frac{1}{n_2} \right)},$$

where p_c is the proportion in the total sample, q_c is $1 - p_c$ and n_1 and n_2 are the sizes of the two groups to be compared.

Significance is tested by calculating $Z = d_{prop}/s_{prop}$, where d_{prop} is the difference between the two proportions.

---

this, or more extreme, arising by chance. The trick is to calculate the *Z statistic* – defined as the difference divided by its standard error – and look this up in a table of probabilities of the normal curve, which will tell you the likelihood of getting a *Z* this large as a random deviation from zero difference in the population. Five per cent of values of the curve lie outside the bounds defined by ±1.96 times *Z*, and a 5 per cent probability of error (odds of 19 to 1, if you like) looks unlikely enough to be worth betting on. Longer odds still, if we want to be more certain, would be the 1 per cent level (odds of 99 to 1), which would be given by a *Z* value of 2.58, as only 1 per cent of the normal distribution lies outside the boundaries set by ±2.58 times *Z*.

If you are finding this difficult to follow, look back over Chapter 3 and remind yourself about standard deviations, standard errors and the normal distribution of probabilities.

You can pull a similar trick quite simply for comparing proportions or percentages (Box 8.2). The standard error of a difference between proportions is calculated by multiplying the proportion in the whole sample (the combined proportion for both groups added together) by (one minus the proportion), multiplying this by the sum of the reciprocals of the two group sizes and taking the square root. For percentages, first divide by 100 to reduce them to proportions. (This sounds complicated when you write it out in words, but the formula is reasonably simple and clear – see Box 8.2). You should note that smaller differences come out as significant if the overall proportion is around 50 per cent than if it is very small or very large. It is also notable that the size of the population does not matter – it is the size of the sample groups that makes the difference. This is because the population is assumed to be infinitely large. Provided it is larger than about 100 this assumption is more or less valid. Differences between other statistics which you might calculate can be handled in the same way; formulae for the

---

Box 8.3: Standard errors for comparing a range of statistics

Difference between	Formula	
Means	$\sqrt{s_{m1}^2 + s_{m2}^2}$ or	Z test
	$\dfrac{n_1 + n_2}{n_1 n_2} \sqrt{\dfrac{(n_1 - 1)s_{m1}^2 + (n_2 - 1)s_{m2}^2}{n_1 + n_2 - 2}}$	t test
Proportions	$\sqrt{p_c q_c \left(\dfrac{1}{n_1} + \dfrac{1}{n_2}\right)}$	Z test
Correlations	$1/\sqrt{n}$	Z test
Median	$1.253 s_m / \sqrt{n}$	Z test
Standard deviation	$\sqrt{0.5(s_{m1}^2 + s_{m2}^2)}$	Z test

In general, whenever samples are reasonably large and standard errors can be calculated for a measure, the standard error of a difference between measures is given by

$$\sqrt{s_1^2 + s_2^2}.$$

When the population is finite and less than about 20 times the size of the sample, the Z-test formulae should be multiplied by

$$\sqrt{1 - \frac{n}{n_T}}.$$

In the above the following subscripts are used: 'c' refers to the complete sample (so p_c is proportion of the total sample and q_c is $1 - p_c$); 'm' refers to the mean (so m_1 refers to the mean of group 1 and s_{m1} its standard deviation; s_m is the standard deviation of the total sample); n is the number of cases (so n is the sample size and n_1 is the size of group 1); and 'T' refers to the total population (so n_T is the population size).

---

standard errors of the differences, or reasonable approximations to them, can be found in Box 8.3.

The statistic you have been looking at so far is the Z statistic. Another similar statistic you are very likely to come across in published papers is the t statistic, and this is what you will usually be given if you are using a computer statistics package. The t statistic is very similar to the Z statistic – and for large samples the two are identical – but it gives more trustworthy results when samples are small or the trait being examined is very rare or very frequent. On the other hand, it is more difficult to

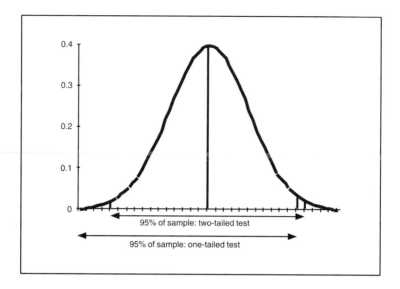

FIGURE 8.1   *One-tailed and two-tailed probabilities*

calculate by hand (see Box 8.3 for the formula). You should definitely use *t* rather than *Z* if your sample is smaller than 100 or the characteristic you want to compare holds for less than about 20 per cent of the overall sample or more than about 80 per cent.

The figures of 1.96 and 2.58 given above, as critical values of the normal distribution, correspond to what is known as 'two-tailed probabilities'. If we are looking at the sample value and asking what the probability is of obtaining a result this large or larger as a deviation from a true population value of zero, we have to take into account that the mistake could occur *in either direction*; the 'fake' difference could as easily have been negative as positive. Very occasionally it is legitimate to assume that the deviation could have occurred in only one direction: for example, when comparing two drugs both of which are known to have *some* curative effect, with the research question being whether drug A does significantly better than drug B. In these cases we can look at probabilities in just one tail of the distribution, and the critical values become 1.65 for the 5 per cent level of significance and 1.96 for the 1 per cent level (see Figure 8.1). Situations such as this do not often occur in survey work, however.

Non-sampling error

Understanding our results and interpreting them to understand the research topic or question, we have to be constantly alert to take account of every element of the data-collection process. *Survey Research* has three elements – the finder; the process of finding; and what is found. An apparent 'result' may not be 'what is found' – a true/useful statement about the social or material world – but a product of the nature of the researcher or the nature of the research process.

Spend a few minutes thinking and looking back over the book so far, and list the elements we have considered which can distort the findings, or which need taking into consideration before we can give the findings due weight.

Sampling

It seems odd to talk about errors in sampling under the heading of 'non-sampling error'. However, we tend to reserve the term 'sampling error' for the calculable likelihood of drawing an untypical sample by correct means from a complete and correct sampling frame – the *mathematical* error inherent in the sampling process. If the sampling frame is not correct and complete in the first place and/or the sampling processes non-random, errors can creep in which are *not* calculable, though we may be able to estimate the direction of their effect.

Questions we must ask ourselves about the sample include the following:

- *Was the sampling frame (or equivalent process of sampling) complete, or does some portion of the population stand less chance of being selected?* Even when sampling from supposedly complete lists, such as the UK electoral registers, errors may occur. The lists are not up to the minute, so some people will be on the list who have died or moved away. Some people may deliberately avoid appearing on the list – as part of a tax or benefit 'fiddle', for instance, or to avoid the police or divorce investigators – and some will fail to make a return out of sheer laziness, despite the legal penalties. Those who do not have an address may well not appear on the register. Thus a sample based on the registers will be biased against the transient population and the poorest part of it. Other sources of listings, such as telephone directories, may embody more extreme and more obvious biases.
- *What is the effect of refusal and non-contact?* A random sample of addresses might give, in principle, a random sample of the population, but the achieved sample is likely to be biased against those who will not co-operate with the research, those who cannot understand or cope with the questionnaire or interview and those who are away from home so often and for so long that they cannot be contacted. These people are unlikely to be a random subset of the population.

    This effect is much stronger still with volunteer samples achieved, for example, by putting up an advertisement and interviewing those who reply to it. These are very unlikely to be a random sample of the population.

personal bias in the sampling? This is most evident in quota and haphazard samples, where the interviewer chooses the cases ~~s~~etimes within predefined quotas – and is free to seek out the ~~eas~~t ones to locate and approach and to avoid those who it is thought ~~migh~~t be difficult or hostile. In the worst circumstance, however, the ~~rese~~archers may have picked the sample themselves and consciously or u~~n~~consciously used the research hypothesis as a basis for the selection. For this reason 'blind' procedures are sometimes employed in survey research, as in experiments: the person who selects the sample and has contact with them does not know the underlying research questions and the kinds of answer the researchers are expecting.

None of this necessarily *invalidates* the surveys in which it occurs; validation is not a yes/no state, but a process admitting of degrees. However, we do have to think carefully about the effects of exclusion on the interpretability of the results and the extent to which non-random exclusion may bias them.

Measurement

I would want to ask the following questions:

- *How accurate are the answers or readings or counts?* To what extent are respondents likely to be lying, or putting the best interpretation on their actions/beliefs? To what extent are they likely to have mis-interpreted the question? To what extent can I expect genuine mistakes? For example, if I asked 'How often did you experience this in the last year?', to what extent will I be given a genuine year's worth of data, as opposed to 15 months or 9? (It is better practice to *anchor* questions about the past – 'How often have you experienced this *since Christmas*?') If I am using a composite indicator as a measuring tool – a scale of intelligence or personality, for example – to what extent can I expect accuracy and precise discrimination between people, as opposed to rough rank ordering? If direct observation is the basis of the survey, how reliable is the recording into categories? In other words, how much 'noise' is there around the 'signal'?
- *How good is the operationalization,* if we are using indirect measures as indicators of concepts? For example, in some deprivation studies car ownership has been used as a proxy for the affluence/poverty dimension (because access to a car is collected in the British Census and income level is not). However, this works as an indicator only in urban areas; rural deprivation is not well correlated with car ownership, because in rural areas you need a car to get to work at all, irrespective of your income (see Abbott et al., 1992). And, in general, are the measures of demonstrable validity?

Collection

The questions here concern the nature of the interviewer, the interviewer's behaviour and the way the task was presented.

- *Did the interviewer build a relationship of confidence and trust?* Was it the right kind of interviewer to inspire trust – not of an inappropriate class or gender or ethic group or age? Was a relationship built in which the respondent could relax and speak without unduly 'considering the answers'? Was there adequate prompting and explanation to ensure that the answers were full, that all relevant aspects were covered and that the respondent really did understand what was meant by the questions in the same way as other respondents?
- *Was the interviewing sufficiently standardized to ensure that variation between cases was not due to variations in the interviews?* Was there more than one interviewer and, if so, are there systematic differences between groups which might be ascribed to the identity of the interviewer? Was the manner of the interviewer constant – the same for all kinds of respondent, and the same for a hostile reception as for co-operative respondents? Was there prompting or explanation which differed among respondents?

We noted earlier that these two groups of questions are mutually antagonistic; ensuring a relaxed and trusting performance and an equal understanding among informants may weaken the claims of the interviews to be a standardized data-collection instrument.

- *Is there the possibility of reactivity as an explanation for results?* In other words, how was the nature of the task presented, how did the interviewers present themselves as people, and could this in any way bias the answers given? (Social desirability effects are very likely, for example, but others may also occur – such as men's unwillingness to say certain things about women to a female interviewer.) Direct observation could also cause reactivity, if the presence of the observer is obvious: people may not behave in the same way when observed as in the observer's absence.

Most of these possible effects are hidden, though the good researcher will use his or her imagination to identify what they might be and eliminate them by features of the design or investigate them as part of the data-collection or analysis. We have always to bear in mind, when interpreting our own findings or those of other researchers, that the data-collection phase is an interaction between people and that social interactions have (often unexpected) effects of their own.

This subsection has been written as though all survey data were collected by interviewers or observers. This is patently not the case: many surveys use self-completion questionnaires, often sent through the post. Just because there is no interviewer present, however, we should not imagine that no social interaction takes place. Answering questions is a task that makes no sense unless there is someone asking them. If we cannot see the person who is answering them, we supply one or imagine one; filling in questionnaires and forms is a process of interacting with an invisible interviewer 'in the head'. We have also seen that self-completion questionnaires have problems of their own, in terms of lessened control over the presentation of the questions.

Codification

Finally, we should remember that what the researcher analyses is *not* straightforwardly the answers to questions. A lot of construction work goes on before the questions are even asked, and a lot more before the data set is ready for analysis (see Swift, 1996).

- *Do the predetermined answers provide the sort of information needed for the analysis?* We precode as much as possible, reducing the answers to predetermined categories even as the respondents give them. Sometimes, if the precodes have been misjudged or the question changes as a result of analysis, the recorded data may not be adequate for answering questions which the researcher wants to ask.
- *Does the structured format inhibit the respondents from answering in the most helpful way?* Surveys are very good instruments for obtaining data to confirm or deny questions which the researcher has in mind. They are generally very bad for 'finding out what is going on' when it is not clear what questions should be asked; 'qualitative' methods are generally much more appropriate for this. The usefulness of a survey analysis depends crucially on the researcher having envisaged the possible answers and therefore deduced what the proper questions are; if the key question is not there, the respondents cannot answer it. (Open-ended questions get round this problem to some extent but have problems of their own.)
- *Where open-ended questions were used (or an 'other' response allowed), how was the coding done?* This kind of coding is not a mechanical process but depends on decisions taken by the researcher. These may be shaped by preconceptions, deliberate or quite unconscious.
- *Finally, was the coding accurate?* Surveys require a great deal of transfer of information from schedules or questionnaires to means of analysis such as computers. Where humans are involved in the transmission, errors can and will occur. (Even 'mechanical' means of transmission such as optical readers are not fault-free.)

Again, these decisions and stages at which error can occur or preconception can be imposed on the data are largely invisible to the reader and mostly invisible even to the researcher. We have, simply, to remember that they are there and treat any kind of analysis with a healthy degree of scepticism, however clear-cut the results may appear to be.

The political uses of measurement

This chapter has looked at the interpretation of results by considering possible sources of error. Beyond errors, however, lies the question raised in the last section of the previous chapter – the disputable nature of the concepts in which our results are framed. This will be the subject of the rest of this chapter.

A first point to note is that we have a strong tendency to turn grammatical nouns into substantive ones – to suppose that because we can name something it has a real existence – and then to act on that existence as real. (This process is called *reification.*) We tend not to remember how much our theories are bound up in the way we create names. For example, a manufacturer will commission market research to explore 'attitudes' to coffee with the intention of changing them. This may or may not be an appropriate way to behave, but what it certainly does is to declare as true a theory about the world – that attitudes lead to intentions which lead to behaviour. The manufacturers would not be glad to find that they had changed attitudes successfully but were selling no more coffee as a result. (This was an element of the 'focusing' process we explored in Chapter 2: determining what the research question is by determining what counts as a successful outcome – in this case buying behaviour, not verbalized attitudes.) To take a real case from market research, research-based advertising campaigns of the early 1980s were quite successful in changing heavy smokers' beliefs about the safety and dangers of tobacco, but they made little or no direct difference to whether they smoked.

When we build a 'scientific' measure of some human characteristic, one of the things we do is 'solidify' it – give it a real, scientific existence. The measurement of IQ, for example, helped to *create* intelligence as a basis for selection and manipulation, by a reverse process of construct validation: if you can measure it, then it must exist, and so the theories about it must be correct. The concept is then available, along with its associated measuring instruments, for use in social policy: for the regulation of United States immigration in the early years of the twentieth century, or for the regulation of school selection in the United Kingdom in the years after the Second World War. Personality inventories are routinely used for job selection and even as a basis for putting people of opposite sexes in touch with each other via dating agencies. Diagnostic schedules determine whether potential mental hospital patients are worth the attention of psychiatrists and psychologists. When we create a scientific measuring instrument we tend to conceal rather than make explicit the theories on which it is based and their necessarily tentative nature. Once the instrument exists, it will be taken as measuring something real and something useful. Indeed, it is not just complex measuring instruments which have this property. Some of our most everyday ways of describing and classifying people have this same 'common-sense' but theory-laden nature and are used to make political judgements under the guise of factual description. We shall look at them in the next section.

The political uses of description

Where descriptions are predictive, they may also lend themselves to management or manipulation. This is obvious in the case of the market research survey or the government statistical survey; the one is used for managing the market, the other for economic or social planning, but both are conducted to provide the evidence on which rational management can proceed. In other cases, however, the collection and publication of material about intentions can change these same intentions. The most obvious case is the political opinion poll, where publication of statistics on people's declared voting intentions can suggest which party is likely to win and mobilize undecided voters in its favour or against it. For this reason such polls are banned just before elections in some European countries.

Beyond intentional manipulation and the side-effects of publishing material on intentions, there are some perfectly 'ordinary' variables whose everyday use tends to have an impact on the social world. Gender, for example, looks like a straightforward descriptive variable; we do not even have to ask about it but can code it 'on sight' as in Example 6.1. 'Race', similarly, is taken as a simple descriptive variable. However, we need to ask ourselves the purpose for which such information is collected and the reason for including it in an analysis, because both gender and race are ascribed as well as biological characteristics. (Indeed, we may validly question whether they are biological characteristics at all; there is no set of biological features which unifies all the different people described as 'Black' except a white Anglo-Saxon point of view which considers them 'not like us'.)

By 'ascribed characteristic' I mean one which is used for purposes of social classification and control and therefore has a political importance. It is *important* that people are female or Black, in a way that it is not important that they are tall or have brown hair. We treat gender and ethnic group as fundamental facts about people – part of their substance, not accidents, to use mediaeval terminology. If women are more or less intelligent than men, or more or less patient, or more or less caring, this makes the news. Similarly, the intelligence and scholastic ability of Black people is continually being re-examined, their criminality is a matter of more than just research interest and people still seem to be looking for a gene for 'a natural sense of rhythm'. There *are* some genuine biological differences: women tend on average to be shorter than men, though there are many women taller than many men; Afro-Caribbean people tend on the whole not to make champion swimmers (which I gather is something to do with floating and the distribution of body fat). There *could* in principle be psychological differences also. We should ask, however, why we are so keen to find them. Many would argue that it is not by accident that gender determines relative power, with women confined in principle to childcare and the support of working men, and 'race' is a historical determinant of power and affluence in formerly imperial and slave-owning countries.

If we do not want to contribute further to building the social stereotypes of women and of Black people, we probably need to ask ourselves, on every occasion, *why* we are analysing by gender or ethnic group. There are many legitimate reasons for doing so – to monitor the effects of equal opportunities legislation, for example. For many activities, however, gender and skin colour are just *not* inherently relevant, unless we make them so by our analysis.

The politics of survey research

To sum up, research involves an exercise of power, to whatever small extent. We have already noted in Chapter 2 the power relations implicit in the conventional practice of research, and particularly survey research – researchers extracting the data *they* want by the means *they* want to employ from respondents *they* select, with the role of respondents being simply to comply with honesty. Beyond this, however, researchers are among those who categorize the world – what Foucault (1979b: 304) has called 'the judges of normality':

> The judges of normality are present everywhere. We are in the society of the teacher-judge, the doctor-judge, the educator-judge, the 'social-worker'-judge; it is on them that the universal reign of the normative is based.

We might add 'the researcher-judge': the person who takes and uses the power to describe things as they are and in the process determines the categories of description and declares how things are to be understood. In describing the world we determine what is to count as a valid description of it, and we legitimate the practice of other judges by the provision of evidence that we and they deem to be relevant. It would be wrong to boast of great control – we are creatures of our culture and stand ourselves within a complex power structure – but within our limitations we claim and exercise the right to describe.

Surveys themselves come out of a history of counting, measuring and putting to good use. The discovery of the population as an exploitable resource for industry and agriculture, of the health of the people as the concern of its managers, of the nation's children as a future resource in need of protection and improvement, and of mothers as agents of the state for this purpose forms one single history, and survey research was invented (in the form of the Census, health statistics and the great surveys of the life of the poor) as a tool for the proper management of human resource. In their turn, surveys offer construct validation: they demonstrate that the population *is* countable and assessable and assignable. In the process, political arguments tend to become technical ones – not *whether* people are to be described and handled in this way, but *how many* of them there are and what the results are of their treatment:

> taking what is essentially a political problem, removing it from the realm of political discourse, and recasting it in the neutral language of science. Once this is accomplished the problems have become technical ones. (Foucault, 1982: 196)

This is not intended as an attack on survey research or a prohibition on conducting surveys. Rather, it is a suggestion that when we carry out our little pieces of technically correct research, we need to remember that the activity we undertake is located in a society organized in terms of power relations, as are all societies, and that all our thoughts and actions may have consequences for ourselves and others, as may anybody's.

Further reading

Further reading for this chapter would be Foucault (1979b) and/or Rose (1985). The latter is 'a difficult read' but rewarding.

PART D

EXPLORING DATA

---

9   Keeping it simple: Tabular analysis

In the first of three chapters on the analysis of survey data we shall look at
the simplest form of complex analysis, using tables to explore relationships.
No paradox is intended here in the juxtaposition of 'simple' and 'complex'.
Tables are just about the simplest way of describing a sample: they just
present the counts. In my family, three quarters of the members are female,
and half – all female – cannot vote. There is a clear association at the level
of the sample, therefore, between gender and being able to vote. In reality,
however, gender is not the important factor here; half the family are under
the age of 18 – both female, as it happens – and there is a perfect
association between age and having the franchise (Table 9.1). This is what I
mean by complex analysis – being able to reason from apparent associations in samples to actual associations in the population, taking account
of more than two variables and allowing for sampling error – and all this
can be done using tables.

Significant association in tables

There is little that can be concluded from Table 9.1; it does not contain
enough cases to allow much in the way of analysis. Consider Table 9.2,
however, which looks at measurements taken from a mythical random
sample of 200 students in a particular university. The sample has been
divided at the mid-point into the 100 more extravert students and the 100
more introverted – on the basis of questionnaire scores, let us say – and
their performance on a simple reaction-time task has been used to split
them into three roughly equal groups – the slowest 65, the fastest 65 and
the 70 people in the middle. There are enough cases here for conclusions to
be drawn, so what do we want to say about the table?

    There is an obvious relationship, in this sample, between extraversion/
introversion and speed of reaction time. There are about twice as many
extraverts as introverts in the 'slow' third, and substantially more introverts

TABLE 9.1   *Gender, voting and age in one family*

Gender	All ages Male	All ages Female	Under 18 Male	Under 18 Female	18 or older Male	18 or older Female	
Can vote	1	1	–	–	1	1	
Cannot	–	2	–	2	–	–	
Total	1	3	–	2	1	1	N = 4

TABLE 9.2   *Extraversion and speed of reaction in a mythical sample*

Speed	Extraverts	Introverts	Total
Fast	27	38	65
Medium	30	40	70
Slow	43	22	65
Total	100	100	200

in the other two rows. (The two columns have the same total, so we can validly compare them.) This is factual information and needs no testing; *it is the case* that the extraverts are on average slower than the introverts *in this sample*. What can we say about the population from which the sample is drawn, however?

Well, first we have to acknowledge that the sample is not likely to be representative of the general population, because it consists entirely of students, who tend to come from a very restricted age range and are likely to differ from the population in background, education and motivation. We cannot even treat the sample as representative of students as a whole, because it comes from a single university and is therefore covertly selective. The best we would say, of these larger populations, is that the results may be suggestive but would need checking on different samples.

As a sample of the cohort of students in this one university this group might be reasonably representative, as it was randomly chosen. Even a random sample might not be representative, however; unrepresentative samples can be drawn by random means (see Chapter 3). Given the relationship between extraversion/introversion and reaction times in this sample, how likely is it that there is a similarly strong relationship in the parent population? How likely is this to be an untypical sample drawn by chance from a population in which the relationship does *not* hold? This is the question of *statistical significance*, discussed in earlier chapters, and it can be decided by statistical means. The statistic we shall be using mostly in this chapter is *chi-squared* (written χ^2, where χ is the Greek letter 'chi', pronounced to rhyme with 'why'). It involves *model-fitting*: working out what the table would look like if there were no association between the variables, and then assessing how different the observed figures are from these 'expected' ones. If the difference is sufficiently large the *null hypothesis* of 'no difference' will be rejected and we shall assert that the sample difference probably reflects a real difference in the population – with a designated probability of being in error.

If there is no association between the two variables – if your score or position on one does *not* predict where you will score on the other – then the numbers in each row, or each column, will be distributed in the same proportions as the table's marginal totals. In Table 9.2 we have equal numbers of extraverts and introverts, so if there is no association – if extraversion is not predictive of reaction time – then we should have equal numbers in each row as well. These are the *expected values*, on the basis of the null hypothesis – the model of 'no association'. The expected vales associated with Table 9.2 are shown in Table 9.3.

You might like to work them out for yourself before looking at Table 9.3. (*Hint*: don't worry if some of the answers are not whole numbers.)

TABLE 9.3   *Expected values for Table 9.2*

Speed	Extraverts	Introverts	Total
Fast	32.5	32.5	65
Medium	35	35	70
Slow	32.5	32.5	65
Total	100	100	200

Now, our measure of difference between the null hypothesis model and the observed (actual) figures starts with the subtraction of each expected value from its observed counterpart. So, in the first cell we have an observed value of 27, an expected value of 32.5 (half of 65) and so a difference of –5.5. Next we square this figure, so that larger differences have proportionately more impact on the result than small ones, giving a figure of 30.25. Finally, it is evident that the importance of a difference depends on how big the numbers were – the difference between 7 and 5 is more important than the difference between 102 and 100 – so we scale the result by dividing by the expected value. This gives us a chi-squared value of $30.25/32.5 = 0.931$ (to three decimal places). This is the first component of the statistic. You now do precisely the same for every cell and add up the resulting figures, to obtain the overall value of chi-squared for the table, which is 10.07. The calculations are shown in Table 9.4.

Again, you might like to do the calculation for yourself before looking at Table 9.4.

Now we look up the value of chi-squared in a special table of probabilities, to find the significance level of the result. A small version of the

TABLE 9.4 *Calculating chi-squared for Table 9.2*

Speed	Extraverts	Introverts	Total	χ^2 components
Fast	30.25/32.5 = 0.931	30.25/32.5 = 0.931	65	1.86
Medium	25/35 = 0.714	25/35 = 0.714	70	1.43
Slow	110.25/32.5 = 3.392	110.25/32.5 = 3.392	65	6.78
Total	100	100	200	$\chi^2 = 10.07$

TABLE 9.5 *Critical values for the chi-squared statistic*

Significance level	Degrees of freedom							
	1	2	3	4	5	6	7	8
$p < 0.05$	3.84	5.99	7.81	9.49	11.07	12.59	14.07	15.51
$p < 0.01$	6.63	9.21	11.34	13.28	15.09	16.81	18.48	20.09
$p < 0.001$	10.83	13.82	16.27	18.47	20.52	22.46	24.32	26.12

table is reproduced as Table 9.5. We need one more concept before we can do this, however – the notion of *degrees of freedom*. In a table with only four cells – two rows and two columns – we can work out every figure in the table, given the marginal totals and one other number (see Figure 9.1). The table is therefore said to have one degree of freedom. With a 3 × 3 table (Figure 9.2) we need four figures, as well as the marginal totals, before we can work out the rest by subtraction, so the table has four degrees of freedom. The general rule is that the number of degrees of freedom is given by $(R-1) \times (C-1)$, where R is the number of rows and C is the number of columns.

So how many degrees of freedom does Table 9.2 have?

There are three rows and two columns, so there are $(3-1) \times (2-1) = 2$ degrees of freedom. This is the last thing we need to determine the significance of the association between the two variables. We look at Table 9.5, in the column for two degrees of freedom, and we find that we need a chi-squared value of 5.99 or higher for significance at the 0.05 level, and 9.21 or higher for significance at the 0.01 level. Our chi-squared value of 10.074 from Table 9.2 is therefore significant at the 0.01 level, so we can assert that we ought to get a sample with this large an association, from a population where there is *no* association, less often than one time in a hundred ($p < 0.01$).

An important limitation on the use of chi-squared is that it is not valid – it does not necessarily give the right answer – if numbers are too small. The

a	R1 − *a*	R1
C1 − *a*	R2 − (C1 − *a*) or C2 − (R1 − *a*)	R2
C1	C2	

FIGURE 9.1 *One degree of freedom*

a	*b*	R1 − (*a* + *b*)	R1
c	*d*	R2 − (*c* + *d*)	R2
C1 − (*a* + *c*)	C2 − (*b* + *d*)	R3 − (C1 − (*a* + *c*)) − (C2 − (*b* + *d*))	R3
C1	C2	C3	

FIGURE 9.2 *Four degrees of freedom*

usual rule of thumb is that every *expected* value must be at least 5, though in large tables a few expected values less than 5 can be tolerated provided they are randomly scattered. (If they form a pattern – run along a row or column, for example – then you probably need to combine categories to increase the expected values.)

There are a number of other tests of the significance of association in tables which are in common use. Two of them are briefly described in Box 9.1, along with a summary of information about chi-squared.

Box 9.1: Tests for significant association in tables

Chi-squared (χ^2)

This is a useful general-purpose test, applicable to any size of table provided that expected values are at least 5 in each cell (or most of them, on large tables). To calculate: for each cell, compute $\chi^2 = (O - E)^2/E$, where O is the observed value in the cell, and E is the expected value under the null hypothesis of no association, calculated by dividing the row total by the proportion of cases in the column (or the other way about – whichever is most convenient).

When working with 2 × 2 tables (two rows, two columns) the value of chi-squared should be reduced slightly by applying a *correction for continuity*. The simplest way to calculate the corrected chi-squared is to use an overall formula rather than calculating cell chi-squared. If we label the four cells of the table as A to D (A and B in the top row, C and D in the bottom), then the corrected chi-squared is given by

$$\chi^2 = ((A - D) - 1)^2 \, / \, (A + D),$$

taking the absolute value of $(A - D)$ – that is, ignoring any minus sign.

McNemar's Q

This is used where we have dichotomous information ('yes/no', 'pass/fail') for a number of individuals (N) on a number of measures/questions (C), or for N individuals under C conditions for a single measure, or N sets of C matched individuals on a single item. The formula is

$$Q = \frac{(C - 1)(\sum T_n^2 - (\sum T_n)^2)}{C \sum X_n - \sum X_n^2},$$

where T_n is the total in the nth column and X_n is the total in the nth row. Provided N is larger than about 30 the statistic follows the chi-squared distribution with $C - 1$ degrees of freedom.

Z-test for difference between proportions

In a 2 × 2 table the simplest test is to look directly at the significance of the difference between the proportions in one category of the dependent variable by categories of the independent variable – in other words, to compare the percentages who have a particular score on the dependent variable. (This works only for 2 × 2 tables; with more categories the procedure yields more than one measure of association.) The test is not safe – it may not produce valid results – if sample size is less than about 40 or if the 'split' is too extreme; it should not be used if one category of the independent or dependent variable has less than about 10 per cent of the cases.

How to perform a test is outlined in Box 8.2.
If you have forgotten which is the dependent and which the independent variable, see Box 2.3.

TABLE 9.6 *Gender and reaction time in a mythical sample*

Reaction time	Observed figs.			Expected figs.		χ^2 components		
	M	F	Total	M	F	M	F	Total
Fast	25	40	65	39	26	5.026	7.538	12.56
Medium	40	30	70	42	28	0.095	0.143	0.24
Slow	55	10	65	39	26	6.564	9.846	16.41
Total	120	80	200			χ^2 (2 d.f.) = 29.21		
%	60	40				$p < 0.001$		

Three-way analysis and statistical control

So we have a clear result: reaction time is linked to extraversion in our mythical study. This appears to be true of the population of students in the university, not just the sample, and it could well be true of the population at large. The job of analysis does not stop there, however. The mythical study did not collect much information about participants, but one thing the researchers did note was their gender. (Psychologists generally do take note of gender, even when there is no good reason *a priori* to expect any difference. This is probably because they see it as one of the simplest and least controversial of descriptive measures – but see the discussion in Chapter 8.) The difference in reaction times by gender is shown in Table 9.6, and it leads to a significant result, with a higher chi-squared value than the value for extraversion/introversion. (Normally you cannot compare chi-squareds directly, because the size of the figure varies with the number of cells in the table, but in this case the two tables have the same shape and number of cells and it is therefore valid to compare them.)

I have included the 'workings' with the table, as an example of calculating a chi-squared with unequal column totals. Work through the figures and make sure you can see what I am doing here.

The result needs to be examined further. The first thing to check is whether gender is associated with introversion. There is little or no evidence in the literature to suggest such an association, and none is particularly obvious when we look at the figures (Table 9.7), but the statistical calculation shows a significant association at the 1 per cent level – which shows the importance of doing the tests, not just trusting our judgement. This being so, it is possible that gender rather than introversion may be the explanation of the results: the apparent relationship between speed and introversion may be a product of a gender imbalance in the sample, with women's greater introversion being responsible for the spurious apparent relationship.

One simple way of exploring the relationships between *three* variables is to do three-way tables – in other words, to split the sample on the basis of

TABLE 9.7 *Gender and extraversion in a mythical sample*

	Gender		
E/I	M	F	Total
Extr.	70	30	100
Intr.	50	50	100
Total	120	80	

$\chi^2 = 8.33$ with 1 d.f., $p < 0.01$.

one variable and look separately at the tabulations of the other two. This enables us to see whether the variable we use for splitting the tables:

1 *is a more important determinant* of variation in the dependent variable than the one we were originally examining (in which case the 'sub-tables' will show little or no statistical significance);
2 *has an independent effect* (in which case the significances of the sub-tables will be virtually unaffected, except for a slight decline due to smaller numbers); or
3 *shows an interaction* with the other independent variable (in which case the pattern of significance will be *different* among the sub-tables).

This process is an example of *statistical control* – using the relationship between variables to tease out overlapping or contrary effects, after the data have been collected and by statistical means. (It should be contrasted with *design control*, the control of potentially confounded effects by the selection of the sample or the design of the study.) A three-way analysis of the data from our mythical study is illustrated in Table 9.8.

What we appear to have here is an interaction effect. The definite significance of the overall table of extraversion/introversion with reaction time disappears if we look at just the men in the sample; the relationship in the 'males' table is not statistically significant. On the 'females' table, however, we appear to have a very definite relationship. We would therefore probably conclude (subject to all the warnings about sampling that were discussed above) that there is definitely a gender effect on reaction times, and that introversion/extraversion is also probably important, but only among women. However, the second half of this conclusion has to be treated with some caution. The basic requirement of the statistical test, that every expected value should be greater than 5, is breached in the last row of the 'female' table, and it is this row in which the really large effect is shown, so we would be reasoning from very few cases to a conclusion about the population. Safer would be to put this forward only tentatively and carry out a further study (collect more cases) to confirm it.

Box 9.2 summarizes the kinds of effect that you can look for using this form of analysis and how to spot it. Example 9.1 is a further 'worked

TABLE 9.8 *Gender, extraversion and reaction time in a mythical sample*

Reaction time	Total sample			Males			Females		
	E	I	Total	E	I	Total	E	I	Total
Fast	27	38	65	15	10	25	12	28	40
Medium	30	40	70	20	20	40	10	20	30
Slow	43	22	65	35	20	55	8	2	10
Total	100	100	200	70	50	120	30	50	80
χ^2 (2 d.f.):		10.07			1.78			12.64	
		$p < 0.01$			NS			$p < 0.001$	

Note: Results should be treated with caution; one row in the last block of the table has an expected value of less than 5.

example' of a three-way analysis which I constructed for an Open University methods course in the late 1980s from five years of the data from the People in Society survey.

Example 9.1: The People in Society survey (3): the pay-off of education

To what extent, and for whom, does educational level 'pay off' in terms of salary/wages? What follows is a crude attempt to explore these questions, using data from the 1980–84 responses to the People in Society survey. (Row percentages have been used throughout in the tables, but the chi-squared statistics were of course calculated using the raw numbers.) Table 9.9 shows the relationship between wages (split at the median into 'low' and 'high') and educational level, in total and separately for men and women, for those who were in full- or part-time work.

There is a strongly significant relationship between income and education in all three blocks of the table – in each we notice that the larger figures are in 'low income, low education' and 'high income, high education'. We note also an independent effect of gender: the relationship with education holds for both genders, but women earn *less* on average than men do – more women are in the 'low' column. An obvious influence on level of earnings, however, is whether people are in full-time or part-time work, and it is known that more women than men work part-time. It will be worth decomposing the sample further to explore the influence of type of occupation, and this is done in Table 9.10.

The table confirms that very few men, relatively speaking, are in part-time employment, and for those the relationship between educational level and income does not hold up – the chi-squared value is not significant. We have significant associations in all the other blocks of the table, but we might note that the chi-squared value is very much

Box 9.2: Statistical control: effects to look for

Main (independent) effects

These occur where an independent variable has an association with a dependent variable which is not the product of or influenced by the association of both with a third variable. An example would be the relationship between physical fitness and running speed over a given distance. This is tested in analysis by showing that no other independent variable which correlates with speed also correlates with physical fitness. If a third variable did correlate with both, three-way analysis could be used to see whether splitting the sample by one variable abolished significant association between the other and the dependent variable.

Interaction effects

Here the pattern of interaction between an independent and a dependent variable is different for different levels of a third variable. An example might be the weight of a bicycle: while this would make little or no difference for an unfit rider, the fittest riders ought to be able to go faster on the lighter machines. Test: three-way analysis should reveal the difference in the pattern of association.

Suppressor effects

Very occasionally one variable has the effect of concealing the relationship of another with the dependent variable because it works in the opposite direction. An example might be differential reward according to lack of fitness: if the unfit cyclists were on a behaviouristic 'exercise on prescription' programme and given a substantial reward for cycling fast, while the fit ones were just cycling for the fun of it, the effect of the reward might be to make the unfit cyclists cycle faster than the fit ones.

  More often, one variable suppresses the effect of another because its effects are very much larger and swamp any other effect. An example is the gradient of a track – even an unfit cyclist should be able to cycle faster on a steep downhill incline than the fittest cyclist can cycle up a steep hill. In a test (for both), three-way analysis should allow the relationship to emerge in the sub-tables (e.g. analysing uphill, level and downhill gradients separately). If the sub-tables show roughly equal effects then we have two independent main effects, one of which is suppressing the effect of the other. If they are not roughly equal then the suppressor variable is interacting with the other one. For example, fitness might have more effect on uphill gradients than on downhill ones.

Note

The analysis does not determine which is the dependent and which the independent variable, but only that there are interacting or non-interacting patterns of association. The direction of causation has to be supplied by the researcher, on the basis of other evidence or argument.

TABLE 9.9 *Wages and educational level by gender in the People in Society survey*

Education	Total		Males		Females	
	Low wages	High wages	Low wages	High wages	Low wages	High wages
O level						
or less (%)	62.9	37.1	44.2	55.8	82.3	17.7
Higher levels (%)	31.2	68.8	15.9	84.1	46.8	53.2
N	4632		2307		2325	
χ^2 (1 d.f.)	472.02		220.81		324.70	
	$p < 0.001$		$p < 0.001$		$p < 0.001$	

TABLE 9.10 *Education, employment type, gender and income in the People in Society survey*

Education	Males				Females			
	Full-time		Part-time		Full-time		Part-time	
	Low wages	High wages	Low wages	High wages	Low wages	High wages	Low wages	High wages
O level								
or less (%)	35.3	64.7	86.4	13.6	66.2	33.8	94.0	6.0
Higher levels (%)	11.4	88.6	76.5	23.5	27.4	72.6	85.3	14.7
N	2028		279		1223		1102	
χ^2 (1 d.f.)	164.21		3.34		182.37		21.60	
	$p < 0.001$		NS		$p < 0.001$		$p < 0.001$	

smaller in the 'part-time, female' block. This suggests a possible inter-action: educational qualifications are not as productive of income, or as important for level of occupation, among part-time workers as among those in full-time employment. The chi-squared value is some-what higher for women than for men even among those in full-time employment, which again suggests a possible interaction. Other litera-ture suggests that 'credentialism' is more important for women than men – that educational qualifications determine women's level of employment, with men succeeding more often in getting 'on-the-job' promotion. A final table (Table 9.11) tests this to some extent by splitting the full-time workers by marital status. Given that married women may sometimes take employment below their 'natural' level for reasons to do with childcare, and if credentialism is a good explanation of observed variation, then we would expect single women to show a much greater association between educational level and income than any groups of men, and a greater one than married women. This prediction is not born out, however; while unmarried women show a substantially higher chi-squared value than married ones, the highest value is obtained for married men and the lowest for unmarried men.

TABLE 9.11 *Education, gender and income among full-time workers in the People in Society survey*

	Males				Females			
	Married		Not married		Married		Not married	
Education	Low wages	High wages	Low wages	High wages	Low wages	High wages	Low wages	High wages
O level or less (%)	27.4	72.6	49.0	51.0	58.8	41.2	74.4	25.6
Higher levels (%)	5.1	94.9	25.8	74.2	22.7	77.3	31.3	68.8
N	1356		672		593		630	
χ^2 (1 d.f.)	129.72		37.40		78.60		112.43	
	$p < 0.001$		$p < 0.001$		$p < 0.001$		$p < 0.001$	

Advantages and weaknesses of tabular analysis

Major advantages of this kind of tabular analysis are its simplicity and flexibility. People can understand tables, in a way that they do not necessarily understand more complex and technical forms of analysis. You never become remote from the data; at each stage you are presenting tables of actual figures from samples or subsamples, not sophisticated indices or derived measures. The idea of chi-squared itself is not very difficult to understand – the rejection of the idea that the figures in the table could be randomly distributed between the cells. You can tailor your analysis to precisely the topic you want to explore, introducing variables as they are needed and perhaps following only one line of a dichotomy (exploring the employment of women, say, without further reference to men's employment). It is a superficially very crude method of analysis, but it can detect all the effects that more sophisticated methods can identify.

It has several disadvantages however. Among the most practical is the sheer bulk of paper it produces. When doing three-way or higher-order analysis we usually work on 2 × 2 tables, or at most 3 × 3, because the number of tables produced expands geometrically as you go up to higher levels of interaction (Figure 9.3). Five-way analysis using variables with two categories to 'split' the sample yields 15 blocks of table; using variables with three categories yields 42 blocks! Admittedly the same technique can be used with more compact means of describing samples than tables – means, medians, variances, correlations (standard errors for testing significances of differences can be found in Box 8.3) – but it is not well adapted for dealing with a large number of variables.

A second problem is that while this technique can *identify* all the effects, it cannot *say how big they are*. There *are* ways of estimating the size of effects in tabular analysis, and we shall discuss them in the next chapter, but in general there are better ways of estimating contributions to variance, if that is your problem.

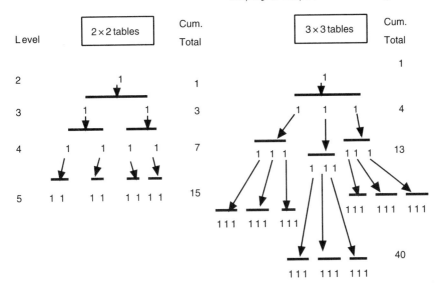

FIGURE 9.3   *Tabular analysis – numbers of tables produced*

Finally, it is inherent in the nature of statistical inference that if you do a large number of independent statistical tests you will make some mistakes. To say that something is statistically significant is to say that there is one chance in 20, or one in 100, that you will reject the null hypothesis incorrectly when there is in fact no association in the parent population. So if you do 100 separate chi-squared tests, or even 20, the odds on one of them producing a false result are very good indeed. For this and other reasons more sophisticated statistics have sometimes to be used, and these are discussed in the next two chapters.

Further reading

Marsh (1979) gives a similar account of tabular analysis as this chapter, but using the significance of difference in proportions as the indicator of association. Maxwell (1961) is a classic account of partitioning tables which goes well beyond the level reached in this chapter.

10   Correlation and its friends

We saw in the previous chapter that the major problems faced by tabular analysis were the difficulty of assigning percentages to the amount of variance explained by a given effect and the sheer bulk of output produced when working with large numbers of variables. In this chapter we look at much more compact means of analysis – correlation coefficients and the related technique of regression analysis.

Correlation

Correlation and *regression* are used for *linear modelling* – seeing how much of the variation in the dependent variable can be explained by positing a straight-line relationship with an independent variable. For example, in the ideal world of the physicist we can perfectly predict the distance travelled by a car as a straight-line function of its speed and elapsed time (illustrated in Figure 10.1(a)). The distance travelled (Y) is given by elapsed time (X) multiplied by the speed of the car (b):

$$Y = bX.$$

(Note that the car's speed (in miles per hour) is the *gradient* of the line – the rate at which it goes up on the Y axis (in miles) for every unit of time (in hours) on the X axis.) This is a *regression equation* for the special case where the line intercepts the zero on the graph – in zero time the car travels no miles. More often in life there is also an *intercept coefficient* to take into account, because at the beginning of the process the starting value is not zero. For example (Figure 10.1(b)) when we heat water its temperature (Y) is a straight-line function of the amount of power used to heat it (X, times some multiplier, b, which represents the amount the temperature of the water rises for every unit of power supplied). However, the water starts off at room temperature (a), not at zero, so the equation is

$$Y = a + bX.$$

The quantities a and b in this equation are known as *regression coefficients*.

The regression coefficients measure the strength of association, but they are difficult to interpret because they are in the original units (miles and hours, degrees and units of power). If we had used kilometres instead of

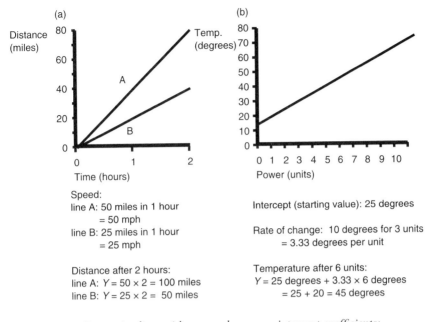

(a)

Distance (miles)

Time (hours)

Speed:
line A: 50 miles in 1 hour
= 50 mph
line B: 25 miles in 1 hour
= 25 mph

Distance after 2 hours:
line A: $Y = 50 \times 2 = 100$ miles
line B: $Y = 25 \times 2 = 50$ miles

(b)

Temp. (degrees)

Power (units)

Intercept (starting value): 25 degrees

Rate of change: 10 degrees for 3 units
= 3.33 degrees per unit

Temperature after 6 units:
$Y = 25$ degrees $+ 3.33 \times 6$ degrees
$= 25 + 20 = 45$ degrees

FIGURE 10.1 *Regression lines with zero and non-zero intercept coefficients: (a) distance travelled versus time elapsed; (b) water temperature versus power supplied*

miles, the same degree of relationship would give us different regression coefficients. What is needed is some form of *standardization* – like using percentages instead of raw figures in tables – so that like can readily be compared with like, and this is what the *correlation coefficient* provides. The one in most common use (called the *product-moment coefficient*, and devised by the statistician Karl Pearson) works by standardizing both the measurement scales, so that scores are expressed in standard deviation units rather than miles or degrees or hours. In other words, every score is expressed as a deviation from the mean on each of the two variables, and the distance from the mean is expressed in standard deviations. Some of these scores will be positive, therefore, and some will be negative, and most but not all will be rather small, if the scores on the variables are normally distributed. What we then do (or what we can get a computer to do) is take each point of data (each case) and multiply the X value (in standard deviation units) by the Y value, and then add all these new figures together. Now if there is no association between the two variables – if a high value of X, for example, is just as likely to predict a low value of Y as a high one, or any point in between), then if the sample is reasonably large the sum of the new values should be zero or close to zero – there will be as many positive scores as negative ones, and they should add up to similar totals. If high scores on X predict high scores on Y, and low scores on X predict low scores on Y, then the new figure should be large and positive, because where the larger original scores are concentrated you will (almost) always be multiplying a positive figure by a positive figure or a negative figure by a negative figure (and two minuses produce a plus in multiplication). If the opposite is the case, and high scores on *X* go with low scores on *Y* and vice versa, then you will produce a large negative figure, because you will (almost) always be multiplying a positive score by a negative score. To produce the correlation coefficient, the computer rescales these numbers so that:

- the highest possible positive score produces a coefficient of +1.0 (*perfect positive correlation*);
- the highest possible negative score produces a coefficient of −1.0 (*perfect negative correlation*);
- a score of zero produces a coefficient of 0.0 (*no association*); and
- other numbers produce an appropriate number between −1.0 and 0.0 or between 0.0 and +1.0.

So the correlation coefficient varies between +1 and −1, via zero (no association). This is the case *whatever the original units of measurement*, so correlation coefficients can be compared. (The equation for the correlation coefficient is given in Box 10.1.)

Returning to Chapter 9's mythical study of extraversion and reaction time, Table 10.1 gives the associations between variables, expressed as correlation coefficients. You can see how much more compact this presentation is by comparing this table with the ones in Chapter 9.

Each figure in Table 10.1, is the correlation coefficient measuring the association between two variables. So, in the first row:

- the first figure (1.00) is the correlation of variable *A* (reaction time) with itself – necessarily perfect and positive;
- the second figure (0.22) is the correlation of variable *A* with variable *B* (extraversion/introversion); and
- the third figure (0.35) is the correlation of variable *A* with variable *C* (gender).

The correlations of variable *B* with itself and variable *C* are given in the second row, and so on. The other half of the table could be given – the correlation of *A* with *B* is the same as the correlation of *B* with *A*, for example, so you could fill in 0.22 in the appropriate place. This is redundant, however, and is generally omitted.

Note that, with one exception, you can calculate correlation coefficients validly only if your variables are measured at the interval or ratio level (see Box 3.2). Extraversion/introversion is at least at the interval level, and reaction time is a ratio variable. The exception, which allows us to include gender in this analysis, is that dichotomous variables (those with only two

Box 10.1: The product-moment correlation coefficient (*r*)

For two variables *x* and *y* measured for the same sample, Pearson's correlation coefficient *r* is calculated as:

$$r = \frac{\text{sum of squares for } xy}{\sqrt{(\text{sum of squares for } x)(\text{sum of squares for } y)}},$$

where *xy* is the 'cross-product' – the *x* value multiplied by the *y* value. An alternative formulation is

$$r = \frac{\sum(x_i - m_x)(y_i - m_y)}{(n-1)s_x s_y},$$

where x_i is the value of *x* for the *i*th case, m_x is the mean of the *x* values and s_x is their standard deviation. (You will find computationally easier formulae in most statistics textbooks, if you need to calculate *r* 'by hand'. It is better, however, to use a computer.)

A third formulation is that

$$r^2 = \frac{\text{explained sum of squares}}{\text{total sum of squares}}$$

(in other words, squaring the correlation coefficient gives the proportion of variance explained).

The statistic *F* is the ratio of explained variation to the rest:

$$F = \frac{\text{mean explained sum of squares}}{\text{mean residual sum of squares}}.$$

So it can be shown that

$$F = \frac{r^2}{(1 - r^2)(n - 2)}.$$

Each component of the formula has an associated 'degrees of freedom' figure: 1 for r^2 and $n - 2$ for $1 - r^2$.

Hints on using the computer program:

- Most statistical packages offer you a choice of output, between a *correlation matrix* and *pairwise correlation* (each individual pair of variables yielding a single correlation coefficient).
- Most statistical packages will give the significance of correlation coefficients, but you may have to ask for this.
- You need to be careful about 'don't know', 'refused' and 'information missing' cases. You probably coded these at one extreme or the other of your code list, and leaving them in the analysis will badly distort the

results. You can (a) recode them to the mean/median (which will somewhat reduce the size of the correlation), or (b) make an intelligent guess as to what the value ought to be (but this inevitably introduces non-sampling bias, and the basis of estimation will have to be justified in the report), or (c) omit them from the analysis. The last of these is the usual course. Most statistical packages will allow you to flag code values as 'missing' and have them omitted from the analysis. If yours does not, you will have to exclude them by some other means.

• Most statistical packages default to *listwise deletion* of missing values – a case is omitted if it has a missing value on *any* of the variables in the current analysis. (So if you have one variable with a lot of missing cases, think carefully before including it.) You are often offered the alternative of *pairwise deletion* – omitting cases only from the correlations where they have missing values – but this gives you a different sample size for correlations in the same matrix, and you will have to get the software to tell you on what numbers each correlation is based.

TABLE 10.1 *Reaction time, gender and extraversion/introversion in a mythical sample: correlations*

		A	B	C
A	Reaction time	1.00	0.22	0.35
B	Extraversion/introversion		1.00	0.20
C	Gender			1.00

categories) behave like ratio variables for most statistical purposes and may be included here.

The same question arises with correlation coefficients as with tables of differences between means or proportions – the question of sampling error. How likely is it that we could achieve a correlation of the size of the one calculated from the sample, if it were drawn randomly from a population in which the overall correlation was zero – in which, in other words, the two variables were not associated? We need a test of statistical significance, to decide whether the coefficient is sufficiently larger than zero for it probably *not* to be an aberrant result. One has already been given, in Box 8.3 – a Z test – but here we shall consider a more sophisticated means of testing which has wider applications.

The correlation coefficient, like a regression coefficient, can be drawn as a line on a graph. If the correlation is a good fit to the data, then it will be a good way of predicting where the individual cases will fall on the graph. This is true by definition; what we mean by high correlation is that high scores on one variable predict high scores on the other (in the case of positive correlation), so the data points lie somewhere on or near a line

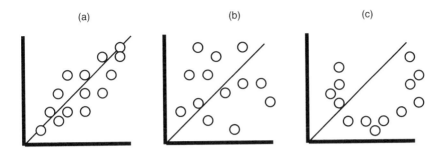

FIGURE 10.2 *Fits of correlation lines: (a) good fit; (b) poor fit; (c) non-linear configuration*

which joins the 'low *X*, low *Y*' part of the graph to the 'high *X*, high *Y*' part. So if we use the correlation coefficient to predict where a given case ought to fall, we can measure the 'goodness of fit' by recalculating each score as a squared deviation from the correlation line. A 'good fit' will minimize the sum of these squared deviations. Various kinds of fit are illustrated in Figure 10.2. Figure 10.2(a) shows a very good fit, with all the points lying reasonably close to the line and equally (randomly) divided between points above the line and points below. (One way of telling whether a correlation is worth calculating is to get the computer to plot all the data points on a graph – known as a *scattergram* for obvious reasons – and look for the cigar-shaped distribution characteristic of high correlation.) Figure 10.2(b) shows a relatively poor fit; the points are still randomly scattered around the line, but the deviations are large. Figure 10.2(c) shows a distribution where the 'linear model' approach of correlation is not suitable at all; the relationship is actually U-shaped. (An example would be the relationship of anxiety to examination performance, where both very low levels of anxiety and very high levels tend to lead to poor performance.)

What we have to explain (account for) is the variance in the figures – the sums of squared deviations from the means, multiplied together. A proportion of this is accounted for by the correlation; assuming that the figures lie along the line of correlation gives us a better prediction of them than the means alone, if the correlation (r) is large and significant. This proportion can be obtained, quite simply, by squaring the correlation coefficient: a correlation of 0.5 accounts for 0.25 (a quarter) of the variance, and a correlation of 0.9 accounts for 81 per cent of it. So in Table 10.1 two of the correlations each account for about 4 per cent of the variance, and the third accounts for rather more than 10 per cent.

What is left over $(1 - r^2)$ is the variance that still has to be explained – error variances of various kinds, and the effects of other variables. Comparing the two gives us our index of significance. If r accounts for a large proportion of the variance it will be statistically significant, and if it

TABLE 10.2 *Computing* F *values for the correlations in Table 10.1*

Variables	Sample size	r	r^2 (a)	$1 - r^2$ (a)	df	a/df	F
$A-B$	200	0.22	0.0484	0.9516	1	0.0484	
					198	0.0048	10.07
$A-C$	200	0.35	0.1225	0.7775	1	0.1225	
					198	0.0044	27.64
$B-C$	200	0.20	0.0400	0.9600	1	0.0400	
					198	0.0048	8.25

does not then it will tend not to be – depending on the sample size, as smaller effects show up as significant with larger samples. What we calculate, therefore, is the ratio of variances (a statistic conventionally labelled *F*).

However, the 'error variance' will itself vary with the number of cases – the more, the larger – so we need some way of scaling it down in proportion to the size of the sample. What we use for this is a version of 'degrees of freedom', for which we need two values; the logic behind them is similar to the calculation of degrees of freedom for chi-squared. The size of the sample (*n*) gives us our starting point. If we know all the values except one, and the mean or total, then we can work out what the final value must be, so we have ($n - 1$) degrees of freedom to play with. We allow one of these for the correlation, which therefore has one degree of freedom. The remainder ($n - 2$) is the degrees of freedom for the error variance. So we show our correlation as having (1, $n - 2$) degrees of freedom. Now when looking up its significance we divide each of the terms in the equation by its degrees of freedom before looking up the *F* value in the table.

Table 10.2 shows the calculations for the correlations in Table 10.1. Looking up the resulting *F* values in Table 10.3, we can see that all three of the correlations are significant at the 1 per cent level ($p < 0.01$).

When you use tables of *F* values, you will notice that there is a separate table, or block, for each level of significance. (Table 10.3 has blocks for $p < 0.05$ and $p < 0.01$.)

Having selected the required level of significance, the first of the two 'degrees of freedom' figures is located along the array which has the lower figures (generally forming the column headings of the table, and often labelled ν_1, as in Table 10.3).

The second and larger 'degrees of freedom' figure should be located in the other array (generally forming the rows of the table and often labelled ν_2).

The intersection of the column and row thus selected gives you the critical value of *F* at that level of significance – the smallest value that will indicate statistical significance at that level. Any *F* value smaller than this figure fails the test (but may pass it on a table with a lower critical value).

TABLE 10.3 *Values of the* F *distribution*

	$\nu_1 = 1$	2	3	4	5	6	12	24	Infinity
$p = 0.05$									
$\nu_2 = 1$	161.4	199.5	215.7	224.6	230.2	234.0	243.9	249.0	254.3
2	18.5	19.0	19.2	19.2	19.3	19.3	19.4	19.5	19.5
3	10.1	9.6	9.3	9.1	9.0	8.9	8.7	8.6	8.5
6	6.0	5.1	4.8	4.5	4.4	4.3	4.0	3.8	3.7
12	4.7	3.9	3.5	3.3	3.1	3.0	2.7	2.5	2.3
20	4.4	3.5	3.1	2.9	2.7	2.6	2.3	2.1	1.8
40	4.1	3.2	2.8	2.6	2.4	2.3	2.0	1.9	1.4
Infinity	3.8	3.0	2.6	2.4	2.2	2.1	1.8	1.5	1.0
$p = 0.01$									
$\nu_2 = 1$	4052.0	4999.0	5403.0	5625.0	5764.0	5859.0	6106.0	6235.0	6366.0
2	98.5	99.0	99.2	99.2	99.3	99.3	99.4	99.5	99.5
3	34.1	30.8	29.5	28.7	28.2	27.9	27.1	26.6	26.1
6	13.7	10.9	9.8	9.1	8.8	8.5	7.7	7.3	6.9
12	9.3	6.9	6.0	5.4	5.1	4.8	4.2	3.8	3.4
20	8.1	5.8	4.9	4.4	4.1	3.9	3.2	2.9	2.4
40	7.3	5.2	4.3	3.8	3.5	3.3	2.7	2.3	1.8
Infinity	6.6	4.6	3.8	3.3	3.0	2.8	2.2	1.8	1.0

So when we were looking up the correlation of 0.22 between extraversion and reaction time, which yielded an *F* value of 10.07, we start with (1, 198) as degrees of freedom. Looking at the '$p < 0.01$' block of the table, we need to be in the first row ($\nu_1 = 1$) and in a row labelled 198 for ν_2. The table does not have such a row, but we note that for 40 degrees of freedom the critical value is 7.3, and for infinity – the highest possible value for ν_2 – the figure would be 6.6, so the value for 198 degrees of freedom lies somewhere between the two. Our figure of 10.07 is clearly larger than both, so the null hypothesis may be rejected and we can declare the correlation to be significantly different from zero at $p < 0.01$.

Actually you will not often have to work things out in this detail; your computer will generally give you the significance values for the correlations. You need to understand the *F* test, however, because it is important for other statistical procedures in this and the next chapter. The background to it is summarized in Box 10.1.

Various other correlation coefficients are used as approximations to the product-moment value under particular circumstances. The biserial correlation coefficient, for example, can be used when we have scores on two variables (measured on an interval or ratio scale) for a dichotomous variable (for example, 'at school' and 'at home', Test 1 and Test 2, 'before treatment' and 'after treatment'). Where the scales do not achieve interval or ratio status but do count as ordinal, a common tool is Spearman's rho (ρ), which works on ranked data. Tables of two dichotomous variables (2 × 2 tables) can yield a phi (ϕ) coefficient which is derived from the chi-squared value (which gives us a way of assessing the *size* of effects in tabular analysis: ϕ^2 is the proportion of variance explained). Another useful tool is Kendall's coefficient of concordance W, which measures the average agreement between judges. These and others are listed and briefly described in Box 10.2.

Multiple and partial correlation

Any given correlation coefficient is like a table (though much more compact); it measures the association between a single pair of variables. A matrix of correlations does this for a set of such pairs, two variables at a time. It is also possible, however, to use correlation to assess the relationship of *more than one* independent variable with a dependent variable. By a relatively simple calculation (the equation is given in Box 10.3) you can work out how two variables *together* influence a third. The extra information you need to do so, apart from the two *zero-order* correlations (the coefficients for the correlation of each independent variable separately with the dependent one) is the correlation of the two independent variables with each other. This is because, to the extent that the two are correlated, the influence that they have on each other may be 'passed on' to the dependent variable and so 'counted twice'. This is illustrated in Table 10.4, using our fictional study of reaction times, and in Figure 10.3. If the independent variables were uncorrelated – as in Table 10.4 and Figure 10.3(a) – then the whole of each can be 'brought to bear' on the dependent variable: the total 'area of influence' is the whole of both variables, and we can work out their joint influence just by adding their squared values. As they are correlated, however, they share variance, and the total 'area of influence' is reduced by the overlap. The multiple correlation coefficient for these three variables, taking account of the overlap between the two independents, is 0.38, explaining about 14 per cent of the variance (not 17 per cent, as it would if they were uncorrelated).

So the multiple correlation coefficient calculates, if you like, the area of the independent variable circles in Figure 10.3(b), taking due care not to count the region of overlap twice. This is the second step of a multivariate analysis using correlation: having ascertained the *separate* relationships of independent variables to dependent ('at zero order'), you look to see what they *all* contribute, taken together and making due allowance for their intercorrelation. The next step is to look for the *independent* effects of the variables – what they contribute when all other influences have been allowed for, what they add distinctively to the analysis. For this task we can use the *partial correlation coefficient* (Box 10.3). The partial correlation coefficient expresses the relationship between two variables with the effect on both of a third variable subtracted (that is to say, *controlling for* a third variable). In the case of our fictional study, the two partial correlation coefficients for the independent variables, controlling in each case for the effect of the other variable, are given in Table 10.5. We can see that both the zero-order coefficients 'shrink' when the effect of the other variable is

Box 10.2: Other correlation coefficients

Data measured at the interval or ratio level (*see Box 3.2*)

The *biserial correlation coefficient* is used where we have two sets of scores on the same people or matched groups.

$$r_b = (M_2 - M_1)(p_1 p_2)/ZS_y,$$

where M_1 and M_2 are the means of the two groups defined by the dichotomy, p_1 and p_2 are the proportions the two groups form of the total, S_y is the standard deviation on the continuous variable as a whole and Z is the Z value given in a table of the normal distribution for p_1 or p_2 (whichever is smaller).

The sampling error of r_b is given approximately by

$$SE = \frac{\frac{\sqrt{p_1 p_2}}{Z} - r_b^2}{\sqrt{N}}.$$

The coefficient should not be used if p_1 or p_2 is larger than about 0.9.

Data measured at interval level

Spearman's rank-order coefficient (ρ) is used where we have two sets of scores on the same people or matched groups, but one or both is not measured at interval or ratio level.

Arrange the data so that columns are scores and rows are cases. Rank each column separately (1 is the highest score and tied cases are given the average of the ranks they would cover) and calculate the difference (D) between column 1 and column 2 for each case. Then

$$\rho = 1 - \frac{6 \sum D^2}{N(N^2 - 1)}.$$

The test of significance is

$$t = \sqrt{\frac{N - 2}{1 - \rho^2}}$$

with 2 degrees of freedom.

Kendall's coefficient of concordance (*W*) is used where there are more than two columns (judges). Arrange the data and rank each column separately, as for ρ, and add up the rows to give a *T* score for each case. There are *C* columns and *R* rows.

The maximum variance that a given number of judges and cases could produce is

$$s^2_{max} = \frac{C^2(R^2 - 1)}{12}.$$

The actual variance is given by

$$s^2_{sum} = \frac{1}{R^2}(R\sum T^2 - (\sum T)^2).$$

W is the ratio of these two variances:

$$W = s^2_{sum}/s^2_{max}.$$

Provided R is greater than 7, the significance of W may be tested by

$$\chi^2 = \frac{12Rs^2_{sum}}{CR(R + 1)}$$

with $R - 1$ degrees of freedom.

For use with tables

Here we have phi (ϕ) and Cramér's V. The former is given by

$$\phi = \sqrt{\chi^2/N};$$

the latter by

$$V = \sqrt{\chi^2/n(k - 1)},$$

where k is the number of rows or columns in the table, whichever is the smaller. Phi is used for 2 × 2 tables and Cramér's V for larger tables. Both coefficients are significant if the χ^2 value is significant.

partialled out. Gender remains a significant influence and explains about 2 per cent of the variance, controlling for extraversion, but extraversion itself loses its significance. We are therefore inclined to say that gender has an independent effect on reaction time, in this fictional study, but extraversion influences it only via gender.

Thus we have used correlation – at zero order and by calculating multiple and partial correlation coefficients – to explore the structure of the data in the mythical survey. We have shown that two variables show a significant relationship with reaction time at zero order, but that the effect of one of them (introversion/extraversion) fails to reach significance when we control for the other. Its effect, therefore, would appear to work only in interaction with gender. Overall we have explained about 14 per cent of the variance in the reaction time scores, with a multiple R of 0.38.

Box 10.3: Multiple and partial correlation

The multiple correlation of variables 2 and 3 with variable 1 — the joint overall effect of variables 2 and 3 on variable 1 — is given by

$$R_{1.23} = \sqrt{\frac{r_{12}^2 + r_{13}^2 - 2r_{12}r_{13}r_{23}}{1 - r_{23}^2}}.$$

Its standard error is given by

$$\frac{1 - r_{1.23}^2}{\sqrt{N}}.$$

Using this formula in a Z test is valid, however, only where N is reasonably large (greater than 500, say) and R is reasonably low (less than about 0.3). On the other hand, you will seldom have to use it; if your zero-order correlations are all significant and have the same arithmetical sign, then the multiple correlation is significant.

The *partial correlation* of variable 2 with variable 1, controlling for (eliminating) the effects of variable 3, is given by

$$R_{12.3} = \frac{r_{12} - r_{13}r_{23}}{\sqrt{(1 - r_{13}^2)(1 - r_{23}^2)}}.$$

Significance is tested by a t test with $N - 3$ degrees of freedom:

$$t = \frac{R_{12.3}}{\sqrt{\frac{1}{N-3}(1 - R_{12.3}^2)}}.$$

TABLE 10.4 *Multiple influence of two independent variables on reaction time in a mythical study*

		Variance explained (%)	
Variable	*r*	If independent variables were uncorrelated	As independent variables are correlated 0.20
Zero-order explanations			
Extraversion	0.22	4.84	4.84
Gender	0.35	12.25	12.25
Multiple explanation		17.09	14.59
			($R_{1.23} = 0.382$)

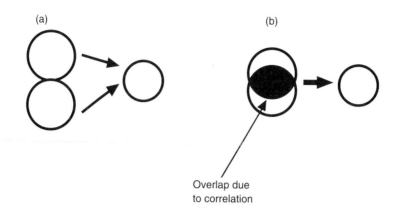

Overlap due
to correlation

FIGURE 10.3 *Relationship to dependent variable of (a) uncorrelated and (b) correlated independent variables*

TABLE 10.5 *Partial correlations for the effects of two independent variables on reaction time in a mythical study*

	Zero-order correlation	Partial correlation	t value	Significance of partial coefficient
E/I	0.22	0.08	1.13	NS
Gender	0.35	0.16	2.81	$p < 0.01$

Note: E/I and gender are correlated 0.20.

This kind of analysis can be extended to four or more variables, but the formulae and calculations become very unwieldy. Better for the purpose, given access to a computer's statistical package, are techniques based more directly around the concepts of regression and multiple regression. It is to these that we turn in the next section.

Regression

As we saw earlier, a regression equation is the simplest form of linear modelling other than predicting that all cases will lie on the mean. It attempts to explain as much variance as possible by fitting a straight line as close to all the data points as possible. A zero-order regression line is specified by

$$Y = a + bX$$

where a is the value of Y when X is zero and b is the gradient of increase in Y as we progress along the X values. Regression is closely related to correlation – a correlation line is a regression on standardized variables – and as a form of multivariate analysis it can be used for all the purposes for which correlation can be used. The statistical significance of the *b* coefficient – the coefficient of slope, or relationship – is tested by the variance ratio *F*:

$$F = \frac{\text{explained sum of squares}}{\text{residual sum of squares}}.$$

Multiple regression

Turning a zero-order regression equation into a multiple regression is simply a matter of adding more terms:

$$Y = a + b_1X_1 + b_2X_2 + \ldots,$$

where X_1, X_2, . . . are independent variables and b_1, b_2, . . . are the regression coefficients associated with them.

Multiple regression is extremely tedious to calculate 'by hand' (as is correlation!), but easy to do on a computer with the aid of a statistical package. All you have to do is specify which is the dependent variable and to give a list of independent variables, and the machine will do the rest. (Remember about missing values, however – see Box 10.1.) What the machine will produce for you is some or all of the following:

- The components of the equation – the value of *a* (the intercept) and the *b* coefficients. (These will not be of much interest to you unless you literally want to predict the value of *Y* from values of the *X*s – when planning housing supply, for example, and so estimating population growth in particular age bands.)
- The multiple correlation coefficient *R*, which is the first and most useful product, and probably a significance level based on an *F* ratio. This can be compared with the original zero-order coefficients to see what combining variables adds to the explanation, and the package may test whether the multiple *R* is significantly larger than the largest of the zero-order *r*s. Squaring the R gives proportion of variance explained; the package may even do this for you!
- A *beta coefficient* for each variable in the equation, derived from the *b* coefficients. These are *standardized partial regression coefficients* (akin to partial correlations) and give an idea of the size of each variable's independent effect, controlling for all the other variables. If you square the betas you obtain the proportion of variance explained by any one of the variables when all the others in the equation are controlled for.
- A test of each component's significance, as a contributor to the equation (probably by a *t* test).

Note that most packages will also calculate and display for you (perhaps by plotting them around the line of best fit) the *residuals*, the amounts of each variable's variance left over after the multiple regression equation has explained as much as it can. These should (if the regression is a successful predictor) be fairly small, and they should be randomly scattered around the prediction line. If they are *not* random but show some pattern, it is likely that an important causal influence remains unmeasured or at least not entered in the current analysis.

Stepwise regression and testing effects

One interesting and informative way of going about multiple regression is to take the analysis one step at a time. Starting from the highest correlation, which by definition indicates the variable explaining the greatest proportion of variance, most packages will allow you to add the next most important when the effects of the first have been controlled, and then the next after taking account of the effects of the first two, and so on until nothing more of significance is being explained. This enables you to see how few variables you need to explain most of the variance which is going to be explained and what, in the particular sample, seems to have independent effects on the dependent variable. The order of entry (or indeed, the composition of the list of variables which enter) is not always straightforwardly interpretable, because it tends to be somewhat unstable between samples. Replication is always needed to confirm the membership of the list and the order of entry – either between years or, with a very large sample, between randomly selected halves of the data file. However, the stepwise pattern of proceeding does give more insight into the 'workings' of the analysis than just putting all the variables in at once.

You should remember, however, that one thing the order of entry does *not* tell us is which variables have the greatest independent effect. This is because of shared variance – correlation between independent variables. When the first variable enters the equation, its contribution to the prediction is taken as including the whole amount of its association with the dependent variable, including any which is shared with other variables. When the second enters, therefore, it can contribute only what is left over when its association with the first is controlled; when the third enters, it can contribute only what is left over after the first and second have entered; and so on. (See Figure 10.4, and note particularly the visible area of the circle corresponding to variable *C*, which indicates the amount of variance it apparently explains.) Typically, therefore, the *increase* in the multiple correlation coefficient becomes smaller and smaller as each variable is added. If you want to know the independent contributions made by variables at each stage you must look at the beta coefficients and their associated tests of significance.

Another way of proceeding which can sometimes offer insights is to have the process done *backwards* – to start by putting every variable into the

(a)   (b)   (c)

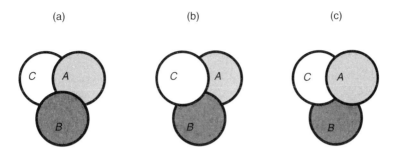

FIGURE 10.4 *Share of variance in multiple regression, with order of entry:*
(a) A, B, C; (b) C, B, A; (c) A, C, B

equation and then removing, at each step, the variable which makes the
least difference to the proportion of variance explained. Remember, however, that it is still the beta coefficients which tell us how much the variable's independent contribution was; the multiple *R* itself may not shrink
much, because of the effects of correlation among independent variables.

Stepwise regressions can also be performed in an order of insertion (or
deletion) chosen by the researcher on theoretical grounds. (Where this
occurs it is sometimes called *hierarchical regression.*) For example, if we
had used regression instead of tabular analysis to examine the problem of
income, education and gender explored in Example 9.1 above, we might
have started by computing a multiple *R* with income of background and
social/class variables, to see how much of the variance could be explained
without reference to either gender or education – taking account of part-
or full-time working as another rather simple determinant of amount
earned. Then we might try entering gender, or education, or both, and
seeing how much the prediction of income is *improved*. Another common
reason for manipulating the variable list 'by hand' instead of leaving the
choices to the package's computation of variance explained is to test the
effect of a given variable. If you have a set of variables which gives a
satisfactory prediction of a dependent variable, you can test the importance
of key variables by removing them from the equation and seeing how much
R declines and how the pattern of betas readjusts itself. In looking at
women and social class in the People in Society data, for example, we were
interested in the influence of women's own occupations and education (as
opposed to husband's occupation) on women's subjective class identification. One simple way to explore this problem was to build regressions of
own occupation, husband's occupation, father's class, education and so on
on class identification, then remove husband's class and see how much R^2
fell as a result and/or which variables rose to take its place. Many statistical packages have a TEST routine in the regression analysis which does
precisely this and gives a useful evaluation of the effects of the removal.

Causal modelling

An alternative interpretation of intercorrelation, if one of the correlated variables is temporally or logically prior to the other, is that one is having an indirect effect on the dependent variable through its effect on the other independent one. Regression can be used, in an elaboration of the kind of analysis described above, to devise and test models of direct and indirect causal influences. This process is called *causal modelling*, or sometimes *structural equation modelling*.

What we need first is a temporal and/or logical order for the influence of variables. We can then regress each on its supposed determinants, across the model, to decide which paths of influence appear to be statistically significant and which are trivially small, and from this we can build up a picture of how each independent variable influences the ones after it in the causal chain and ultimately the dependent variable. We proceed, from an initial hypothetical pattern or map of causal links, via regression analysis to test their existence in the sample and determine whether they are likely to be a product of sampling error or to represent links in the parent population, through to a 'trimmed' model which constitutes our best estimate of how the variables are linked in the population and what has influence on what.

This is best explained by use of an example. Read Example 10.1, an analysis of beliefs about social class in the People in Society survey originally carried out by Liz Atkins, and make sure you follow the chain of argument.

Example 10.1: The People in Society survey (4): influences on a belief about social class

What follows is a summary of an analysis of one year's People in Society data originally prepared by Liz Atkins as teaching material on an Open University research methods course. The dependent variable is an early question on the schedule, 'How many social classes are there?', included in the schedule because other research had suggested it is an indicator of certain models of society. The independent variables included in the analysis are:

- *class of origin* (father's class, measured on the Social Grading Schema);
- *highest educational qualification achieved*;
- *own occupational class*, again measured on the Social Grading Schema; and
- *age* at the time of the survey.

'Age' is not just a biological and maturational variable but also a social one – different cohorts or generations will have had different upbringing, different educational experiences and different job opportunities, in different economic climates – and it is in this sense that the variable was used here. It was therefore decided to recode it into two variables – 'young/not' and 'old/not' – to bring out generational differences. 'Young' was defined as 'under 35' and 'old' as 'over 55'.

The first stage is to lay out the full preliminary model, with all the possible causal paths, and this is illustrated in Figure 10.5(a). Age ('generation') and father's class clearly precede and probably influence education and so are shown on the left of the diagram. There is necessarily a correlation between the two 'age' variables in that each predicts the absence of the other. A correlation with father's class is also shown; there has been a change in the class composition of the labour market over the years such that younger people are much more likely than older ones to have had middle-class fathers. Education is likely to be a determinant of the informant's current job, but it may also be influenced by age (older people have had more time to be promoted) and father's class (people with middle-class parents are more likely than people from working-class origins, proportionally, to finish up in middle-class jobs). Any or all of these variables may have a direct effect on the ultimate dependent variable, belief about number of classes in society, which comes on the right of the diagram. Note also the arrows pointing at each of the variables from outside the diagram; these represent extraneous influences and error variance – the amount which the model will *not* explain.

This gives us three blocks of regression analysis to carry out:

Dependent variable	Independent variables
Education	Father's class
	Young
	Old
Occupational class	Education
	Father's class
	Young
	Old
No. of classes	Occupational class
	Education
	Father's class
	Young
	Old

The initial intercorrelation of variables is given in Table 10.6.

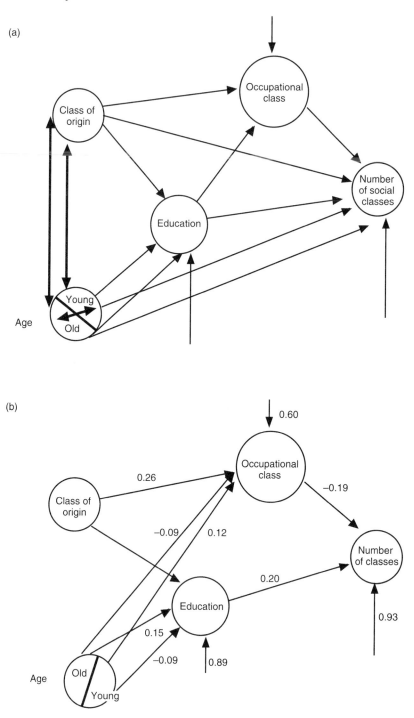

FIGURE 10.5   *A causal model of beliefs about social class: (a) preliminary model; (b) final model*

TABLE 10.6 *Correlations with a class belief in the People in Society survey*

		A	B	C	D	E	F
A:	No. of classes	1.00	−0.34	0.34	−0.16	−0.06	−0.12
B:	Occupational class		1.00	−0.74	0.58	0.18	0.22
C:	Educational qualifications			1.00	−0.45	−0.14	−0.20
D:	Father's class				1.00	0.18	0.18
E:	Old					1.00	−0.45
F:	Young						1.00

Note: It should be remembered that the two 'class' variables are coded 'upside down' from the point of view of interpretation – a higher number means a *lower* social class.

The first stage of the analysis, paradoxically, is to start at the end and look at the possible direct influences of each variable on class belief, ignoring indirect effects, so we enter all the independent variables into a regression equation with 'number of classes' as the dependent variable. The results are shown in Table 10.7. Overall, the equation explains about 14 per cent of the variance ($R^2 = 0.142$) – not a lot, but at a highly significant level, so the effect is unlikely to be a chance one – leaving 86 per cent unexplained. Own class and education appear to have the largest effects, as judged by the beta coefficients, and the *t* values indicate that they are the only variables making an independent and statistically significant contribution, though one of the 'age' variables comes close.

Similar analyses give us the influences on 'own class' and 'education' (Tables 10.8 and 10.9). All four preceding variables contribute significantly to the substantial multiple correlation (0.80) with 'own class', the largest independent contributor being education, followed by father's class. 'Education' is less adequately explained ($R = 0.46$), but the correlation is significant and still reasonably high; father's class and one of the 'age' variables make a contribution, the former having by far the larger beta coefficient. Thirty-six per cent of the variance in own class remains unexplained by the variables used in this model ($1 - 0.80^2$, as a percentage), and 79 per cent of the variance in education.

The final stage is to 'trim' the model by removing connections which do not appear informative, and this involves a mix of analysis and theorizing. We have three near-zero paths on the initial model, connecting father's class and the two 'age' variables directly with the ultimate dependent variable.

1 *Father's class*: we can use the procedure of removing a variable from the equation to look at whether a direct link with the criterion variable 'number of classes' should be posited in addition to its indirect links via own class and education. Its initial, zero-order correlation with the criterion is −0.16, which is small, but stable and significant. In a regression equation with education and own class the path coefficient is even smaller and positive rather than negative

TABLE 10.7 *Regression of all variables on 'number of classes'*

		Variable	Beta	t	Sig.
Multiple R	0.377	Occup. class	−0.20	2.84	$p < 0.01$
		Education	0.21	3.28	$p < 0.01$
R^2	0.142	Father's class	0.08	1.49	NS
		Young	−0.09	1.85	$p < 0.10$
		Old	−0.06	1.10	NS

Analysis of variance:

	d.f.	Sum of squares	Mean square	F
Regression	5	109.09	21.81	15.90
Residual	481	660.00	1.37	$p < 0.0001$

TABLE 10.8 *Regression of background, age and education on occupational class*

		Variable	Beta	t	Sig.
Multiple R	0.80	Education	−0.59	19.25	$p < 0.0001$
		Father's class	0.26	8.33	$p < 0.0001$
R^2	0.64	Young	0.15	4.72	$p < 0.0001$
		Old	0.12	3.67	$p < 0.001$

$F = 218.5$ (d.f. 4, 482), $p < 0.0001$

TABLE 10.9 *Regression of background and age on education*

		Variable	Beta	t	Sig.
Multiple R	0.46	Father's class	−0.42	9.79	$p < 0.0001$
		Young	−0.09	1.89	$p < 0.10$
R^2	0.21	Old	−0.10	2.13	$p < 0.05$

$F = 44.10$ (d.f. 3, 483), $p < 0.0001$

(0.06), and the equation yields an R^2 of 0.136. If we remove it from the equation, the R^2 (variance explained) drops by only 0.003. What it is adding may therefore be considered trivial. Now we can calculate the *indirect* effect by multiplying the coefficients along a given indirect path, and for father's class this yields:

Indirect effect via own class:	$0.26 \times -0.20 = -0.052$
Indirect effect via education:	$-0.42 \times 0.21 = -0.088$
Indirect effect via effect of education on own class:	$-0.42 \times -0.59 \times -0.20 = -0.050$
Total	-0.190

TABLE 10.10   *Testing for zero path coefficients in a causal model**

Variables removed:	R^2 change	F	Degrees of freedom	Significance
Old, Young	0.0061	1.72	(2, 484)	NS
Old, Young, Father's class	0.0088	1.65	(3, 483)	NS
Old, Young, Father's class, Education	0.0260	3.65	(4, 482)	$p < 0.01$

* The variables in the original equation were: number of classes (dependent); own class, education, father's class, young, old (independent).

The three components are all in the same direction, and their total is substantially greater than the posited direct effect of 0.08, so the latter may be dropped without abolishing the influence of father's class.

Check back over the last three tables and make sure you can locate all the figures used in this calculation.

---

2 *Age*: here we shall use a more formalized procedure, employing the SPSS TEST routine (which will also allow us to check the effect of removing the direct link with father's class). Table 10.10 gives an extract from the output and shows the test for R^2 changing as variables or combinations of variables are dropped from the analysis. The result is that dropping the two 'age' variables makes no significant difference to the prediction, and nor does dropping father's class. (If we tried to drop education, however, R^2 would drop noticeably and significantly.) We may therefore delete the direct paths in the final model and leave age and father's class as represented only by indirect effects.

The multiple R with 'number of classes' now has to be recalculated, as we are deleting two variables from it, but the change is only minor. The final figures (including the estimates for variance not explained by these variables) may now be inserted in the modified causal model (Figure 10.5(b)).

Thus it is possible to trace the effect of antecedents on dependent variables through a causal chain of influence, looking both at direct effects and at the effect one variable has via another of whose variation it may be seen as a cause. Variables which appear to have little or no direct effect may be seen as relatively influential once indirect paths are calculated. Father's class, for example, appears to have little or no direct effect on the number of classes perceived, but via education and own occupational class it shows a total beta value of 0.19, not a trivial amount.

Three things need to be remembered about causal modelling, however, and about correlational analysis in general:

1   It cannot be overemphasized that *correlation does not establish causation*. All the data supply is associations; the causal inference is made by the researcher. He or she may be wrong, because both the variables in the equation have an extraneous cause – remember the storks and babies!

2   Even if we have a pair of variables which do form a causal chain, what we have *in the data* is *directionless* associations. The direction of the relationship is for us to determine, on the basis of theory, and is not given by the form of analysis. Even 'obvious' temporal precedence may not guarantee the direction of causation. For example, schooling precedes type of job, so current occupation cannot influence past schooling. On the other hand, many people will have taken the degree course they did in order to become teachers or doctors or nurses or social workers, so in a sense the eventual occupation is responsible for the prior education. (Alternatively, perhaps both are a product of a third variable 'intention to become a teacher'.)

3   Any analysis is only as good as its operationalization. In Example 10.1 we take 'class of origin' and 'father's class' as interchangeable terms, as has been the tradition in class analysis. There is a great deal of sound evidence, however, that class of *mother* is more influential than class of father on the children's education (see Willis, 1977; Miller and Hayes, 1990).

Discriminant function analysis

You will sometimes find regression analysis used when the dependent variable is a dichotomy; this practice has been quite common in social class analysis, for example. However, it is incorrect and on the whole to be avoided. The problem is not with the dichotomous variables themselves; as we have seen in earlier chapters, dichotomies do behave like ordinary interval-level numbers and can be used in arithmetic. However, in regression analysis a vital test of goodness of fit of the linear model is that any residual variance shall lie randomly around the prediction line. (If it does not, the supposition must be that an important variable has been left out of the analysis or that the relationship is not linear.) The residual variance from a dichotomous variable *cannot* be randomly distributed along the continuum of regression scores; the variable can take one of only two values. (Regression of the kind discussed in this chapter cannot handle nominal dependent variables with more than two categories at all – but see the discussion of *logistic regression* in Chapter 11.)

One way of dealing with analyses where the dependent variable is a dichotomy (or, indeed, a nominal variable with more than two categories)

– *loglinear analysis* – is outlined in the next chapter. A second method is *discriminant function analysis*. This is based on similar ideas to those of regression discussed above and centres around computing the likelihood of a given case lying in a given category of the dependent variable, given its scores on independent variables. It takes a dependent variable which is expressed on a nominal scale (as categories), and attempts to produce the best prediction of the category to which a given case will belong on the basis of the available independent variables (the null hypothesis being that the independent variables do not help with the prediction). The analysis is of use wherever the dependent variable is inherently nominal (categorical). It was originally developed for problems such as the assignment of archaeological material to cultures or periods: given two islands with excavated pottery shards which differ in measurable ways (size, thickness, colour, and so on), and a third whose shards have not yet been assigned and which are somewhat mixed, do the shards from the third island conform more closely to those of the first or the second?

In use the analysis proceeds like multiple regression. If the available independent variables are not related to the dependent variable, then using them to predict which case belongs in which group will not improve the prediction above the level of chance. (The chance level of prediction is that the likelihood of a case belonging to a given category is proportional to the relative size of the category – if we have two equal categories, any given case is 50 per cent likely to be in either category, and if one category is twice as large as the other then the likelihood of being in the larger category is 67 per cent.) We then try building predictions using the independent variables which will improve our 'success rate' over the chance level. The analysis is often carried out *stepwise*, entering the variable first which makes the greatest single improvement over chance, then the one which most improves the prediction once the effects of the first have been controlled, and so on. For example, if we were predicting the wearing of skirts we would probably find that gender was the main predictor, but that among the men nationality also had something to contribute – some Scots wear kilts. (We must bear in mind, however, that the *amount* by which the prediction is improved at each step does *not* reflect the independent contribution of the variable, just as in regression analysis, because of the intercorrelation of independent variables, and that the order of contributions is in any case somewhat unstable and needs to be replicated before it can bear the weight of elaborate interpretation.)

The usual statistic produced by most packages for assessing the 'goodness of fit' of the prediction is *Wilks' lambda* (λ). This works the other way up from most statistical measures: the *smaller* the value, the *higher* the variance explained. A λ of 1.00 means that the prediction is no better than random, and a λ of 0.00 would mean perfect prediction. The *F* statistic (ratio of variance explained to residual variance) can be used to assess the statistical significance of each variable's inclusion, and many packages test the overall significance of λ by means of the χ^2 statistic. Most packages will also produce a 'hits and misses' table of actual categories against predicted categories, which enables us to assess the proportion of cases correctly classified.

Factor analysis

Although it is a rather different kind of animal from the ones discussed above, this chapter ends with a discussion of *factor analysis*. It is included here because, like regression, factor analysis tries to 'explain' the variance in correlation matrices. Unlike the other analyses discussed in this chapter, however, factor analysis does not have a dependent variable whose variance is to be explained by independent variables. Instead, it aims to build 'metavariables' and to summarize the variance of the associations between variables in a more economical manner than by treating the original variables as independent entities.

If you have taken a large number of measurements on a population, you can present the way in which they are associated with each other in a matrix of correlations. If the variables all 'have lives of their own' – none of them 'behaves' like any of the others – then their intercorrelations will be low and the matrix will not lend itself to simplification. More likely, however, is that some of the variables will show similar patterns: if a given person is high on one of them, he or she will also be likely to have a high score on others. If we were measuring income, social class of head of household's occupation, cost of family home, engine size of the family's first car, amount of money spent annually on children's education and amount spent on accountants annually, these variables would probably show a high degree of correlation. Indeed, we could usefully replace them, for many purposes, by a single index of wealth or status to which all of them contributed. Similarly, if we were measuring whether the person felt well most of the time, whether he or she suffered from a range of diseases or disabilities, how often he or she visited a doctor for reasons unconnected with child health, how much time he or she had spent in hospital in the last year and whether any medical condition impaired his or her ability to work, we should expect a high degree of correlation – those who feel ill probably visit the doctor, may well have been in hospital and are likely to constitute the majority of those who have a diagnosed complaint and are hindered in their working ability by poor health. Again, the cluster might profitably be replaced with a single index of ill health. If we had collected both sets of data, however, there is no *prima facie* reason why the items in either cluster should correlate with those in the other cluster as highly as with each other, so we might need two separate indices to do justice to the data.

Factor analysis is a method of constructing indices such as these on a systematic basis, rather than just 'by eye', and assessing the contribution of each single variable to each index. It has three major uses:

1 The most common use is as an exploratory tool for simplifying a mass of data and picking out the important dimensions for further analysis.
2 It is relatively often used, also, for demonstrating the unidimensionality of a complex measurement instrument ('test' or 'inventory') – showing that all the items can reasonably be seen as measuring 'the same thing'.
3 More rarely, factor analysis is used for hypothesis testing, where the hypothesis specifies the number of dimensions which are to be found in the data – as, for example, where someone has constructed a test to measure a single factor of 'general intelligence' or two separate factors of 'verbal ability' and 'non-verbal performance'.

The results of a factor analysis are presented as 'factor loadings' which are like correlations: the loading of the factor as a whole (squared) is the proportion of overall variance explained, and the loadings of individual items are their contribution to the factor. The significance of contributions to the explanation of variance will be tested, generally by means of the F statistic (variance ratio).

The first stage of factoring a correlation matrix is called *principal components analysis*. Here the statistical package will construct as many components as there are original variables. The first component, however, will take account of the intercorrelation of variables to select those which together constitute a single component accounting for as much as possible of the variance (somewhat like stepwise multiple regression, where the package picks the variable which makes the single greatest contribution, but in this case the 'variable' is a *component* made up of several variables, weighted so that they form, together, as good a single predictor of all the different scores as can be formed). Then the second component is constructed to account for as much as possible of what is left over, and the third to account for as much as possible of what is not explained by the first two, and so on.

If there is no useful way of simplifying the matrix of variable correlations into a smaller number of factors, then all the components will be roughly equal. Normally, however, the first is by far the largest and only a small number are sizeable. We may therefore go a step further and select out, for further analysis, just the factors which are large enough to be explaining appreciable proportions of the variance. (Three methods of determining how many factors to extract are described in Box 10.4. They all depend to a large extent on the concept of *eigenvalues*, which is defined in the box.) We may then *rotate* these components, to improve the fit still further; the package will look for the best way of constructing the specified number of factors *orthogonally* ('at right angles to each other' – in other words, so that the factors are not themselves correlated with each other). This will then give a set of factors – metavariables – which are not correlated with each other and which explain as much as can be explained of the variance in the original correlation matrix. What is left over is the residual variation in the original individual variables.

Box 10.4: Eigenvalues and deciding on number of factors

Eigenvalues represent the proportion of variance explained by a given variable. If you have ten variables in a correlation matrix, then the sum of the eigenvalues in a corresponding principal components analysis will be 10.00; 1.00 – the whole of the variance to be explained – is contributed by each variable. However, if there are extractable factors then the principle components will not have equal eigenvalues. A more typical split is illustrated in Table 10.11, which gives figures from a fictional study of personality. Here you will see that the first factor has a much higher eigenvalue than any of the others, but that the next two all have eigenvalues greater than 1.0 (the value that each of the original variables has to contribute). Three factors, therefore, are contributing more than any variable by itself to the explanation of variance.

There are two main methods of deciding how many factors to extract. One is simply to extract all the factors which have an eigenvalue greater than 1.0 – all that are explaining more of the variance than a single variable ought to explain. In this example this would give us a three-factor solution. The second, known as the *scree test* by analogy with the shape of the pebbles pushed ahead of a glacier or an ice field, is to plot a graph of percentage of variance explained and take as a cutting point the point at which the slope appears to be changing into a rubble of minor decrements. Such a graph, for the fictional example, is illustrated in Figure 10.6. This suggests taking the first two factors only; after that the line evens out and becomes virtually straight. In practice, we should probably compromise, look at the loadings of the variables on the second and third components, and decide which combination was likely to be the most interpretable.

TABLE 10.11 *Eigenvalues from a fictional study of personality*

Factor	Eigenvalue	% of variance	Cum. % of variance
1	3.95	39.5	39.5
2	1.70	17.0	56.5
3	1.18	11.8	68.3
4	0.91	9.1	77.4
5	0.54	5.4	82.8
6	0.48	4.8	87.6
7	0.35	3.5	91.1
8	0.33	3.3	94.4
9	0.31	3.1	97.5
10	0.25	2.5	100.0
Total	10.00	100.0	

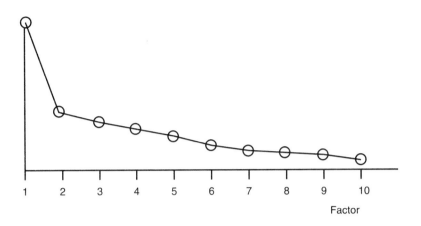

FIGURE 10.6 *Percentage of variance contributed by factors in a fictitious study of personality*

The effects of rotation are illustrated in Figure 10.7. Here we have the position on two sets of variables of three groups of informants – those who score highly on factor 1 (athletic performance, say) and also on factor 2 (academic performance, say), those who score high on factor 1 and low on factor 2, and those who are about average on both. Two orthogonal factors minimize the deviation of these groups from the two lines in Figure 10.7(a), but they are not in themselves particularly easy to interpret. If we move the lines round (as in Figure 10.7(b)) we get a much more interpretable pattern.

It is possible to go a step further beyond the creation of rotated orthogonal factors. These factors have been constructed, deliberately, to be uncorrelated with each other. For some purposes, however, you may *want* them to be correlated; your theorized description of what is going on may *specify* that they should be correlated. In the example above, for instance, it is *not* the case in real life that wealth and health are uncorrelated. Instead of rotating the components to yield orthogonal factors, therefore, we could specify non-orthogonal (correlated) ones. These will normally explain a little more of the variance than orthogonal factors, at the cost of a little loss in interpretability (because of the same problem as with multiple correlation and regression – that correlated variables have indirect as well as direct effects on each other, via the variables with which they are correlated).

Three important points need to be made about factor analysis before we leave the topic.

1   The factor structure which emerges from the analysis is specific to a given data set, and its reliability cannot be guaranteed. Some form of replication or check on reliability is therefore essential if it is to be used to make claims beyond 'this is a convenient way of summarizing the

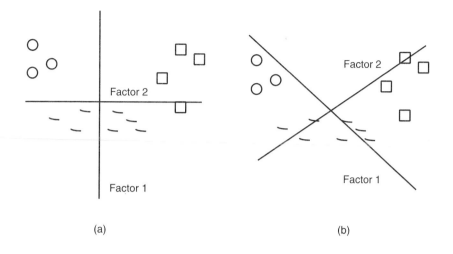

FIGURE 10.7 *(a) Unrotated and (b) rotated factors*

pattern of correlation in this data set' – claims about the nature of the population. With a large enough data set it is possible to construct factors using one randomly chosen half and replicate using the other. Where the set is not large enough for this, collecting a further sample for replication is highly recommended.

2 Modern statistical packages will churn out principal components, the first stage of a factor analysis, for *any* set of figures, whether or not it is appropriate to do so. If your analysis is to stand any chance of being reasonably stable and interpretable, you *must* have more cases than variables in the set, and preferably many more; otherwise the principal components at the end of the list are in essence based on fractions of a case.

3 Factor analysis (and principal components analysis) tells you how to summarize your data most economically, but it does *not* tell you what the factors or components *mean*. (As we have seen, it does not even tell you unequivocally how many factors you should extract – the number of factors extracted is a matter of judgement.) The meaning of factors is deduced – or rather, *constructed* – by looking at the variables which make the greatest contribution to them. So you may have a factor which loads on a test of aggression, a test of emotional strength and a test of intelligence. You might want to interpret this as, perhaps 'angry intellect' or 'rational emotionalism'. If these were the only psychometric tests among the variables, however, all the others being background or behavioural variables, an alternative interpretation might be 'scores on paper-and-pencil tests'. It is very easy to read our preconceptions into the results of a factor analysis, by thoughtless naming of factors which we have determined beforehand 'ought' to be there.

The final example in this chapter is a study by Mary Anne Taylor and Lynn Shore of the factors which predict retirement age and whether psychological elements add anything to 'objective' variables such as financial status when predicting whether people will take early retirement. It uses factor analysis to simplify the matrix of explanatory variables and demonstrate the validity of the indices used – that they are reasonably unidimensional and not confounded with each other. It then uses hierarchical regression to test hypotheses about which variables will be useful in the prediction.

Example 10.2: Predictors of planned retirement age

To be able to predict in advance which staff would opt for early retirement would be of substantial benefit to personnel departments in industry and commerce, but little solid information on organizational, personal and psychological factors making the decision more or less likely has been available to them. An analysis by two researchers in the United States (Taylor and Shore, 1995) goes some way towards remedying this deficit.

The subjects of the analysis were 303 employees (247 men and 56 women) of a large multinational firm with its headquarters in the south-eastern United States. They held a variety of positions within the firm – roles such as mechanic, secretary or supervisor. Eighty-nine per cent were white, 7 per cent were black, 1 per cent were of other ethnic background and 3 per cent did not report on this. Mean age was 47 years (with a range from 19 to 71), and mean tenure of present post was 12.5 years. Given the eligibility requirements for early retirement in the firm, 134 were eligible and 169 ineligible.

Standardized measures of job satisfaction, satisfaction with pay and organizational commitment were filled in by all participants, plus measures (devised on the basis of past research) of health, financial status, retirement attitudes and the extent to which the organization provided retirement support and counselling. Health was measured by self-rating (including an item asking whether respondents thought their health would allow them to work as long as they wished) and financial status/comfort was measured by items asking about whether they expected their pension to be adequate and their life after retirement financially comfortable – plus a measure of satisfaction with current pay. Organizational factors were covered by a validated organizational commitment questionnaire, a three-item job satisfaction scale and a four-item scale exploring the extent to which the firm provided retirement counselling and phased schemes for retirement and early pension. Psychological factors included beliefs about their ability to make the transition to retirement successfully, a social interaction/satisfaction scale and a measure of leisure orientation –

10.12 *Factor analysis of scale scores in a prediction study of early*
ent

Item	Factor						
	1	2	3	4	5	6	7
Current satisfaction							
with work interactions	0.67	−0.11	0.02	0.13	0.00	0.04	0.20
with outside interactions	0.71	0.00	−0.09	0.11	0.08	0.03	0.05
with amount of family time	0.61	0.05	−0.24	0.21	0.04	0.04	−0.04
Expected satisfaction							
with work interactions	0.67	0.04	0.06	0.07	−0.04	0.02	0.08
with outside interactions	0.77	0.15	0.12	0.02	0.07	0.07	0.07
with amount of family time	0.66	0.13	0.13	−0.03	0.04	0.14	−0.07
Retirement							
Confident will adjust	0.00	0.74	0.20	0.00	−0.21	0.15	−0.05
No trouble handling	0.06	0.83	0.14	0.01	−0.22	0.04	0.04
Expect to enjoy	0.06	0.81	0.16	0.01	−0.05	0.04	0.18
The thought depresses (−)	0.09	0.79	0.05	−0.01	0.00	0.08	0.08
Leisure time							
Look forward to more	0.07	0.45	0.62	0.10	−0.01	−0.12	0.05
Work prevents	−0.20	0.08	0.69	0.13	−0.23	−0.10	−0.05
Enjoy spending time on it	0.11	0.06	0.78	−0.02	−0.07	0.02	0.02
Retirement will allow more	0.04	0.25	0.78	0.08	0.05	0.06	0.08
Organization fulfils needs							
Early retirement	0.22	0.00	0.06	0.61	0.08	0.32	−0.06
Counselling for retirement	0.22	0.10	−0.14	0.71	0.13	0.12	0.04
Opportunity to phase in retirement	0.01	−0.01	−0.11	0.83	0.09	−0.08	0.05
Higher pension for late retirement	0.05	−0.05	0.21	0.67	−0.19	0.02	0.04
When plan to retire?	0.02	−0.22	0.07	0.01	0.90	−0.06	0.06
When prefer to retire?	0.11	−0.17	−0.13	0.06	0.88	0.05	0.03
Finance							
Pension adequate	0.01	0.15	−0.07	0.09	0.07	0.84	0.09
Will be comfortable	0.24	0.07	0.00	0.17	−0.01	0.80	0.07
Health							
Allows continuing work	0.17	0.21	0.09	−0.03	0.19	0.04	0.79
What is level of health?	0.07	0.04	−0.01	0.03	−0.07	0.11	0.87
Eigenvalues	4.45	3.74	1.85	1.70	1.58	1.22	1.14
Variance explained (%)	19	16	8	7	7	5	5

whether participants looked forward to retirement as an opportunity
to follow their leisure interests.

Because the scales overlapped to some extent in their conceptual
content, and to ensure and demonstrate independence and unidimensionality of measures, a factor analysis of scale scores was carried
out. This demonstrates (Table 10.12) that there were reasonably high
correlations between related scales, yielding interpretable factors, and
low correlations with scales contributing to other factors. The one
slightly doubtful item was the leisure orientation scale, which had a
correlation of only 0.45 with the factor consisting of items related to
adjustment to retirement, but it was retained because it made sense

TABLE 10.13 *Hierarchical regression analysis of data in a prediction study of early retirement*

Variable	Step	R^2	β	t	Significance
Age	1	0.12	0.34	5.83	$p < 0.001$
Personal variables	2	0.15			
Health			0.16	2.66	$p < 0.001$
Finance			0.04	0.72	NS
Satis. pay			−0.07	1.12	NS
Psy. variables	3	0.23			
Adj. to retirement			−0.25	3.81	$p < 0.001$
Leisure orientation			−0.08	1.21	NS
Social expectations			0.08	1.32	NS
Organizational variables	4	0.26			
Retirement needs			0.01	0.11	NS
Job status.			0.07	0.88	NS
Org. commit.			0.17	2.28	$p < 0.001$

Note: all R^2 values are significant at $p < 0.001$.

within the factor and had lower loadings with scales in the other factors.

A hierarchical regression analysis was carried out on the resultant data. Variables were entered in a planned order, to test their expected effects. *Age*, as an obvious determinant, was entered first so that its effects could be controlled. The second group to enter were personal factors which research has shown to be consistently related to retirement decision, concerning health and financial concerns. The third group were psychological factors, to see what they added to the prediction. Finally, job and organizational factors were entered.

The results are shown in Table 10.13. It will be seen that age proved a significant predictor, as would be expected, accounting for 12 per cent of the variance. Personal factors added another 3 per cent to the prediction, but health was the only significant item here – finance and satisfaction with pay did not contribute to the prediction. With these elements controlled, psychological factors still added a substantial and significant amount to the prediction, but 'adjustment to retirement' was the only factor to make a significant contribution; leisure orientation and social interaction did not contribute. Finally, organizational commitment, among the organizational factors, added another 3 per cent to the variance explained.

The last task was to enter 'retirement status' – whether the subject was eligible for the early retirement scheme. This was strongly correlated with several of the other variables, which precluded its entry straightforwardly into the multiple regression: either its effects would already be 'spoken for' by other variables or it would dislodge them, and in neither case would we know which was responsible for the effect. We can note, however, that the significant correlations were with pay satisfaction, retirement needs and organizational commitment. Those who were ineligible for early retirement were likely to set a later date for their probably retirement if they were dissatisfied with their pay and, paradoxically, if they were satisfied with the company's provision of counselling and support on retirement, opposite effects to those to be seen in the 'eligible' group.

The results do not, therefore, throw up anything surprising. However, they do show that retirement decisions are to some extent predictable and that attitude variables can improve the prediction.

Further reading

The full account of this research is given in Taylor and Shore (1995).

Further reading

A good and non-mathematical introduction to regression and factor analysis and how to do them on the computer will be found in Bryman and Cramer (1997). For the more advanced student, Everitt and Dunn (1991) covers regression, factor analysis and discriminant function analysis. On factor analysis, see also Kim and Mueller (1978a; 1978b).

11   Getting complicated: Explaining variance

This is the last of the three statistics chapters. We have looked at analysing relationships and differences using tables and the chi-squared statistic, and at assessing the size of relationships and the underlying patterns in the data using correlation and regression. Both of these approaches involve *model-fitting*; we see how well we can recreate the pattern of the actual observations by making theoretical assumptions about what the pattern *ought* to be if the assumptions were true. In the case of tabular analysis the model is a simple one – simply the null hypothesis, that the underlying distribution is a random one. From this model we derive expected figures, and then we compare these with the actual observations; if the model of 'no association' fits too badly, we discard it and feel free to assert that there probably *is* an underlying association. In correlation and regression the model is a straight line; we see how far we can get in finding a line, defined by additive components of variables, from which the variance is as small as possible. This is one way of thinking about analysis: 'How well can I predict the values of a dependent variable?'. In this chapter we shall be looking at the other major approach, in which the variance is partitioned and assigned to the effects of independent variables of their interactions. The question here is not one of prediction but of how much of the variance is due to each of the possible causal factors. The two approaches resemble each other and have the same underlying mathematics, but they represent different ways of approaching the problem of analysis. The 'regression' approach is much used in survey analysis; the 'partitioning of variance' approach has often been more typical of experimental research.

Analysis of variance

Univariate analysis

One-way analysis of variance is, quite simply, the F test which you have met already (Box 10.1). It operates with one independent variable, which is nominal – divided up into categories or groups – and one dependent variable which is at the interval or ratio level. F is calculated as the explained sum of squares divided by the residual sum of squares, and this is the key to the concept of analysis of variance. What is to be explained is the variance of scores – the squares of their deviations from the mean value. If the amount which can be explained is sufficiently larger than the amount left still to be explained, then we may call the result of the explanation statistically significant.

In the simplest case, we want to know if differences between groups on some variable are sufficiently large to be statistically significant – whether the differences in our sample are likely to represent true differences in the population. An obvious example to take is gender and height among adults. In a sample of the population whose height we happen to have collected, men are on average a little taller than women – the mean value of height for men is larger than its mean for women. However, there is a fair amount of 'spread' in both groups, and a non-trivial proportion of women are taller than a non-trivial proportion of men. We proceed to argue as follows:

1   If there were no association between gender and height, the best single predictor of anyone's height would be the mean height of the whole sample; if all we know is that we have a sample of people whose average height is 5 ft 10 in, then our best guess (though not very good!) about the height of any given person in it will be that he or she is 5 ft 10 in, give or take a bit. The standard deviation of the sample heights will allow us to calculate how large this 'bit' has to be to make it a fairly safe prediction.

2   If there is a real (significant) difference between men and women, then we can improve this prediction if we know the gender of the person. If the average for women in the sample is 5 ft 8 in for example (and, say, 5 ft 11 in for men), then if we know that the person whose height I am predicting is a woman, my best guess is 5 ft 8 in plus or minus a bit, not 5 ft 10 in. My best estimate of the safe size of error margin will be based on the standard deviation for the women in the sample, not the standard deviation of the whole sample.

3   What we are hypothesizing here, effectively, is that the women are on average more like each other in terms of height than they are like the group of men. So the model we are fitting says that there is a large variation *between* the two groups and a smaller amount of difference *within* each group.

4   So we can test the significance of the fit of this hypothesis (or, more accurately, we can try to reject the null hypothesis that dividing the sample into these groups does *not* give a better fit to the data than just basing the estimate on the overall sample mean). The 'variance explained' in the equation for the F statistic is the between-groups variance, and the residual is the remainder, the within-group variance. The *between-groups* variance is the variance of the group means about the overall mean, and the *within-group* variance is the sum of the variance of the individual cases in each group around that group's mean. If dividing the cases into groups really does improve prediction then the between-groups variance will be large and the within-group

variance small. If it does not, then cases will be scattered up and down the scale, irrespective of group membership, and the sum of variances around group means will be not much smaller than if we had calculated the variance from the overall sample mean.

Obviously just adding up the sums of squares will yield a between-groups variance which is very much smaller than the sum of within-group variances, because very many fewer data points contribute to it. We need to apply scaling to the figures, therefore, and what we use is *degrees of freedom* – the same concept as degrees of freedom used with chi-squared in Chapter 9, but calculated in a different way. When working with chi-squared we counted cells of the table, and we noted that in each column and each row the information from one cell was redundant – the cell was not free to vary, given that we knew the marginal totals. With analysis of variance we count individual cases, but again some cases are redundant, so the degrees of freedom figure is always smaller than the total number of cases. The total degrees of freedom for a given analysis is the sample size minus 1 (because the last case is redundant – if we know the mean, the sample size and all the other cases we can calculate what the last case has to be). The degrees of freedom for the between-groups variance is the number of groups minus 1 (because, again, one of the group means is redundant – we can calculate it, given the other two means, the overall mean and the group sizes). What is left – the degrees of freedom for the within-group variance, or *residual variance*, is then obtained by subtracting this figure from the total degrees of freedom.

We can use these degrees of freedom to scale the sums of squares. Dividing the between-groups sum of squares by its degrees of freedom gives the mean square for between-groups variance, and dividing the within-group sum of squares by its degrees of freedom gives the mean within-group square. Then dividing the between-groups figure by the within-group figure gives the F statistic, the ratio of variance explained to residual variance. We can look this up in a table of F values (Table 10.3), using the two degrees of freedom figures to locate the correct critical value. Box 11.1 summarizes all this and gives the components of each term in the calculation, but it is unlikely you will ever have to work out even this simple form of analysis of variance for yourself; we really do use computers for this kind of thing nowadays.

Bivariate and multivariate analysis

With *two* independent variables, analysis of variance performs much the same job as we did using three-way tables in Chapter 9, but more powerfully. As with univariate analysis, the figures in the cells – the values of the dependent variable – are not just counts of cases, but mean values on an interval- or ratio-level variable.

Box 11.1: One-way analysis of variance

In a one-way analysis of variance, variance is partitioned as follows:

Source	Degrees of freedom	Sum of squares	Mean square	F ratio
Between groups	$g - 1$	SS_b	$SS_b/g - 1$ $= MS_b$	
Within groups	$n - g$	SS_w	$SS_w/n - g$ $= MS_w$	
Total	$n - 1$	SS_T		MS_b/MS_w

Here n is the sample size, g the number of groups, SS = sum of squares, MS = mean square and the suffixes b, w and T refer to 'between groups', 'within groups' and 'total'.

An analysis of a variance table with two independent variables will show the main (independent) effects of each variable separately – how much the prediction is improved by knowing the location of the case on the one or the other. To extend the example above, suppose we had measured heights not just for adults but for a sample of people aged 10 and over. Two predictive variables might then be gender and age – younger people are shorter, on average, than adults, and men are taller, on average, than women. Again there will be some variation about each group mean – there are some very tall 12-year-olds and some very short adults – so for each variable we assess the significance of its effect by comparing the mean between-groups square with the mean within-group square, yielding two F ratios to be looked up. The components of the table are shown in Box 11.2.

As well as main effects, however, there could be an interaction effect – the effect of one variable could vary according to the value of the other. For example, we might find a partial reversal of the gender effect on height according to age: girls of 10 or 11 might tend if anything to be taller than boys of the same age. The analysis will therefore also show an interaction term and assess its significance by producing an F statistic.

Box 11.2 looks complicated, but we can unpick it without too much difficulty if we take it in stages.

- The mean total variance, just as for one-way analysis, is the sum of squared deviations from the overall mean of the dependent variable, divided by the total degrees of freedom (number of cases minus 1).
- What we are trying to do is improve our prediction by looking at the effects of the two 'treatments' – the two independent variables. We can think of these as forming a table, with g columns (the number of categories in variable 1) and h rows (the number of categories in

---

Box 11.2: Two-way analysis of variance

Source	Degrees of freedom	Sum of squares	Mean square	F ratio
Total treatments	$c - 1$	SS_c	$SS_c/(c - 1)$ $= MS_c$	MS_c/MS_w
Variable 1	$g - 1$	SS_g	$SS_g/(g - 1)$ $= MS_g$	MS_g/MS_w
Variable 2	$h - 1$	SS_h	$SS_h/(h - 1)$ $= MS_h$	MS_h/MS_w
Interaction	$T - ((g - 1)$ $+ (h - 1))$ $= I$	$SS_c -$ $(SS_g + SS_h)$ $= SS_I$	SS_I/I $= MS_I$	MS_I/MS_w
Residual (error)	$(n - 1) - (C - 1)$ $= E$	$SS_T - SS_c$ $= SS_w$	SS_w/E $= MS_w$	
Total	$n - 1$	SS_T		

Here n is the sample size, C the number of cells in table, g and h are the number of categories in each of the two independent variables, and $SS =$ sum of squares, $MS =$ mean square and the suffixes c, g, h, I, w and T refer respectively to 'between cells', 'between groups (variable 1)', 'between groups (variable 2)', 'interaction term', 'within groups' and 'total'.

variable 2). This gives us *gh* cells in the table, each of which has a mean value on the dependent variable. The overall *treatment effect* is the mean variance of these cell means about the overall mean – the sum of squared cell deviations divided by the treatment degrees of freedom, which is the number of cells minus 1.

Why is the number of degrees of freedom not calculated using the same formula as with chi-squared: $(r-1)(c-1)$?

The calculation is different from the one for chi-squared because different pieces of knowledge are assumed and therefore different pieces of information are redundant. In a 3 × 2 table, for example, we have six cells, and we saw that when the cells contain counts of cases and we know the marginal totals then four of the cells contain redundant information – their contents can be worked out from the values of the other two and the marginal totals. In analysis of variance, however, what we have is six *mean values* and knowledge about the sample sizes and the overall mean. In this case only one of the means is redundant – we need all the other five to calculate what the sixth must be.

- Now, the *effect of variable 1* is given by the mean squared deviation of its category means from the overall mean. This is the sum of squared deviations divided by the degrees of freedom, which is one less than the number of means.

- The *effect of variable 2* is calculated in just the same way, for the other variable.

- If there is an *interaction effect*, the effects of variables 1 and 2 will not add up to the whole effect of treatment – there will be something over. (More accurately: when we add up the squares of deviations of the various treatment-category means, they will not account for all the sums of squares from adding up the squared deviations of the cell means.) What is left over is the interaction effect, given as the remaining sums of cell squares divided by the remaining degrees of freedom for the treatment as a whole.

- The *within-groups mean square*, or *residual*, or *error term*, is what is left – the remainder of the sums of squares divided by the number of degrees of freedom left over when we have subtracted all the ones already used.

- Each of these terms, except the total and the error term, has a corresponding F statistic which is its mean square divided by the error term, so the significance of each effect can be assessed.

The analysis also yields an F ratio which assesses whether there is *any* significant effect of treatment at all. This is important because there are dangers in doing repeated tests of zero-order significance. All that significance levels guarantee is that you ought not to get a falsely significant result more than one time in 20 ($p < 0.05$) or one time in a 100 ($p < 0.01$). So if you get 20 results significant at $p < 0.05$, one of them is quite likely to be false! The effect of the overall F test is to assess *in a single test* whether there is *anything* worth looking at. Then you can go on to do tests of main and interaction effects with the confidence that there *is* significance in the table somewhere.

This pattern of analysis can be extended to cope with any number of independent variables in just the same way, by working out an overall treatment variance and partitioning it between the main effects and interactions of the different variables. With three independent variables you would have three main effects and four possible interaction terms (effects of variable 1 and variable 2, variable 1 and variable 3, variable 2 and variable 3, and the interaction of all three variables). You would work out the two-variable interaction terms from tables of their joint effects irrespective of the third, and when all three had been worked out in this way then the left-over 'treatment' variance would form the three-way interaction. Sorting out interaction terms can get very complicated indeed when you have a number of independent variables (see Box 11.3), and third- and higher-order effects are often treated as part of the error term unless there is a very good theoretical reason for treating them as a real effect.

Good analysis of variance computing packages can deal with some very complex analyses. It is usual, for example, to find routines for dealing with

---

Box 11.3: Effects to be tested in a four-variable analysis of variance

In the analysis of variance of four independent variables (A, B, C, and D) and their effects on a dependent variable there are 16 terms to consider:

4 main effects: A, B, C, D;
6 two-way interactions: AB, AC, AD, BC, BD, CD;
4 three-way interactions: ABC, ABD, ACD, BCD;
1 four-way interaction: ABCD;
+ an error term — the residual variance.

---

multiple dependent variables and repeated measurements within cases. Most packages can also deal with covariates – extraneous variables correlated with the independent and dependent variables whose effects have to be controlled in order that the effects of the independent variable can be isolated. Discussion of these is beyond the scope of this book; a good and simple account will be found in Bryman and Cramer (1997).

Restrictions on the use of analysis of variance

A first assumption in the use of analysis of variance procedures is that the data are normally distributed on all the independent variables and that the variances are roughly equal across groups. The *F* test for significance is little affected by a mild breach of the first of these assumptions, but it will seriously under- or overestimate significance if the data are seriously non-normal or if the variances are very discrepant. Sometimes it is possible to transform the data arithmetically so that they more closely approach normality; this kind of statistical technique is covered in many textbooks – see, for example, Snedecor and Cochran (1967). (The effects of non-normality are the more acute if groups are of very unequal size. In general, it is best to keep sample sizes as equal as possible.) Where sample sizes are unequal it is necessary to use a computing procedure which applies weighting factors to the figures to allow for this.

Often the variance on a given variable is grossly affected by one or two *outliers*, very discrepant cases with very large or small values – sometimes due to errors in measurement or recording. It is good practice to eliminate such outliers before starting the analysis.

Loglinear analysis

Loglinear analysis follows a pattern of thought more nearly akin to tabular analysis and χ^2, using one of the mathematical transformations which

---

Box 11.4: Odds ratios

Comparative data are sometimes represented, particularly in loglinear analysis, in the form of *odds ratios* — the ratio of two probabilities. For example, if 20 per cent of men in a sample were over 6 ft in height but only 5 per cent of women, we could say that the odds on being over 6 ft tall are 4:1 if you are a man and 19:1 if you are a woman. The *ratio* of these two figures is $\frac{1}{4}/\frac{1}{19} = 4.75$, and this is the odds ratio. It may be interpreted as meaning that you are a little less than five times more likely to be taller than 6 ft if you are male than if you are female.

---

render data more nearly 'normal' in the statistical sense. An expected value is computed for every cell of the table and all possible 'effects' (row differences, column differences, differences between blocks, interaction effects) on the presumption that all of the effects are zero and the cases are randomly distributed. Differences from this null hypothesis can then be tested. A series of χ^2 statistics is often used to test the significance of any observable differences or correlations, and the results may be presented in a form similar to the output from an analysis of variance table. The data themselves may be presented as raw figures, percentages, proportions, rates or *odds ratios* (see Box 11.4).

The power of the technique, for survey analysis and theory testing, is that it will allow us to build a model specifying which effects ought to be significant and to see by how much these predict different results from the null hypothesis of no association, to see how well the model fits the observed data and to compare the performance of different models (perhaps embodying different theoretical assumptions).

Logistic regression

The general loglinear model will accommodate variables with any number of categories and does not posit independent and dependent variables; you use it to explain all the variance in the figures, privileging one variable as 'dependent' by your choice of interaction models (see below). The most used version for survey analysis, however, *logistic regression*, is a hybrid between loglinear and regression analysis and is used for explaining variance in a dependent variable which is expressed in the form of a dichotomy.

Logistic regression (also known as *logit analysis*) depends on the notion of calculating the odds – probabilities – of a given case lying in one rather than the other of the two categories of the dependent variable. (Can we improve this prediction by knowledge of scores on the independent variables?) The *logit* is the logarithm of the odds or probabilities. Probabilities form an interval-level variable and can therefore be used in a form of regression which assesses how much a given variable contributes in terms of lengthening or shortening the odds of belonging to a given category. A similar transformation is the *probit*, which is calculated by reference to the normal distribution as the basis for computing probabilities – part of the calculation involves looking up the value in a normal distribution table which would generate odds of the observed magnitude.

Either form of analysis will produce tests of the significance of the overall effect and also of each single variable and of their interactions, or a designated subset of all these effects. The test involved is generally a version of χ^2, comparing the observed distribution on the dependent variable with the distribution predicted on the basis of the independent variables. Similar methods can also be used to produce a causal path analysis of the direct and indirect effects of each independent variable (see below).

The great analytic strengths of all loglinear analysis are that it works on categorical (nominal) data – more common in survey research than any other kind – and that it will allow you to test the fit of different hypotheses to the data. You could, for example, specify a model in which all main effects are significant, and *only* main effects, and assess the fit to the data. This can then be compared with models in which only some of the main effects are significant, or models which also contain one or more significant interaction terms. Example 11.1 illustrates an analysis of this kind.

Example 11.1: Determinants of income (1): an example of logistic regression

The data for this example come from the British Household Panel Study (BHPS), a longitudinal study which collects data every year from over 10,000 individuals in a nationally representative sample of over 5000 households. The data used come from the first wave of data collection, in 1991, and the analysis is restricted to persons currently in paid employment. The dependent variable is own annual income from paid employment. The potential explanatory variables are current employment status – full-time (30 or more hours per week) or part-time – father's social class (Registrar-General) at age 14, highest educational qualification obtained, gender, marital status (married/cohabiting or not) and age at date of interview. Income has been dichotomized at the median, and codes on other variables have been combined to give categorical data with reasonable numbers in each category. Table 11.1 shows the numbers in each category of the independent variable and the significance of their zero-order association with the dependent variable.

The first stage is to explore the main effects of the variables in combination. The first logistic regression to be run, therefore, specifies the dichotomized income variable as dependent and the five

TABLE 11.1 *Determinants of income: zero-order associations**

	Income level			
	Low (%)	High (%)	Total (%)	Significance (χ^2)
Age				
< 31	60.1	39.9	28.2	
31–45	41.8	58.2	28.6	
46+	59.0	51.0	43.2	$p < 0.001$
Educational level				
No qualifications	63.6	36.4	33.6	
Below O level	58.7	41.3	11.2	
O level or equivalent	58.4	41.6	21.2	
A level, equivalent or nursing qualification	46.3	53.7	12.2	
Degree, teaching qualification, other higher qual.	29.0	71.0	21.8	$p < 0.001$
Marital status				
Not married or cohabiting	61.9	38.1	34.8	
Married or cohabiting	45.0	55.0	65.2	$p < 0.001$
Employment status				
Part-time	92.0	7.8	22.4	
Full-time	33.6	66.4	77.6	$p < 0.001$
Gender				
Male	31.3	45.1	47.1	
Female	70.8	29.2	52.9	$p < 0.001$
Father's class				
Semi-/unskilled	54.9	45.1	20.5	
Skilled manual	49.9	50.1	44.4	
Routine non-manual	49.0	51.0	9.0	
Professional/managerial/technical	44.5	55.5	26.1	$p < 0.001$

* Sample size 6327, of which 3164 were low-income and 3163 high-income.

possible independent variables. The method specified is a forward stepwise procedure in which the variables are added one at a time until no further improvement in fit can be obtained.

Results are shown in Table 11.2. Note that the figures do not tally exactly with those shown on the crosstabulations in Table 11.1 because of the differential effect of missing values when variables are combined. For example, we appear to have lost slightly more cases in the 'below average income' category than in the 'above average' category, so that we now have 54 per cent of the sample rather than 50 per cent in the higher category.

As with multiple regression, the package produces several pages of printout and a lot of figures, all of which mean something to somebody. The trick is to pick out the ones that mean something to *you* and are useful for your current purposes. Table 11.2 gives the figures that I find useful for the purpose of examining the effects of a range of independent variables on income. There are four sets of figures on which I have concentrated:

TABLE 11.2 *Predicting income: stepwise logistic regression using main effects only*

Step	Variables entered	−2 log likelihood*	Model $\chi^{2\dagger}$	R	% correctly predicted	Sig. of change
0	Constant only	6847.21			54.24	
1	Work status	5471.67	1375.67	−0.32	72.93	$p < 0.001$
2	Work status			−0.26		
	Gender	5108.03	1739.18	0.23	72.83	$p < 0.001$
3	Work status			−0.27		
	Gender			0.22		
	Education	4822.94	2024.27	0.19	77.14	$p < 0.001$
4	Work status			−0.28		
	Gender			0.22		
	Education			0.20		
	Age	4642.55	2204.66	0.16	77.22	$p < 0.001$
5	Work status			−0.28		
	Gender			0.22		
	Education			0.21		
	Age			0.12		
	Marital status	4553.52	2293.68	−0.11	77.60	$p < 0.001$

Variable not in the equation at step 5: Father's class
Significance of relationship if included: $p = 0.0534$ (NS)

* −2 log likelihood: a measure of predictive power.
† Model chi-squared: a measure of the extent to which the prediction is better than when only the constant is used.

1　I asked for a stepwise fit to the data, and the first thing I look at is the variables which entered the equation and the order in which they did so.

(a)　The package will first fit a constant, which corresponds to the proportion of cases in the 'reference category' – generally the larger of the two categories (coded 1 for the purposes of the analysis, with the other category coded 0). So in the current model the machine assigns every case a score of 0.54 – equivalent to saying that without other information our best guess is that any given case will have the mean score.

(b)　I then asked the package to add variables in a stepwise progression (like stepwise multiple regression).

(i)　It has selected work status (whether the individual works full- or part-time) as the most important determinant, and this comes as no surprise; obviously you earn more on a whole salary than half a salary, all other things being equal.

(ii)　The second variable to enter is gender; even controlling for work status, men earn on average more than women.

(iii)　The third variable is educational level, so education does appear as a determinant of earnings, as in Example 9.1, but only after gender has entered.

(iv)   The fourth variable to enter is age. In the 'variables in the equation' block of the output the package will give a correlation for each category of a categorical independent variable; this is not reproduced in Table 11.2, but inspection of it showed me that the effect was due to lower wages in the youngest age group.

(v)   Finally, marital status enters the equation; married people tend to earn more than single people (see Table 11.1), and this effect persists even when the effects of the other variables have been accounted for.

(vi)   The variable on the original list which has *not* entered the equation is father's class. In the 'variables not in the equation' block of the output a significance level is given for its potential contribution to the prediction, and this just exceeds the 5 per cent level.

At each step of the procedure a 'model chi-squared' is produced which assesses the significance of the change since the last step. This is consistently significant in this analysis at $p < 0.001$, so each variable is making a significant contribution.

2   Next we look at a figure mysteriously labelled '–2 log likelihood', which measures the predictive power of the loglinear regression equation – its ability to determine which category a person falls in on the dependent variable. The –2 log likelihood figure is a comparison of the quality of this prediction with the residual deviation from it; the larger the figure, the worse the prediction. We can see that this decreases from step to step of the procedure, from an initial figure of 6487 to a final figure of 4553, with two large decreases when the first two variables are entered, a fairly substantial one for the third variable and less for the fourth and fifth. (The final figure is still very large, however, and significant at $p < 0.001$. This means that the prediction is still not very good – a lot of variation remains unexplained.) An alternative measure of fit we might have used – appearing generally in the same part of the computer output – is the 'goodness of fit' chi-squared, which is also shown as significant if the fit is poor. This statistic measures not *whether* a given person will fall in one category or the other, but the *probability* of that person doing so. The two figures will not always agree in their significance levels, and you will need to think about which is best for your purposes.

3   A further way of looking at the quality of the prediction is to follow the percentage of cases correctly classified at each stage of the procedure. As I said above, the package first fits a constant and gives every case the same score, which means that all the cases will appear in one predicted category of the 'hits and misses table' which is produced (not shown in Table 11.2). The baseline

prediction, therefore, will correctly assign every case in one category and misassign every case in the other; in the current analysis this means that we start with about 54 per cent of cases correctly allocated. Adding the effects of the first variable immediately raises this percentage to about 73 per cent, an improvement of nearly 20 per cent. Thereafter the prediction is refined but not much is added to its overall accuracy; the final equation correctly assigns about 77 per cent of cases. (There is a larger increase for the effects of education than for the other variables after the first, however.)

4   Finally, the 'variables in the equation' block of the output yields a correlation coefficient for each variable, which allows us to assess their effects relative to each other. These are multiple partial correlation coefficients and give us an estimate of the independent effect of each variable or term in the equation. In the final equation of the current analysis they range from 0.28 for work status to 0.11 for marital status – explaining respectively about 8 per cent and not much more than 1 per cent of the variation.

Now let us see if we can improve the prediction by exploring the effects of interactions between the independent variables. My particular interest here is in looking at effects of gender, and particularly testing ideas about factors which structure women's wages. I shall therefore be adding four interaction terms to the equation.

1   One reason why women earn less than men is because very many more of them are in part-time work. This is controlled in the regression above – gender entered even after the effects of part-time working are accounted for – but it could be the case that women finish up in part-time jobs which are poorly paid in comparison to the part-time jobs that men might do. I shall therefore add 'gender × work status' to the equation to test for this.

2   Do married women earn less even than single women? I can test for this by adding 'gender × marital status' to the equation.

3   It has been argued that men get more on-job promotion, while women's work level is more determined by educational credentials which they have on entry to the labour market. If this is the case, then the interaction 'gender × education' should make a significant contribution to the prediction, because women will tend to have higher qualifications than men at a given salary level.

4   Finally, I shall add the three-way interaction 'gender × education × work status' to see if men's part-time jobs tend to be at a higher level than women's or if women in part-time work are seriously overqualified for it. (I should have to run tables to see which of these explanations was the case, if the term came out as significant in the logistic regression.)

The results of this analysis are shown in Table 11.3. (Note: the percentages in each category have changed slightly again, because 'father's class' has been omitted from the analysis and this slightly changes the number of cases omitted because of missing values.) The results are not much different. The same main variables enter, in the same order. The final model predicts the observed figures very slightly better than the model using main effects only, but only slightly. All three of the two-way interactions do enter the equation, but as 'late entrants' and contributing very little to the prediction. The three-way interaction does not enter the equation at all. For most purposes, then, unless we were testing interactional effects and were interested in statistical significance even if the substantive significance is slight, we would accept the 'main effects only' model as the most parsimonious.

A final stage we might usefully put the figures through is to control for employment status by looking only at the full-time workers. (Part-time working can have many different causes: it can be forced on one, as in short-time working, or taken for want of better, as where only part-time jobs are available, or deliberately chosen to fit in with childcare.) The results of such an analysis are given in Table 11.4. They are broadly similar, except that age becomes less important, dropping down the list to fall after the interaction of gender and marital status.

Example 11.1 illustrates how you might proceed with definite hypotheses in mind. If you were 'exploring the data' in a more general way you would probably work with all four of the independent variables and their interactions, introducing main effects and interactions one at a time to see what provides the best fit to the data. (In all these analyses we should remember, as with any other complex multivariate approach, that the ordering of variables and the amount of variance explained by each is not necessarily stable. It might be good practice to fit a model to a random half of the data set and check its stability by subsequently applying it to the other half.)

Whether the analysis is exploratory or aimed at testing particular guesses or hypotheses, what we are looking for is a *parsimonious* explanation. The acceptable model will be one which provides a good fit to the data using the minimum of information. On the other hand the solution must also be an *interpretable* one – one which will make good sense – and a slightly poorer fit which is readily interpretable will be preferred to a better one which is unduly complicated. This is particularly the case when we move away, in the next subsection, from logistic regression to full-blown loglinear analysis.

Loglinear modelling

Logistic regression is a hybrid technique, combining the use of the logit transform to estimate odds according to the influence of specified variables

TABLE 11.3 *Predicting income: stepwise logistic regression using main effects and selected interactions*

Step	Variables entered	−2 log likelihood	Model χ^2	R	% correctly predicted	Sig. of change
0	Constant only	7767.85			53.65	
1	Work status	6276.15	1491.70	−0.32	72.16	$p < 0.001$
2	Work status			−0.27		
	Gender	5866.57	1901.21	0.23	72.46	$p < 0.001$
3	Work status			−0.27		
	Gender			0.22		
	Education	5561.86	2024.27	0.19	77.14	$p < 0.001$
4	Work status			−0.27		
	Gender			0.22		
	Education			0.20		
	Age	5352.48	2415.36	0.16	76.60	$p < 0.001$
5	Work status			−0.28		
	Gender			0.22		
	Education			0.20		
	Age			0.12		
	Marital status	5249.84	2518.01	−0.11	77.65	$p < 0.001$
6	Work status			−0.26		
	Gender			0.18		
	Education			0.20		
	Age			0.11		
	Marital status			−0.11		
	Interaction: gender × marital status	5202.29	2565.56	−0.08	77.39	$p < 0.001$
7	Work status			−0.24		
	Gender			0.15		
	Education			0.20		
	Age			0.11		
	Marital status			−0.11		
	Interaction: gender × marital status			−0.07		
	Interaction: gender × work status	5180.19	2587.66	0.05	77.35	$p < 0.001$
7	Work status			−0.24		
	Gender			0.15		
	Education			0.20		
	Age			0.12		
	Marital status			−0.11		
	Interaction: gender × marital status			−0.06		
	Interaction: gender × work status			0.06		
	Interaction: gender × education	5148.55	2619.30	0.05	78.60	$p < 0.001$

The three-way interaction falls very far short of the significance level needed to enter the equation.

TABLE 11.4 *Predicting income for full-time workers: stepwise logistic regression using main effects and selected interactions*

Step	Variables entered	-2 log likelihood	Model χ^2	R	% correctly predicted	Sig. of change
0	Constant only	5596.42			66.54	
1	Gender	5262.91	333.51	0.24	66.92	$p < 0.001$
2	Gender			0.24		
	Education	5016.24	580.18	0.20	72.23	$p < 0.001$
3	Gender			0.23		
	Education			0.20		
	Marital status	4827.79	768.63	-0.18	72.00	$p < 0.001$
4	Gender			0.19		
	Education			0.20		
	Marital status			-0.17		
	Interaction: gender × marital status	4772.84	823.58	-0.10	72.53	$p < 0.001$
5	Gender			0.19		
	Education			0.21		
	Marital status			-0.13		
	Interaction: gender × marital status			-0.09		
	Age	4684.56	911.86	0.12	72.94	$p < 0.001$
6	Gender			0.19		
	Education			0.22		
	Marital status			-0.12		
	Interaction: gender × marital status			-0.07		
	Age			0.13		
	Interaction: gender × education	4655.57	940.83	0.06	73.85	$p < 0.001$

and the regression model which posits an essentially causal chain from independent variables to values of the dependent variable. Loglinear analysis can also be used in a 'purer' form to model the total variance in a multi-factorial table of results, producing very similar results in the straightforward 'looking for effects of . . .' situation, but with greater potentialities for elaboration. It can also handle 'dependent' variables with more than two categories; logistic regression becomes very complicated indeed unless the dependent variable is a dichotomy. Example 11.2 illustrates the use of the more generalized form of analysis in a straight-forward case; it carries out essentially the same exploration of the same data as in the last part of Example 11.1, looking for determinants of the income levels of full-time workers. As you can see, a useful way to proceed is first to model the total variance: to see how many of the variables you need to reproduce the pattern of results *exactly* – not just the variation in a dependent variable, but the total pattern of variation in the data set as a whole. (This is called a *saturated model*.) We can then limit our attention to the interactions of independent variables with a dependent variable, singly or in combination, and see how close we can come to the same results.

Example 11.2: Determinants of income (2): loglinear modelling

This example uses the same data file as at the end of Example 11.1 – all people in full-time employment in the first wave of the British Household Panel Study (BHPS). However, I have controlled for age by discarding people under the age of 30. (This may leave a very small age effect, but it should not be sufficient to distort the analysis.) Income has been divided into four categories. We shall be looking at the effect on it of education, gender and marital status.

In finding the best-fit explanatory model for the data, the first stage is to produce a *saturated* model – one which exactly predicts the observed pattern of data. This model uses as 'generating class' the interaction of all the variables – in this case the interaction of income, gender, marital status and educational level. The *generating class* is the set of variables to be examined, with lower-order effects automatically considered along with higher ones, so the four-way interaction of these four variables automatically includes all possible three- and two-way interactions as well as the four main effects. (The concept of 'main effect' is a rather odd one in loglinear modelling; we will discuss it shortly.)

The first thing produced (Table 11.5) is an examination of whether effects of a given order – such as four-way effects – are zero. If they are, they can be ignored in subsequent analysis. In this analysis of British Household Panel Study data, Table 11.5 shows that the four-way effect can safely be ignored but all lower-order effects have to be considered (a significant chi-squared here means that the null hypothesis, that the effects at this level are zero, must be rejected). (Remember that at this stage we have not nominated a dependent variable, so we are looking at all possible effects as factors, including the interrelationships of variables with each other which do not include the variable which we shall eventually want to treat as the dependent one. The package will even record single variables as 'effects'. These are referred to as 'main effects', but they are nothing like the main effects of regression or analysis of variance because they do not represent a relationship at all, but residual unexplained variation within a single variable.)

Continuing with the saturated model, the next thing to consider is the 'table of partial associations'. This tells you which factors are making a significant contribution to the saturated model. Table 11.6 shows that three of the effects can be ignored altogether as making no significant contribution – gender × education × marital status (in which we are not interested for this analysis anyway), education × marital status × income, and the 'main effect' of income. These may therefore be 'trimmed' from the model. (We should trim 'main effects' in any case as of no interest, for the reasons given above, and we should want to trim effects which do explain variation in the total

TABLE 11.5 *Loglinear modelling with BHPS data:
whether higher-order effects are zero*

Order of effect	Chi-squared	Degrees of freedom	Probability
1	3647.71	9	0.000
2	1042.25	27	0.000
3	90.05	31	0.000
4	14.20	12	0.288

TABLE 11.6 *Loglinear modelling with BHPS data: variables
contributing to the saturated model*

Order	Variables	Partial χ^2	Degrees of freedom	Probability
3	Gender, education, marital status	4.79	4	0.31
	Gender, education, income	43.12	12	0.00
	Gender, marital status, income	17.87	3	0.00
	Education, marital status, income	13.16	12	0.36
2	Gender, education	44.72	4	0.00
	Gender, marital status	47.41	1	0.00
	Education, marital status	12.60	4	0.01
	Gender, income	352.80	3	0.00
	Education, income	528.33	12	0.00
	Marital status, income	8.43	3	0.04
1	Gender	320.81	1	0.00
	Education	572.51	4	0.00
	Marital status	1277.66	1	0.00
	Income	3.63	3	0.30

data set but do not involve income as a variable.) What is left will be the variables we shall go on to fit in an *unsaturated* model, trimming the model further to produce the most parsimonious solution that is a reasonably good fit and can be interpreted.

Now we shift to unsaturated modelling, and the first stage is to test the trimmed model using only the factors shown as significant in Table 11.6. The highest 'generating class' for these is the two three-way interactions – gender × education × income, and gender × marital status × income. (When a generating class is specified, the package automatically enters not just the terms specified, but all lower-order terms implied by them – in this case the 'effects' of the single variables.) This yields, as a measure of 'goodness of fit', a likelihood ratio chi-squared of 42.224, which is outside the bounds of $p < 0.05$ (because what is being modelled is the total variation in the data set, and we are interested in explaining only the variation in income) but is the statistic which we are trying to minimize, or at least not to allow to grow much larger. We can then experiment with building different models and see what happens. Eliminating the

TABLE 11.7 *Loglinear modelling with BHPS data: experimenting with incomplete models*

	Variables	Likelihood ratio χ^2	Degrees of freedom
A	Gender × education × income + Gender × marital status × income	42.224	32
B	Gender × education × income + Marital status × income	119.603	36
C	Gender × marital status × income + Education × income	133.804	48
D	Gender × income + Marital status × income + Education × income	211.184	52

interaction of gender and marital status (replacing it with a straight-forward effect of marital status) substantially increases the chi-squared figure, and eliminating the gender × education interaction in favour of a straightforward education effect increases it even further. Modelling the effects as three straightforward explanatory variables with no interaction between them increases it further still. It would appear we are best served by an explanation in terms of two inter-acting pairs of explanatory variables, therefore, with gender in common between them. The history of this process is shown in Table 11.7.

The final stage is to examine the selected solution by way of descriptive crosstabulations, and this is done in Table 11.8. In terms of educational level, what we have here is a clear interaction of two factors to influence income. Women are disadvantaged overall, irrespective of income: in every educational category there are more of them in the lowest quartile of income and fewer in the highest. The effect is much larger for those with no qualifications than higher up the educational scale, however. Marital status, similarly, acts to exacerbate disadvantage; both married and unmarried women earn less than comparable men, but the effect is much more dramatic for those who are married. (Note that the element of causality or influence in this interpretation of the results comes from *me*, not from the analysis; the package deals only in *associations* between variables, which do not in themselves prove causation.)

If we were continuing with this chain of analysis the next things to look at would be current occupational class of those in work and previous occupational class for those not currently in work. It could be that horizontal segregation of the labour market leaves women

TABLE 11.8 *Gender by education and marital status: BHPS data (%)**

	Total	Gender		
		Male	Female	
Educational level				
No qualifications	26.7	27.3	25.6	
Less than O level	9.1	8.3	10.8	
O level or equivalent	19.0	16.6	23.9	$\chi^2 = 34.63$
A level/nursing qual.	12.1	12.2	11.8	with 4 d.f.
Degree/other higher	33.0	35.6	28.0	$p < 0.001$
Marital status				
Married/cohabiting	82.0	86.0	74.1	$\chi^2 = 63.09$
Not	18.0	14.0	25.9	with 1 d.f.
				$p < 0.001$

* The sample consists of 2941 people aged over 30 and in full-time employment, 1956 of whom are male and 985 female.

Note: totals may differ in Tables 11.8 and 11.9 because of different numbers of missing-value cases.

TABLE 11.9 *Gender and income by education and marital status: BHPS data*

	Gender	Income (1=low)				
		1 (%)	2 (%)	3 (%)	4 (%)	χ^2 (d.f. = 3)
Educational level						
No qualifications	Male	22.8	38.4	24.9	13.9	173.35
	Female	70.9	22.1	5.7	1.2	$p < 0.001$
Less than O level	Male	12.4	41.0	29.2	17.4	48.87
	Female	48.6	35.2	11.4	4.8	$p < 0.001$
O level or equiv.	Male	16.2	27.1	31.2	25.5	76.64
	Female	43.0	34.3	15.7	7.0	$p < 0.001$
A level/nursing	Male	8.2	18.0	36.1	37.8	58.67
	Female	31.9	32.7	26.5	8.8	$p < 0.001$
Degree/other higher	Male	8.0	13.4	27.5	51.1	45.95
	Female	20.4	18.6	29.4	31.6	$p < 0.001$
Marital status						
Married/cohabiting	Male	12.4	24.8	29.3	33.6	364.88
	Female	45.4	26.5	16.9	11.1	$p < 0.001$
Not	Male	22.3	29.2	24.6	23.9	14.20
	Female	36.5	27.4	20.2	15.9	$p < 0.01$

(and particularly married and/or underqualified women) concentrated in underpaid occupations within occupational classes. It could be that vertical segregation puts them in lower occupational classes or in lower segments within classes. It could be, however, that it is precisely those women who have no qualifications and are earning little money who can least afford to leave the labour market – particularly if low-paid women tend to be married to the lowest-paid men.

Again, what we have chosen here is the *parsimonious* solution – the model which uses as few and as low-level interactions as will provide a fit which is not too far from the 'saturated' value. The example shows the power of loglinear analysis as an exploratory technique. It has 'homed in' on a complex but interpretable pattern of interaction between independent variables which it would have taken luck and labour to find by tabular analysis alone. Note, however, the use of tables at the end of the example, to illustrate the pattern which we have found and to give us some ideas about what it means.

Residuals and the analysis of change

As with regression modelling, it is important when you have fitted a model to look at the pattern of residuals – at the observed variance 'left over' when the model has been fitted – and see if patterns have been detected. Most analysis packages will provide a table of the 'standardized residuals' for each cell of the original data table. These ought to be approximately normally distributed, with a mean of 0 and a standard deviation of 1, so a useful 'rule of thumb' is that a standardized residual greater than 2 in either direction is indicative of a failure of 'fit' – a remaining relationship that we might want to add to the model we are testing. Large residuals clustered in two quadrants of the table and more or less absent in the other two, for example, would be indicative of an important interaction effect.

In a multivariate loglinear model, one of the independent variables can be 'time' – loglinear analysis is well adapted to the measurement of change. Analysis of residuals is particularly important here, to be able to say what *kind* of change is taking place. For example, in analysis of social mobility (Goldthorpe, 1980) survey data were used to compare men's social class position (occupational level) with that of their fathers' when the respondent was aged 14. Fitting a model with no interaction between the two gives a highly unsatisfactory fit, with large residuals along the diagonals (the cells where son's occupational class is the same as father's), which indicates that sons are very likely to end up in the same class as their fathers. If we omit this diagonal, the 'no association' model still does not provide a good fit to the remaining data; even where sons move out of the father's class, father's class has an effect on their class of destination. We can elaborate the model further (see Gilbert, 1993a: Chapter 7) by partitioning the table and fitting models to only part of it – for example, testing the hypothesis that sons' class is independent of fathers' only for those who are downwardly mobile (which means fitting the model to just the triangle of values below the diagonal, on a conventional mobility table). Yet more complex models can be fitted, which specify the amount by which father's class influences son's (for example, more for those in the highest jobs, whose material position strongly advantages their children, and for those in the lowest, whose material position is one of strong disadvantage, than for those in between).

This kind of analysis allows sophisticated hypotheses about social change to be tested, or sophisticated descriptive models to be fitted and assessed.

Cells which are deleted from the analysis are said to have been 'declared to be structural'. In any set of data there may be cells whose size is known in advance as a logical certainty. The example used by Gilbert (1993a) is the analysis of gender and crime, where any model which predicts any cases falling in the cell of 'rapes committed by females' must to that extent be a poor fit to the data, because in law there cannot be any such cases. A better fit is obtained by putting a prior constraint on the model so that it never assigns cases to this cell. The modelling above uses the same principle; it determines beforehand and on theoretical grounds what the values in certain cells shall be and thereby improves the potential for finding a good 'fit' to the others.

This kind of comparison, collecting valid data from one person at one time to cover two or more time periods, is comparatively rare in social analysis. More commonly, this kind of 'one-shot' design compares current states or behaviours or attitudes with others which are *remembered* or *reconstructed* from past time, which has obvious problems for the validity of the 'past' measurements.

The most common design for avoiding this problem is *trend analysis*, comparing figures collected over time on the *same* variables but with *different* informants – regular surveys drawing fresh random samples in each time period (such as the British Crime Survey) or published statistics such as the decennial Census. The problem here is that 'time' is standing as a kind of shorthand for a wide range of possible influences – straightforward temporal location on a calendar, history, climate, economic changes, changes in social attitude, and so on – any or all of which might be the 'cause' of observed difference.

> The fundamental difficulty is that in trend analysis the factor time is used as a substitute for all sorts of events which take place between or during the period of observation. The confounding factor of history can be (partially) controlled by direct measurement of the extent to which the respondents have been exposed to the relevant events or by introducing . . . a control group that has not been exposed to the relevant events. However, only seldom will this kind of data be available to the secondary analyst. (Hagenaars, 1990: 273).

A further problem is that the population from which the samples are drawn is forever changing – through birth, death and migration – so that the successive samples are not, strictly, drawn from 'the same population'. Interpretation of trend data is therefore to be undertaken with some caution. With this reservation, however, trend data can be analysed by loglinear means in much the same way as the analysis of 'one-shot' data, treating time simply as another independent variable to be included. Again the patterns of residuals will be our guide to what kind of model needs to be fitted.

The best design for a study of people over time is the panel or cohort analysis – where the *same* sample is measured repeatedly over time. Here loglinear analysis with time as a variable can help to explain overall changes in marginal totals (for example, differences in voting figures at different elections) by exploring the extent to which the overall changes are mirrored in each relevant section of the population or whether some sections but not others are responsible for the change (for example, differential changes or preference by younger or older voters). Models to be fitted would be the *independence model* (no association), the *quasi-independence model* (assuming some tendency to vote for the same party in the two elections) or various models which posited effects of other independent variables (age, gender, occupational sector and so on) and perhaps their interactions. Fuller designs would include samples from different birth cohorts, all followed up over time, and here it is possible in principle to separate the effects of age, social cohort, 'history' and time. Again some degree of caution is required in interpreting the results of all these quasi-experimental analyses as demonstrating causal influences, however, for reasons which have been discussed elsewhere.

Latent variables

Loglinear analysis can also be used to do for categorical (nominal) variables some of what factor analysis does for variables measured at the interval or ratio level. A frequent problem in social science, as we have seen elsewhere in this book, is the situation where we have a whole range of observed characteristics which are taken to be indicative of a single underlying hypothetical (or 'latent') variable. These might be answers on a test or personality inventory, taken as indicative of intelligence or of a personality trait or attitude, or they might be 'social facts' about a person's work and income and housing conditions and social status, to be combined in a single 'social class' variable, or a set of physical measurements and reported symptoms to be combined in a single diagnosis. Factor analysis is used with interval/ratio variables to explore how many factors underlie the many observed characteristics – what the best way to describe the data set is – and/or to confirm unidimensionality of measurement. Loglinear analysis can be used similarly for variables which are measured at the nominal level.

An example (Hagenaars, 1990: 96) involved political attitudes. Responses were obtained to nine items which had some face validity as indicators of political stance – items such as 'social change is desirable/not', 'I place myself as on the left/the right/in the middle of the political spectrum', 'owners/employees/both should be running business'. A latent class analysis was run, assuming 'local independence' – that there is no correlation between the nine original items which is not explained by their relationship to the underlying variable – and the adequacy of fit of this model to the observed data was assessed. The analysis suggested that an adequate fit was provided by a single variable (a typology) with four mutually exclusive categories which could be interpreted as 'progressive', 'conservative', 'individualist' and 'politically uninvolved'.

The details of how to derive such a model are beyond the scope of this book and involve considerable mathematical sophistication. Those who are numerate enough to follow such arguments will find useful discussions in Hagenaars (1990), Goodman (1974a; 1974b) and Haberman (1974). Others will, like most of us, be using the analysis because it is available on the statistical package which is to hand and fits the analytic problem. It is important, in this case, to explore the manual and be sure that your data and the way in which they are collected fit the assumptions of the form of analysis used. It is also worth replicating your analysis to demonstrate stability – on another data set or on random halves of a single data set.

Further reading

A very good, non-mathematical introduction to the use and computing of analysis of variance is given in Bryman and Cramer (1997).

Gilbert (1993a) is a good general introduction to loglinear analysis. For a more detailed (but very mathematical) description of the application of loglinear techniques to the analysis of change, see Hagenaars (1990).

PART E

FINISHING UP

---

12   Did you need to do your own survey?

This chapter should probably have come near the beginning, but I have put it here as an opportunity to go back over some of the issues we have been exploring in the rest of the book. Its subject-matter is the wealth of information which is already available and how to use it. There would be no point, except as a practice exercise, in carrying out a survey which has already been done by someone else, and the nuisance which surveys inflict on populations is a sufficient reason for not doing so lightly. (Replication is valuable – repeating someone else's research and obtaining the same answer gives you more confidence in the results – but we do not carry out replication just for its own sake. Normally there has to be some special interest in the findings – they are implausible or counter-intuitive on the face of it, or a very important and/or costly decision depends on the results.)

A wide range of information exists already, in libraries or in other places, to serve as evidence for the research or policy questions you want to ask. (You will want to draw on this in any case, even if you *are* carrying out your own survey, to broaden the scope of your discussion or to put your own figures in context.) It may not be perfect for your purposes – as discussed at the end of this chapter – but it is often based on sample sizes which you could not hope to achieve. Any survey researcher should therefore be aware of the need to explore existing sources as well as or instead of designing fresh surveys.

Existing sources

Very many of the surveys you might have carried out have been carried out already, and the results are to be found in libraries. For 'academic' problems, or specific professional ones, the efficient way of locating them is probably to do a search by subject keywords in one of the abstracts – available in book form (use the subject index) or on-line at a computer

---

Box 12.1: Commonly used abstracting services on-line or on CD-ROM

BIDS	(*Bath Information Data Service.*) The on-line equivalent of *Social Sciences Citations Index* – a wealth of abstracts on all aspects of social science theory and research.
CINAHL	(*Cumulative Index to Nursing and Allied Health Literature.*) Covers almost all of the English-language nursing journals and over 3000 biomedical journals.
Econlit	Abstracts of journal articles, dissertations, books, book chapters and conference papers on economics.
ERIC	Index to 775 education journals; also covers some more transitory documents.
Healthplan-CD	Abstracts of journal articles, dissertations, books and conference papers on non-clinical aspects of healthcare.
LegalTrac	Abstracts from 800 legal publications and the law-related articles from a further 1000.
MEDILINE	Abstracts on health and medicine.
POPLINE	Abstracts on population, family planning, family health-care, law and policy.
Psyclit	Indexes and abstracts from over 1300 psychology journals, plus dissertations, books and conference papers.
Sociofile	Abstracts of journal articles, dissertations, books and conference papers in sociology and social policy.

---

terminal from a remote site, or on a CD-ROM. (A small selection of the many abstracts available on CD-ROM or on-line is given in Box 12.1.) For studies which have have hit the public eye – on major policy issues such as housing or on matters of current public interest such as violence and the media – the index of major newspapers might be a good place to start. (In Britain, for example, *The Times* and *The Guardian* both produce annual subject indices, often available in computer-readable form.)

Libraries also contain copies of the annual statistics publications issued by governments (and some other organizations – major charities and commercial bodies such as building societies and banks, for example). Some of these are themselves major surveys – the Census, for example (see Example 1.1), or the General Household Survey (Example 2.2), or the British Crime Survey (which presents time-series figures for crime victimization, fear of crime and attitudes to the criminal justice system), the British Attitudes Survey (attitude data and self-reported behaviours in areas such as enterprise, family, health, welfare and so on) or the European Labour Force Survey. Others are by-product statistics of public administration or collected by governments and others for use in planning and reporting on their work – birth and death statistics, the population and throughput of institutions such as prisons and hospitals, crime statistics, housing statistics, education statistics, prices and sales of houses, and very many more.

One special kind of library worth mentioning here is the data archive. In Britain, for example, the results (and indeed the data) from many large-scale academic and other surveys are deposited with the ESRC Data Archive at the University of Essex and are available for use and reanalysis by any *bona fide* user.

Among what the data archives have to offer are regular time-series studies – British examples would be the General Household Survey and the British Attitudes Survey, both available at the Essex archive – and ongoing panel surveys such as the British Household Panel Survey, which offers a wealth of data on households and families, work and attitudes to work and health and use of health services for a very large sample of households and people. British Census data are also available, for a fee, in the form of 'anonymized' records which have been randomly 'perturbed' to conceal individual identities. Various other government statistical data are also available in principle and sometimes in practice.

Demonstrating validity

Figures taken from libraries or archives have, as much as figures you collect yourself, to be subjected to validity checks. It is not enough to say 'the government's figures show crime as rising' or 'the Labour Force Survey shows that X per cent of people are out of work'. You need to examine how the figures were collected, from whom and under what circumstances, and to look carefully at the questions that were asked, the observations that were made or the incidents that were counted. That is, you need to satisfy yourself that the figures provide valid evidence for the conclusions you want to draw. Where this could be in doubt, you may also need to satisfy the reader or to explain what the limitations are on what can be concluded. In doing so you will need to consider precisely the headings that we considered in Parts B and C of this book: sampling, measurement and interpretation. (We shall take the last two together, as they are closely related in this context.)

Sampling

The first thing we have to ask is who the respondents are and what impact that has on the figures. Is there a bias in who is identified as a member of the population, or in who gets selected for the sample? Television viewing figures, for example, are collected by taking an automated record of what is being shown on a television, supplemented by a manual diary of who is in the room. We may wish to discuss these as measuring instruments and their different strengths and faults. Beyond such discussion, however, we should note that the measurements come only from televisions in 'settled' private homes; there are no recording devices fitted to televisions in bars and public houses, or in prisons or hospitals, or in relatively causal-occupancy rented accommodation (student housing, bed and breakfast establishments, hotel rooms). For the purpose for which the figures are normally required – establishing who is available to watch advertisements – this may be a perfectly adequate sample. For more 'academic' purposes, such as judging who is exposed to television violence, it may not be adequate because it excludes precisely those classes of people whom we might think the most vulnerable.

Refusal rates, as we have seen, are always a problem for sampling. A perfectly designed random sampling design may yield an achieved sample which is seriously unrepresentative of the population, if those who refuse are themselves not a random sample of the population. Those who cannot be contacted, when selected from a sampling frame such as a register or list or directory, are another group who give us this problem. They are most unlikely to be a random subset; the sample will be deficient in people who are geographically mobile (and have moved away) or elderly and/or in poor health (and have gone to hospital or died). Both problems are to be found in panel or cohort data: those who 'drop out' between waves of data collection, whether because they move out of contact with the researchers, or they die, or they just get tired or bored with co-operating, will be people of particular sorts, not a random subset of the sample. Using other people's data, you need to get what information you can from the accompanying manuals or from published work on refusal and non-contact rates, and you need to use your imagination in thinking about what the consequences of these might be for the interpretation of the data.

Even in '100 per cent count' studies, such as the decennial Census, cases are missed, and knowing or guessing *which* cases can be important for interpretation. In the British Census of 1991, for example, a preliminary count estimated the population at about a million (around 2 per cent) less than would be suggested by updating the figures of the previous census (Marsh, 1993). A validation study was undertaken, going back over some of the ground, but this did not account for as much as half of the 'lost population' – perhaps because the same errors or failures of identification recurred (people deliberately avoided being enumerated in the validation study as well as in the Census itself, and/or the same new households were not identified). Mostly the shortfall makes very little difference – and a mere 2 per cent non-response is a very low rate compared with any other source of survey data – but it is believed that those who were not enumerated are likely to have been disproportionately males, so we would want to exercise a degree of caution when using 'gendered' figures for prediction purposes.

Measurement and interpretation

Other people's data can be irritating to use, because they never quite seem to answer *precisely* the question you want to ask. You want to compare middle-class and working-class people aged 55 or older, and you find that the government figures (or the academic survey which you have found) gives only class of current job, with no 'class marker' for all the people over the age of 55 who have taken early retirement. Or perhaps you want to look at people of pensionable age in a period when the 'compulsory retirement age' is 65 for men and 60 for women, and you find their age-breaks give you 60–70 for both genders. There is no cure for this, except to make the best estimates you can and explain carefully what you are doing. The same problem can occur when you want to compare figures you have collected with the broader sample base of a government survey or official statistics. All too often you find that the way you have coded age or income into bands is not compatible with theirs, or that they used a different social class scale. If there is to be comparison with outside figures you always need to check beforehand how they are coded and presented, or to collect maximal detail (exact ages, exact incomes) and degrade into categories later. In Britain a useful book to consult is *Harmonised Concepts and Questions for Government Social Surveys* (Government Statistical Service, 1996), which sets out the form of questions agreed between government departments for common use.

More problematic, especially with official statistics (though the same point may hold for government or other surveys), is precisely *what* is being counted and whether it is valid as an operationalization of the thing you want to explore. Birth and death statistics are good counts of clearly defined events, for example – and there are double-checks in terms of reporting procedures – but 'cause of death' is potentially unreliable; it depends on a doctor's diagnosis – a product of human judgement and therefore liable to variation – and on decisions as to what shall be recorded as the *main* cause where multiple factors are involved. Other statistical 'facts' are more dubious still for analytic purposes. Counts of crime come from victim surveys – susceptible to unreliability of several kinds – or from the count of crimes recorded by the police, a figure very vulnerable to individual and corporate policy decisions made often on an *ad hoc* basis. (The crime statistics, it is often said, are a correct record of 'crimes' *recorded by the police* but not necessarily of anything else.) If your interest is in suicide and you want to make the distinction between 'real' suicides and those where the deceased did not really intend to die, there is no way (even in principle) that the official statistics can help you.

Beyond this, we have always to remember that government and other published figures are collected for a purpose, and that that purpose may not be yours. There is a wide range of measures of unemployment available, for example.

- Some are based on counts of events – registration as unemployed, claiming benefit and so on – and the occurrence of these events can be affected by psychological factors (such as disincentives to registration) as well as by lack of employment. When using them you would need to think about public policy initiatives and decisions as well. For example, in what sense do the various youth training schemes count as 'being in a job' as opposed to 'being kept busy while unemployed', for your particular purposes? What are you to do about other people in full-time education and training? If you decide to count these as unemployed, then what do you want to say about people who are in full-time training but also have part-time employment (to pay for it and/or provide for their subsistence), and do the figures allow you to pick these out? What will you do about people permanently or temporarily sick or disabled? How do you wish to deal with people who are not registered or claiming because they would see themselves as permanent housewives or mothers and not eligible for registration?
- Alternatively, there are figures based on a variety of 'survey' questions, each of which would pick out a different group of people: 'Do you currently have a job?', 'Have you had a job in the last week/month/year?', 'Are you seeking work?', 'Are you unemployed, or sick/disabled, or retired, or in education/training, or a housewife, or . . .?', 'Would you take a job next week if one were available?'. Each of these takes a different reading of the concept of unemployment, and you will need to select between them and add categories together very carefully, if the figures allow you to do so, in order to pick out precisely the class of people you need for your enquiry.

With other people's surveys (and other sources of data) the point made in an earlier chapter about question-phrasing also holds true. We saw in Chapter 5 how vague such questions as 'Do you have a car?' or 'Do you have a TV?' can be when you have a specific enquiry to base on them. Similarly, job title may not allow you to make an exact assignment to social class (because whether the worker directs or oversees others may be an element in the assignment). Very specific questions in other people's surveys, even more, may not fit *precisely* the use you want to make of them. Using the very rich data of the British Household Panel Study to explore the preventive use of health services, for example, we have found that the questions on use of health checks such as cholesterol screening or blood pressure measurement, designed to catch all cases of their use, confound preventive use with their use as a diagnostic aid where a medical condition is already suspected. Standard questions on voting preference ask either which party you would vote for if there were a general election next week (which does *not* measure political allegiance) or which party you generally support (which does *not* necessarily predict next week's voting), and neither allows explicitly for the voter whose decision is based on policies or personalities, which may be what you are interested in. Again, questions are asked for a purpose, and (a) you need to know the purpose in order to understand the question; and (b) the purpose may not map precisely (or at all!) on to the purpose of your own enquiry.

All this having been said, however, there is great merit in looking for other people's figures before proceeding to collect your own. Sometimes they are entirely or mostly adequate for answering your questions, and carrying out a fresh survey becomes unnecessary. Sometimes they can answer preliminary questions or deal with some aspect of the enquiry, leaving more time and space for other matters. Nearly always they give you a feel for the scope of the enquiry and the range of likely answers, they indicate questions worth asking and they give you a basis for testing whether your own sample is likely to be representative of the population.

Further reading

For further ideas, see Hakim (1982) or Ray Thomas's chapter in Sapsford and Jupp (1996).

13   Reporting the results

Different modes of presentation and different audiences mean that a given survey could give rise to many different ways of disseminating the results. You may be reporting at book length – in a book or an academic thesis/ dissertation for a research degree. You may be aiming for a journal presentation – in an academic or professional journal, or in something more 'popular'. You may be planning a conference presentation or a lecture. Each of these modes and media makes its own demands. However, a common structure runs through what has to be presented, which is the structure of the scientific report: Introduction, Methods, Results, Discussion/Conclusions. This is the logical order in which the evidence needs to be presented in order that the argument can be clearly understood and the value of the evidence clearly assessed.

It is not, particularly, the order in which most projects are carried out – they are likely to have a more recursive structure, with ideas cropping up in the course of the research which demand modifications of the design or which have to be explored in order to make better sense of the results. It may not be the order in which the product is read; experienced readers of academic journal articles generally go for the introduction and conclusions first, to see what the problem is and what is being claimed, followed by the Results section for more detail, and the Methods section may only be skimmed through last, unless there is a problem of interpretation which requires more detail of just how the evidence was collected. Nonetheless, it is a useful format for presenting, analysing and contextualizing your results. Below we shall go through what needs to be said, section by section, and while doing so we shall also explore the demands of the medium of presentation and the needs of different audiences.

What was the problem?

An essential first step of any report, whatever the medium, is obviously to say what the research is *about*. You will have started with a question or a problem or an area about which you felt more needed to be known. This you will need to communicate to your audience, and you will probably need to tell them *why* it was a problem, why it mattered, why it should be of interest to them. The amount of detail required will depend on your audience. If you have been doing nursing research for nurses you probably need only to *name* the problem, but an account of the same research for the general public or for non-nursing academics might well need to explain a lot about nursing and about the problem area. A talk on the same research to management might need, politely, to 'remind' them of aspects of the problem which had implications for nurses and patients as well as for finance and efficient management. This could well also be the place for the results of previous research and/or for some general statistics on the size of the problem and the nature of the population in which it occurs – whatever is needed to improve the readers' or listeners' understanding. These would certainly be expected in a thesis or in a journal article.

This is also the place where the problem is 'theorized' – located within a framework which explains the kind of understanding which you are seeking and the assumptions about 'how things work' which are taken for granted in your work. You may feel you have no 'theory' to display (in which case you are accepting the majority way of conceptualizing the area, and you may need to question this in some respects either here or in your Conclusions). You may be defending an orthodoxy or attacking some aspect of it, in which case the 'theoretical' discussion may be among the more interesting parts of the whole account. There may be a conflict of theories – explicit in the past 'literature' or current political discussion, or brought out by you in your analysis of the problem situation – and this will need to be outlined here. How much of this there is depends on the length of the presentation and the nature of the audience. A PhD thesis often devotes over half of its length – several chapters – to theorization and conceptual analysis of the situation and of past research, before coming to the research that was undertaken. In a twenty-minute slide show you cannot, probably, spare more than a couple of minutes.

This may well also be the place, in any length or type of presentation, at which major ethical and/or political issues might be raised. Certainly any such issue which affected the design of the research needs to be raised here, and any issue which might have been seen as a good reason for *not* doing the research. The reader or listener is entitled to go into the main run of the report – the Methods and Results – with all such issues cleared away or at least brought to a provisional solution. (There may not be much space for this kind of discussion in a short lecture presentation or a newspaper or magazine article – but if you skip it, you may expect it to come back and haunt you at question time or in 'letters to the editor'!)

Methods

Three questions need to be covered here:

- What is the source of your data (the sample of people, settings, news-papers – we should remind ourselves that quantified content analysis of text is a form of survey – or whatever)?

- What information did you collect (what was the questionnaire or data collection schedule, and how (and why) was it chosen or constructed)?
- What procedures did you follow? In other words, how was the questionnaire or schedule administered, how was the researcher's presence introduced, and so on?

The sample

You will need, of course, to say how large your sample is and how it was drawn. The sampling method will need justification and perhaps apology. Expediency and lack of choice are potent reasons for a formally poor sampling method, but you may need to explain at this point why we should take the sample seriously *at all* as representative of the population, and probably to indicate that its shortcomings will be discussed and evaluated at length in the Discussion/Conclusions. It is good practice to present what population figures are available from other sources (such as Census figures) as a comparison, to give an idea of how far your sample is likely to depart from representativeness. If the differences are very gross (either by accident or because you have deliberately over-sampled some groups) then you will probably need to weight your figures (see Box 2.2) when estimating probable population distributions, and the basis for doing so can usefully be described here.

Remember that sampling theory does not apply only to samples of people. If you are observing school playgrounds or writing to commercial companies for information or analysing news presentation in the daily press, you will have drawn a sample and the basis of the sampling needs justification. Indeed, in observation research or media analysis it is probably even more important to have thought carefully and clearly about the sampling frame – about the influence of time of day and season of the year on what is there to be observed or of day of the week on what appears in certain newspapers – and to have corrected for likely biases systematically or by random selection of time periods and so on.

The collection schedule

You will need to describe precisely what was collected and to make some reference to evidence for validity and reliability. If you are using established instruments – psychometric tests, for example – this may consist simply of a reference to the literature or the test's manual. If what you have used is a list of very simple and straightforward questions – 'Do you come here often?', 'Do you like the band?', 'Would you like a drink?', 'It's hot in here, isn't it?' – you will have to explain why each question is present and to offer evidence for validity: that the questions, or scales made up from the questions, do measure what you intend to interpret them as measuring. In the case of questionnaires which tap attitudes or beliefs or intentions or personality – something relatively enduring which is seen as internal to the person – you will want to demonstrate reliability: that the traits are reasonably stable on retest or when subjected to split-half comparison. (This holds as much for less 'individualistic' measures – for example, questionnaires on corporate policy – as for measurement of supposed individual traits.) Where a scale or composite measurement is involved you will probably want to use factor analysis or something of similar weight to demonstrate that the internal structure of the scores is as assumed by the theory according to which they are being used.

Where matters of judgement are at stake – ratings of personality, diagnoses of medical conditions, and most of all scores of observed behaviours – you will need to defend yourself against the charge of having written your preferred results into your scoring system. This is not necessarily an accusation of dishonesty – though dishonesty and sloppiness are also to be guarded against – but a reflection of the known tendency for our theories to have an unconscious effect on our perceptions. Preferably you will have a measure of inter-rater reliability – more than one judge will have been used, either at the collection stage or when classifying cases after the event. If not, other arguments will have to be marshalled, or else the possibility of self-serving error will have to be noted as something to bear in mind when assessing the results.

Some of this will belong in the discussion of methods, and some will need to be raised in the Discussion/Conclusions section, when interpreting the results. A rule of thumb is that technical problems with 'good' solutions – for example, measurements of reliability which showed a high degree of it – can be dealt with entirely in the Methods section. Where the design is faulty or open to question, however, the faults should probably be mentioned in the Methods section but will also have to be brought into the Discussion.

Procedures

The foregoing may be complete and lengthy sections, depending on how much there is to say, or they may be brief descriptions offered as part of the outline of procedures. The Methods section as a whole has to give a complete specification of the project – what was collected, from whom and how. It should be sufficiently specific for the reader to identify shortcomings and for another researcher to replicate the procedures.

As well as the data collected and the details of the sampling, we shall need to know how you were introduced to the sample (or how you positioned yourself for observation), what was said about the research which might have affected what was said or done, and how intrusive you were in the situation. This might be another good point at which to cover any ethical issues of data collection – how the sensitivities of the sample were acknowledged, what promises of anonymity or confidentiality were made and what procedures were built in to see that they were kept, how and whether consent was obtained (in the case of observation) and what degree of deception was built into the procedures, and how you handled people who refused to co-operate. Like the reflexive account of a qualitative project, the Methods section of a survey report should give us everything that we (and you) need to assess reactivity and put limits on our interpretation of the data.

This section should also begin to anticipate the analysis of the data. If there is anything important to say about how questions or scales were coded, what was done with particular ambiguous responses, how you dealt with incomplete schedules and what variables were derived from the data (for example, 'time sick in hospital' as 'time in hospital because of accident or illness' minus 'time in hospital for childbirth'), then you should tell us about it here (unless for reasons of narrative style the account belongs better in the Results section when discussing the particular outcomes).

The discussion above assumes interviewer-administered questionnaires or structured observation. The same principles hold for self-administered questionnaires, however, except that you will need to talk more about what you did about people/institutions who did not respond and about mistakes and ambiguities in filling in the questionnaires. (You may also need to discuss, here or later in the report, the problems of not having complete control over the order of presentation and not being able to probe or explain.) The same principles also hold for quantified content analysis of text or visual material (TV, film).

Results and discussion/conclusions

The penultimate section of the report is the Results section, where you say what the outcome was of the research whose methods you have described. The style here is fairly curt and 'factual' (with the inverted commas standing duty for epistemological issues I do *not* intend to discuss here). With the minimum of fuss you work through:

- preliminary descriptive issues – things we need to know about the sample and its parent population if we are to understand what follows;
- each step in the argument which leads from your research question to the conclusions you intend to draw; and
- anything else in the results which is suggestive or starts an important line of thought.

Every factual statement wants some justification from the data. Sometimes this can be done in the form of a short phrase ('and 30 per cent of the females were taller than any male – a difference significant at $p < 0.001$ by chi-squared'). Mostly it will require a table or graph to illustrate it. Tables in the text should be small, clear and readable and contain the minimum necessary to make the point. (There is a place for larger tables which contain the richer information readers would need to check the conclusions for themselves, and that place is an Appendix to the main paper.) Remember that tables do not speak for themselves and that most of us do not read them with any great fluency; every table should correspond to at least a sentence or two of interpretation in the text.

Statistical significance is very important in the Results section. Because some differences between groups are to be expected by chance alone, as sampling errors when drawing groups repeatedly from a population in which the differences do not occur, we *must not* assert that a difference or a correlation does or does not exist in the population until we have shown that the difference or correlation in the sample is too large to be reasonably attributed to sampling error. (The exception is where the difference is so very large or so very small that it is obvious no test is needed.) Nor ought we to fall into the common error of stating that a result is 'nearly significant' because the statistic almost reaches the critical level. It either *is* significant or it is *not* significant, at the chosen criterion level, and if the result is not significant on the sample figures then we *must not* assert that it exists in the population. (You *can*, however, legitimately point out that the sample figures approach significance and that for this and other reasons – small sample size, for example – you are not prepared to rule out the existence of the difference or correlation in the population on the basis of this survey. To do so may be the right thing to do where the *non*-existence of the result is important for the argument.)

The Results section finishes, or the Discussion section begins, with a restatement of the hypotheses or research questions and a succinct summary of the conclusions about them to be drawn from the evidence of this survey. The credibility of the evidence is also assessed here, using evidence which has been adduced in earlier sections to counter alternative explanations – other variables which might have produced the effects, including reactive aspects of the research procedures and/or deficiencies in the sampling which might count as alternative explanations. Where such faults do exist the report assesses their power to undermine the credibility of the conclusions.

Following this research-related discussion will come the further elaboration of theoretical and practice/policy issues raised in the Introduction. Having answered the research questions – to some extent, and to the best of your ability – you have then to say what they mean in a broader context: what difference the answers make to how you see and understand people and social relations, or to how some aspect of government or commerce or private life should be run, or to how practitioners should conduct their practice. This is also the place to consider again the ethical and political framework of the research. This should have been well covered in the Introduction sections, if there are issues worth discussing, but the answers to the research questions will probably call for a restatement, perhaps in modified and developed form. Following all these extensions of the initial ideas, and in the light of the research itself, we may also want to suggest further research which our conclusions make necessary or desirable or interesting.

The audience and the author

As was said earlier, how much of all this you can do depends on your audience and the medium of publication. You should be able to do most of it in an academic journal article or dissertation and all of it in a book or thesis. If your audience consists of neither academics nor relevant practitioners, and/or they are not familiar with issues of research methods, you would need to explain some of it from a more basic starting point than might otherwise be necessary, and this tends to mean that methods issues get left out of newspaper articles and popular presentations. You ought at least, however, to indicate the way in which the data were collected and the kinds of limitation that this imposes, rather than present your conclusions in an unqualified way as 'facts'. (There is no excuse for leaving methods issues out of a book.) Similarly, in an oral presentation (a lecture or speech) something has to be left out – you might be surprised at how little you can put across in an hour's lecture! – and here it is often the detail of the results, as tables cannot easily be presented orally. Slides are a great help here, or photocopied handouts of tables if the audience is small. (Tables on slides need to be as basic and simple as possible; a crowded table cannot be read on the screen.) Whatever the form of presentation, a minimum to try for is: the nature of the question; why it is interesting; main results and key evidence; how the data were collected; and what limitations must be put on the interpretation. If something has to go, the limitations are more important than the evidence.

A proper mood in which to write up a survey report – provided it is not conveyed in the text – is one of apology. You will have made mistakes; we all do. You will have done the best you can with what was available, but your survey is unlikely to be the perfectly designed and executed project that it might have been given unlimited time, staff and resources. Indeed, some problems can never receive the well-planned and well-designed treatment they deserve. Often you suddenly acquire access and have to proceed, however limited the scope for good design, and often it is necessary to deal with a problem while it is timely rather than wait several years for an opportunity to tackle it in a technically perfect manner. If social research had a motto, it might be *to make the best of what is available*.

Having done your best with the report, the rest is up to the reader. It takes both knowledge and imagination to read a survey report for everything that can be got out of it. The technical issues about sampling, validity of measurement, the logic of comparison and the assessment of sampling error (inferential statistics) are not especially complicated, as you have seen, but they do exist, and a knowledge of them helps with the interpretation of data. (As an author it is part of your job to explain the necessary elements of these to audiences that are not familiar with them.) Beyond this, the reader needs the imagination to see how the research could have been done differently and how the research questions could have been differently framed, in order to see why your survey was designed as it was and what can validly be concluded from it.

This element of imagination is a key factor in all research. Techniques are to be learned, but they can answer only the questions which we have the imagination to ask. As was stressed at the very beginning of this book, the most important stage of any survey – or, indeed, work in any other style of research – is the stage at which you sit down to ask what we really want to know about a situation, taking into account the resources and the access which we can muster. If we ask dull questions we shall get dull answers; if the question is not strictly relevant to our theoretical or practical needs, the answers will not be useful. This same imagination, coupled with a strict passion for logical argument, is also what makes for a good report.

References

Abbott, Pamela (1987) 'Women's social class identification: does husband's class make a difference?', *Sociology*, 21.

Abbott, Pamela (1992a) 'Planning research: a case of heart disease', in P.A. Abbott and R.J. Sapsford (eds), *Research into Practice: A Reader for Nurses and the Caring Professions*. Buckingham: Open University Press.

Abbott, Pamela (1992b) *Stage I Report on the Skills Mix Project*. Plymouth: University of Plymouth Community Research Centre.

Abbott, Pamela (1992c) *Rationalising the Skills Mix in Community Care for Disabled and Older People: A Report of Research in Cornwall*. Plymouth: University of Plymouth Community Research Centre.

Abbott, Pamela (1994) 'Conflict over the grey areas: home helps and district nurses providing community care', *Journal of Gender Studies*, 3: 299–306.

Abbott, Pamela (1997) 'Home helps and district nurses: community care in the far South West', in P.A. Abbott and R.J. Sapsford (eds), *Research into Practice: A Reader for Nurses and the Caring Professions* (2nd edition). Buckingham: Open University Press.

Abbott, Pamela and Sapsford, Roger (1986) 'The class identification of married working women: a critical replication of Ritter and Hargens', *British Journal of Sociology*, 37.

Abbott, Pamela and Sapsford, Roger (1987) *Women and Social Class*. London: Tavistock.

Abbott, Pamela and Sapsford, Roger (1993) 'Studying policy and practice: the use of vignettes', *Nurse Researcher*, 1: 81–91.

Abbott, Pamela and Sapsford, Roger (1994) 'Health and material deprivation in Plymouth: an interim replication', *Sociology of Health and Illness*, 16: 252–9.

Abbott, Pamela, Bernie, Joyce, Payne, Geoff and Sapsford, Roger (1992) 'Health and material deprivation in Plymouth', in P.A. Abbott and R.J. Sapsford (eds), *Research into Practice: A Reader for Nurses and the Caring Professions*. Buckingham: Open University Press.

Advisory Council on the Penal System (1968) *The Regime for Long-Term Prisoners in Conditions of Maximum Security*. London: HMSO.

Ajzen, Isaac (1988) *Attitudes, Personality and Behaviour*. Milton Keynes: Open University Press.

Arber, Sara (1993) 'Designing samples', in N. Gilbert (ed.), *Researching Social Life*. London: Sage.

Arber, Sara, Dale, Angela and Gilbert, Nigel (1986) 'The limitations of existing social class classification of women', in A. Jacoby (ed.), *The Measurement of Social Class: Proceedings of a Conference*. Guildford: Social Research Association.

Austin, J.L. (1962) *Sense and Sensibilia*. Oxford: Clarendon.

Bales, R.F. (1950) 'A set of categories for the analysis of small group interaction', *American Sociological Review*, 15: 257–63.

Barrett, Richard (1994) *Using the 1990 U.S. Census for Research*. Thousand Oaks, CA: Sage.

Bryman, Alan and Cramer, Duncan (1997) *Quantitative Analysis with SPSS for Windows: A Guide for Social Scientists*. London: Routledge.

Campbell, Donald (1969) 'Reforms as experiments', *American Psychologist*, 24: 409–24.

Campbell, D. and Ross, H.L. (1968) 'The Connecticut crackdown on speeding: time-series data in quasi-experimental analysis', *Law and Society Review*, 3: 33–53.

Carstairs, V. (1981) 'Small area analysis and health service research', *Community Medicine*, 3: 131–9.

Clarke, Ron (1980) '"Situational" crime prevention: theory and practice', *British Journal of Criminology*, 20: 136–47.

Clarke, Ron, Gladstone, Francis, Sturman, Andrew and Wilson, Sheena (1978) *Tackling Vandalism*, Home Office Research Study No. 47. London: HMSO.

Clarke, W.B. and Midanik, L. (1982) 'Alcohol use and alcohol problems among US adults: results of the 1979 national survey', in US Department of Health and Human Services (ed.), *Alcohol Consumption and Related Problems*, Alcohol and Health Monograph No. 1, Publication No. ADM-82–1190. Washington, DC: US Government Printing Office.

Cohen, S. and Taylor, L. (1972) *Psychological Survival: The Experience of Long-term Imprisonment*. Harmondsworth: Penguin.

Coxon, A., Davies, P.M. and Jones, C.L. (1986) *Images of Social Stratification: Occupational Structures and Class*. London: Sage.

Dale, Angela, Gilbert, Nigel and Arber, Sara (1983) *Alternative Approaches to the Measurement of Social Class for Women and Families*. Report to the British Equal Opportunities Commission.

Dale, Angela and Marsh, Catherine (eds) (1993) *The 1991 Census User's Guide*. London: HMSO.

de Vaus, David (1991) *Surveys in Social Research* (3rd edition). London: UCL Press.

Doll, Richard and Hill, A. Bradford (1950) 'Smoking and carcinoma of the lung: a preliminary report', *British Medical Journal*, 4682: 739–48.

Doll, Richard and Hill, A. Bradford (1954) 'The mortality of doctors in relation to their smoking habits: a preliminary report', *British Medical Journal*, 4877: 1451–5.

Doll, Richard and Hill, A. Bradford (1956) 'Lung cancer and other causes of death in relation to smoking: a second report on the mortality of British doctors', *British Medical Journal*, 5001: 1071–81.

Doll, Richard and Hill, A. Bradford (1964) 'Mortality in relation to smoking: ten years' observation of British doctors', *British Medical Journal*, 5395: 1399–1410, 1460–7.

Everitt, Brian and Dunn, Graham (1991) *Applied Multivariate Analysis*. Sevenoaks: Edward Arnold/Hodder & Stoughton.

Eysenck, Hans (1953) *The Structure of Human Personality*. London: Methuen.

Fishbein, Martin and Ajzen, Isaac (1975) *Belief, Attitude, Intention and Behaviour: An Introduction to Theory and Research*. Reading, MA: Addison-Wesley.

Flanders, N. (1970) *Analyzing Teaching Behaviour*. Reading, MA: Addison-Wesley.

Foucault, Michel (1979a) *Discipline and Punish: The Birth of the Prison*. London: Allen Lane. (First published in 1975.)

Foucault, Michel (1979b) 'On governmentality', *Ideology and Consciousness*, 6: 5–21.

Foucault, Michel (1982) 'The subject and power', in H. Dreyfus and P. Rabinow (eds), *Michel Foucault: Beyond Structuralism and Hermeneutics*. Brighton: Harvester.

Gilbert, Nigel (1993a) *Analysing Tabular Data: Loglinear and Logistic Models for Social Researchers*. London: UCL Press.

Gilbert, Nigel (ed.) (1993b) *Researching Social Life*. London: Sage.

Godfrey, Christine (1986) *Factors Influencing the Consumption of Alcohol and Tobacco – A Review of Demand Models*. York: University of York, Centre for Health Economics, Discussion Paper 17.

Goldthorpe, John (1980) *Social Mobility and Class Structure in Modern Britain*. Oxford: Oxford University Press.

Goldthorpe, John and Hope, Keith (1972) 'Occupational grading and occupational prestige', in K. Hope (ed.), *The Analysis of Social Mobility*. Oxford: Clarendon Press.

Goldthorpe, John and Hope, Keith (1974) *The Social Grading of Occupations*. Oxford: Clarendon Press.

Goodman, L.A. (1974a) 'The analysis of systems of qualitative variables when some of the variables are unobservable: a modified latent structure approach', *American Journal of Sociology*, 79: 1179–259.

Goodman, L.A. (1974b) 'Exploratory latent structure analysis using both identifiable and unidentifiable models', *Biometrika*, 61: 215–31.

Government Statistical Service (1996) *Harmonised Concepts and Questions for Government Social Surveys*. London: Office for National Statistics.

Graham, Hilary (1993) *Life's a Drag: Smoking and Disadvantage*. London: HMSO.

Haberman, S.J. (1974) *The Analysis of Frequency Data*. Chicago: University of Chicago Press.

Hagenaars, Jacques (1990) *Categorical Longitudinal Analysis: Log-linear, Panel, Trend and Cohort Analysis*. London: Sage.

Hakim, Catherine (1979) 'The population census and its by-products: data bases for research', *International Social Science Journal*, 31: 343–52.

Hakim, Catherine (1982) *Secondary Analysis in Social Research*. London: Allen & Unwin.

Hakim, Catherine (1987) *Research Design: Strategies and Choices in the Design of Social Research*. London: Routledge.

Hall, J. and Jones, D.C. (1950) 'The social grading of occupations', *British Journal of Sociology*, 1: 31–5.

Hammersley, Martyn (1993) 'What is social research?', in M. Hammersley, *Introducing Social Research*, Block 1 of Open University course DEH313 *Principles of Social and Educational Research*. Milton Keynes: Open University.

Hansen, Morris, Hurwitz, William and Madow, William (1953) *Sample Survey Methods and Theory*, Vol. 1. New York: Wiley.

Hathaway, S.R. and McKinley, J.C. (1942) 'A multiphasic personality inventory (Minnesota) III: the measurement of symptomatic depression', *Journal of Psychology*, 14: 73–84.

Heath, A., Jowell, R. and Curtice, J. (1985) *How Britain Votes*. Oxford: Pergamon.

Himmelweit, H., Oppenheim, A.N. and Vance, P. (1958) *Television and the Child: An Empirical Study of the Effect of Television on the Young*. Oxford: Oxford University Press.

Himmelweit, H., Humphreys, P. and Jaeger, M. (1985) *How Voters Decide*. Milton Keynes: Open University Press.

Hosmer, D.W. and Lemeshow, S. (1989) *Applied Logistic Regression*. New York: Wiley.

Kim, J. and Mueller, C.W. (1978a) *Introduction to Factor Analysis: What It Is and How to Do It*. Beverly Hills, CA: Sage.

Kim, J. and Mueller, C.W. (1978b) *Factor Analysis: Statistical Methods and Practical Issues*. Beverly Hills, CA: Sage.

Klassen, Albert and Wilsnack, Sharon (1986) 'Sexual experience and drinking among women in a U.S. national survey', *Archives of Sexual Behaviour*, 15: 363–92.

Marsh, Catherine (1979) 'Two-variable analysis', in *Making Sense of Data*, Block 6 of Open University course DE304 *Research Methods in Education and the Social Sciences*. Milton Keynes: Open University.

Marsh, Catherine (1993) 'The validation of Census data II: general issues', in A. Dale and C. Marsh (eds), *The 1991 Census User's Guide*. London: HMSO.

Maxwell, A.E. (1961) *Analysing Qualitative Data*. London: Methuen.

Mayhew, Patricia, Clarke, Ron, Sturman, Andrew and Hough, John (1976) *Crime As Opportunity*, Home Office Research Study No. 34. London: HMSO.

McNemar, Quinn (1962) *Psychological Statistics*. New York: Wiley.

Miller, Robert and Hayes, Bernadette (1990) 'Gender and intergenerational mobility', in G. Payne and P.A. Abbott (eds), *The Social Mobility of Women*. Basingstoke: Falmer.

Newell, Rosemarie (1993) 'Questionnaires', in N. Gilbert (ed.), *Researching Social Life*. London: Sage.

Oakley, Ann (1981) 'Interviewing women - a contradiction in terms', in H. Roberts (ed.), *Doing Feminist Research*. London: Routledge.

O'Connell Davidson, Julia and Layder, Derek (1994) *Methods, Sex and Madness*. London: Routledge.

Office of Population Censuses and Surveys (OPCS) (1973) *The General Household Survey: Introductory Report*. London: HMSO.

OPCS (1978) *The General Household Survey 1977*. London: HMSO.

OPCS (1980) *Census Topics 1801–1981*. London: HMSO.

OPCS (1996) *Results from the 1994 General Household Survey*. London: HMSO.

Oppenheim, A.N. (1979) 'Methods and strategies of survey research', in *Data Collection Procedures*, Block 4 of Open University course DE304 *Research Methods in Education and the Social Sciences*. Milton Keynes: Open University.

Oppenheim, A.N. (1992) *Questionnaire Design, Interviewing and Attitude Measurement*. London: Pinter.

Procter, Michael (1993) 'Measuring attitudes', in N. Gilbert (ed.), *Researching Social Life*. London: Sage.

Reinharz, Shulamit (1979) *On Becoming a Social Scientist*. San Francisco: Jossey Bass.

Romney, David (1979) 'Evaluation of a data collection method', in *Classification and Measurement*, Block 5 of Open University course DE304 *Research Methods in Education and the Social Sciences*. Milton Keynes: Open University.

Rose, Nikolas (1985) *The Psychological Complex: Psychology, Politics and Society in England 1869–1939*. London: Routledge & Kegan Paul.

Sapsford, Roger (1978) 'Life-sentence prisoners: psychological changes during sentence', *British Journal of Criminology*, 18: 128–45.

Sapsford, Roger (1983) *Life-Sentence Prisoners: Reaction, Response and Change*. Milton Keynes: Open University Press.

Sapsford, Roger and Abbott, Pamela (1996) *Research Methods for Nurses and the Caring Professions*. Buckingham: Open University Press.

Sapsford, Roger and Banks, Charlotte (1979) 'A synopsis of some Home Office research', in D.E. Smith (ed.), *Life-Sentence Prisoners*, Home Office Research Study No. 51. London: HMSO.

Sapsford, Roger and Jupp, Victor (eds) (1996) *Data Collection and Analysis*. London: Sage.

Schofield, William (1993) 'Sample surveys', in R.J. Sapsford et al., *Problem Formulation and Case Selection*, Block 2 of Open University course DEH313 *Principles of Social and Educational Research*. Milton Keynes: Open University.

Schofield, William (1996) 'Survey sampling', in R.J. Sapsford and V. Jupp (eds), *Data Collection and Analysis*. London: Sage.

Seligman, Martin (1975) *Helplessness*. San Francisco: W.H. Freeman.

Smith, F., Bolton, N., Banister, P. and Heskin, K. (1977) 'Investigation of the effects of long-term imprisonment', in European Committee on Crime Problems (ed.), *Treatment of Long-Term Prisoners*. Strasbourg: Council of Europe.

Smith, H.W. (1975) *Strategies of Social Research: The Methodological Imagination*. Englewood Cliffs, NJ: Prentice Hall.

Snedecor, George and Cochran, William (1967) *Statistical Methods* (6th edition). Ames, IA: Iowa State University Press.

Spender, Dale (1982) *Invisible Women: The Schooling Scandal*. London: Writers' and Readers' Publishing Co-operative.

Swift, Betty (1996) 'Preparing numerical data', in R.J. Sapsford and V. Jupp (eds), *Data Collection and Analysis*. London: Sage.

Taylor, Janet (1953) 'A personality scale of manifest anxiety', *Journal of Abnormal and Social Psychology*, 48: 285–90.

Taylor, Mary and Shore, Lynn (1995) 'Predictors of planned retirement age: an application of Beehr's model', *Psychology and Aging*, 10: 76–83.

Thomas, Ray (1996) 'Statistical sources and databases', in R.J. Sapsford and V. Jupp (eds), *Data Collection and Analysis*. London: Sage.

Townsend, P. and Davidson, N. (1980) *The Black Report*. Harmondsworth: Penguin.

Townsend, P., Simpson, D. and Tibbs, N. (1985) 'Inequalities in health in the city of Bristol: a preliminary review of statistical evidence', *International Journal of Health Science*, 15: 637–63.

Wasoff, Fran and Dobash, Emerson (1992) 'Simulated clients in "natural" settings: constructing a client to study professional practice', *Sociology*, 26: 333–49.

West, D.J. (1969) *Present Conduct and Future Delinquency*. London: Heinemann.

West, D.J. (1982) *Delinquency: Its Roots, Careers and Prospects*. London: Heinemann.

West, D.J. and Farrington, D. (1973) *Who Becomes Delinquent?* London: Heinemann.

West, D.J. and Farrington, D. (1977) *The Delinquent Way of Life*. London: Heinemann.

Wicker, A.W. (1969) 'Attitudes vs actions: the relationship of verbal and overt behavioural responses to attitude objects', *Journal of Social Issues*, 25: 41–78.

Wilkins, L. and McNaughton-Smith, P. (1964) 'New prediction and classification methods in criminology', *Journal of Research in Crime and Delinquency*, 1.

Willis, Paul (1977) *Learning to Labour*. Farnborough: Saxon House.

Wilsnack, Richard, Wilsnack, Sharon and Klassen, Albert (1984a) 'Women's drinking and drink problems: patterns from a 1981 National Survey', *American Journal of Public Health*, 74: 1231–8.

Wilsnack, Sharon, Klassen, Albert and Wilsnack, Richard (1984b) 'Drinking and reproductive dysfunction among women in a 1991 National Survey', *Alcoholism: Clinical and Experimental Research*, 8: 451–8.

Wilsnack, Richard, Wilsnack, Sharon and Klassen, Albert (1987) 'Antecedents and consequences of drinking and drinking problems in women: patterns from a U.S. National Survey', in P.C. Rivers (ed.), *Alcohol and Addictive Behaviour: Nebraska Symposium on Motivation 1986*. Lincoln, NE: University of Nebraska Press.

Wilson, Michael (1996) 'Asking questions', in R.J. Sapsford and V. Jupp (eds), *Data Collection and Analysis*. London: Sage.

Zakia (1969) 'Psychological comparison of university students with and without study difficulties'. PhD thesis, University of London.

Author index

Subject index